LEADERS OF THE PACK

★ ★ ★ ★ ★ ★ ★ ★ ★ ★ ★ ★ ★ ★ ★ ★ ★ ★

Starr, Favre, Rodgers, and Why Green Bay's Quarterback Trio Is the Best in NFL History

ROB REISCHEL

TRIUMPH
BOOKS

Library of Congress Cataloging-in-Publication Data

Reischel, Rob, 1969–
  Leaders of the pack : Starr, Favre, Rodgers and why Green Bay's quarterback trio is the best in NFL history / Rob Reischel.
      pages cm
  ISBN 978-1-62937-104-7
  1. Green Bay Packers (Football team)—History. 2. Quarterbacks (Football)—United States—Biography. 3. Football players—United States—Biography. 4. Starr, Bart. 5. Favre, Brett. 6. Rodgers, Aaron, 1983– I. Title.
  GV956.G7R445 2015
  796.332'640977561—dc23

                                                                            2015010786

This book is available in quantity at special discounts for your group or organization. For further information, contact:
  Triumph Books LLC
  814 North Franklin Street
  Chicago, Illinois 60610
  (312) 337-0747
  www.triumphbooks.com

Printed in U.S.A.
ISBN: 978-1-62937-104-7
Design by Patricia Frey
Page production by Amy Carter
Photos courtesy of Getty Images unless otherwise noted

To my wonderful family—wife Laura and daughters Madison and Mia—
who are supportive and patient with my hectic schedule.

To my siblings—Jenni, Ryan, and Jessie—
who have been there for me time and time again.

And to my grandmother, Dorothy, who brings joy into every room she enters.

I love you all!

★ ★ ★
Contents

★ ★ ★

Preface

When the Green Bay Packers offered me the general manager job, all I had to hear was that I was in charge of the entire football operations. I was given that and I was given an opportunity. When they told me that I had full control, I had absolutely no trepidation about coming to work for the Packers.

They hadn't always done it that way. But I think those guys on the board and the executive committee were pretty beat down. They had, what, 20, 21 years of losing up there? I'm sure it wasn't a great thrill to go to Oneida or go out to eat and you're on the executive committee of the Packers and people are saying, "What the hell are you guys doing?"

But we turned it around and turned it around in a hurry. We made Lambeau a very nice place to play, and it's still an incredibly nice place today.

I loved to trade. I really did. I always believed that if I have a player and I can get a player that's better than the guy I'm playing with, then I'm going to go out there and get that player.

And that's one thing I told my guys: when it's all said and done, I'm going to have two six-shooters on me and I've got 12 rounds on me. And I can guarantee you fellows I'm going to fire all 12 rounds. I'm not coming back here with one revolver half full.

The first rule of the game is you have to have a quarterback, and we didn't have one. So I made the trade for Brett Favre, which wasn't very popular at the time. But you look at that trade today, look at all the things Brett did, all the records after that trade, and that's definitely one of the top five trades of all time.

I'm going to the Hall of Fame this year, which I still can't believe is happening. And I'm smart enough to realize that I wouldn't be in there if it wasn't for Brett Favre.

They've always had really good quarterback play in Green Bay, from Cecil Isbell and Arnie Herber to Bart Starr. But they've never had anyone like Brett. I know I'm biased because he was my guy, but to me he's one of the top five quarterbacks of all time. He gave us a chance every game.

People ask me, what if the Favre trade had never happened? What if the queen had balls? She'd be king. I mean, I don't even want to think about it. I don't want to think about what we would have done.

We traded for Brett Favre and it gave us a chance. We had a chance every week. Without a quarterback, we had no chance. They've been pretty lucky up there to have this great tradition of quarterbacks. It's why they've had so much success, because if you don't have one, you really don't have a chance. Well, we got ours and the records kind of speak for themselves.

—Ron Wolf
March 2015

★ ★ ★

Foreword

Playing quarterback in Green Bay is unlike anything else in sports. It's a special place, a remarkable place. It was the perfect place for me to play. And I say it was the perfect place more than anything because that's who wanted me. At that time, things had gone bad in Atlanta. And even though I had no idea they were trying to get rid of me, they were.

So when I say coming to Green Bay was the perfect fit, it was the perfect fit because we had success. But it was also the perfect fit because that's who wanted me and they gave up what they gave up to get me (a No. 1 draft pick).

When I came to Green Bay, I felt like it was a great opportunity. I didn't know a whole lot about the Packers at the time. But I knew a lot about the history of the franchise in general and I knew the franchise was struggling. So I knew this was an opportunity I was lucky to get and then it was up to me to make the most of it. And that's what I tried to do each and every week.

Trying to get that done, trying to do your job each day, is probably easier in some ways when you're in Green Bay than it would be if you're in other cities. We don't have the distractions in Green Bay that you do in some places. We didn't have guys getting in as much trouble as maybe some other teams did. Now, if you want trouble, can you find trouble? Of course you can. But for the most part, we didn't.

And the best way I could sum it up was when you're in Green Bay, you're here to play football. If you're in Chicago, New York, Atlanta, San Francisco, it might not always be the same way. But in Green Bay, you're here to play football. You have very few distractions. It's easy to get from work to your house. You don't have to travel to the other side of town, which can be an hour or two in some places. You're not in the car a long time if all you want to do is get a bite to eat.

Things in Green Bay are simple. You're there to play football. The people in Green Bay are fanatical, and that's great. That's how you want it to be. There was never a problem. And I was home in three, four, five minutes, every day. It was all about football. That's how it should be.

I don't know why Green Bay has had this kind of quarterback success. Part of it, I'm sure, is you have to be a little bit lucky. But you also have to be good at your jobs, too, and the guys finding the quarterbacks certainly have been.

And then I think playing in a town where football is king and the players all realize you're there to play football has to help. You don't want to let anybody down, especially with this tradition now. It's a pretty special thing, to be part of something like that and to play quarterback in Green Bay. I'm just really proud and extremely fortunate I got to be part of that.

—Brett Favre

★ ★ ★

Introduction

Who is the greatest quarterback in NFL history?

It's a debate that's been waged for years.

Sammy Baugh, Sid Luckman, and Otto Graham were the best of their generation. Johnny Unitas and Bart Starr were dominant players in their time.

In the Super Bowl era, the names Tom Brady, Joe Montana, Terry Bradshaw, John Elway, Brett Favre, Peyton Manning, and Dan Marino come up most often.

It's an argument that will never be resolved.

If your case is centered around championships, Starr, Montana, Bradshaw, and Brady reign supreme in the modern era. Graham was a dominant force between 1946 and 1955, winning seven titles in the old AAFC and later the NFL.

If you look deeper than that, maybe the eye-popping statistics compiled by Manning, Favre, and Marino send those players up your list.

What happens, though, when you go beyond just one quarterback? How about two, or even three, with the same franchise?

That's what we've done here with *Leaders of the Pack*.

When you delve deep inside each organization and examine the three greatest quarterbacks every team has had, one thing becomes crystal clear.

No franchise anywhere has had a better trio than Green Bay's threesome of Bart Starr, Brett Favre, and Aaron Rodgers.

Starr was the gold standard for winning football and titles.

Between 1961 and 1967, Starr led the Packers to five NFL Championships in seven years. His career playoff record was a remarkable 9–1.

Starr was a four-time Pro Bowler, won an MVP, and ran Vince Lombardi's offense to perfection.

There were certainly flashier players than Starr—ones with stronger arms who made more highlight-reel plays.

But there haven't been many players who were greater winners than Starr.

Favre was the opposite of Starr in many ways. Favre was an all-time gunslinger, a player with the strongest arm the NFL had seen in years.

Favre had no problem taking chances. But under the guidance of coach Mike Holmgren, he developed into a thinking man's quarterback, as well.

When Favre's mental game caught up with his remarkable physical gifts, Green Bay had the NFL's best player. Favre won three MVP awards, set virtually every passing record that existed, and went nearly 19 years without missing a start.

Favre won one Super Bowl, lost another, and led the Packers to four NFC Championship games. In addition, he endeared himself to fans with a passion and love for the game rarely seen from the modern athlete.

Rodgers has kept Green Bay's great quarterbacking tradition alive. In fact, some would argue he's taken it up a notch.

Through his first seven seasons as a starter, Rodgers ranks first in NFL history in career passer rating. His numbers have bordered on the absurd, and depending how long he plays, Rodgers could eventually break many of the league's all-time passing records.

Rodgers led the Packers to a Super Bowl title in the 2010 season. And including the postseason, Rodgers has gone 76–38 as a starter (.667).

Rodgers' game probably falls somewhere between those of Favre and Starr.

Rodgers' disgust for mistakes is similar to Starr's. His mental skills are off the charts.

But Rodgers' athleticism and arm strength are far better than was advertised when he left California in 2005. And just think: Rodgers may only be halfway through what's already been a brilliant career.

Together, this trio is undoubtedly the best the NFL has ever seen.

Oh, there are a handful of teams that can make a case for No. 1. But where they always fall short is depth.

San Francisco's duo of Montana and Steve Young certainly rivals Green Bay's.

The Top 10 Quarterback Trios in NFL History

1. Green Bay Packers (Bart Starr; Brett Favre; Aaron Rodgers)
2. San Francisco 49ers (Joe Montana; Steve Young; Y.A. Tittle)
3. Baltimore/Indianapolis Colts (Johnny Unitas; Peyton Manning; Bert Jones)
4. Dallas Cowboys (Troy Aikman; Roger Staubach; Tony Romo)
5. Pittsburgh Steelers (Terry Bradshaw; Ben Roethlisberger; Bobby Layne)
6. New England Patriots (Tom Brady; Drew Bledsoe; Steve Grogan)
7. Washington Redskins (Sammy Baugh; Sonny Jurgensen; Joe Theismann)
8. Denver Broncos (John Elway; Peyton Manning; Craig Morton)
9. Oakland Raiders (Jim Plunkett; Daryle Lamonica; Ken Stabler)
10. San Diego Chargers (Dan Fouts; Philip Rivers; John Hadl)

The same goes for Pittsburgh's dynamic duo of Bradshaw and Ben Roethlisberger, or the Colts' terrific twosome of Unitas and Manning.

But when those teams have to play their third card, they don't come close to Green Bay's trio. And when you line up all six men, the Packers always prevail.

In *Leaders of the Pack*, we'll take fans on a ride through the brilliant careers of Starr, Favre, and Rodgers. You'll also learn plenty about the men themselves, the obstacles they overcame in Green Bay, and why they were successful.

We'll also profile the other nine teams in our top 10 list, and their top three quarterbacks. You'll learn what made those players and their franchises great, but also why they fell short of Green Bay's triumverate.

No NFL team has enjoyed greater success than the Packers, who have won a league-record 13 championships. The biggest reason for that success has always been stellar quarterback play.

Keep reading and find out why Green Bay's trio is the best the NFL has ever seen.

Part I

The Green Bay Packers' Quarterback Trio

★ ★ ★
Bart Starr

Bart Starr's first players' meeting with new head coach Vince Lombardi had just ended.

And Starr didn't just think. He knew.

Green Bay would no longer be the doormat of the National Football League.

The Packers, 1–10–1 during a miserable 1958 season, would never be the same after hiring Lombardi—the former New York Giants assistant head coach—on February 4, 1959.

In his initial meeting with quarterbacks and other offensive players, Lombardi made his expectations known.

"He told us, 'I am not remotely interested in being just good,'" Starr explained. "We are going to relentlessly chase perfection, knowing full well that we won't catch it, because nobody is perfect. But in the process, we'll catch excellence."

Those words resonated in Starr's mind.

"I almost jumped out of my chair I was so excited," Starr said. "He said, 'I'm not remotely interested in being just good.'"

When the meeting ended, Starr raced out of the room to use a phone—the rotary variety—to call his wife, Cherry.

"I told her, 'Honey, we're going to begin to win,'" Starr said. "I couldn't wait to get going."

Winning.

That was something Starr had rarely experienced after joining the Packers in 1956 following his collegiate career at the University of Alabama.

The downtrodden Green Bay franchise, holder of six NFL championships under Curly Lambeau from 1921–49, had not experienced a winning season since 1947.

Starr knew the fortunes of the team were about to change. He just didn't know the struggle that loomed to once again prove himself to the second-toughest man in his life.

That is the essence of Starr's football career at every level: proving he was good enough. To his teammates, to his coaches, to himself.

But most of all to his father.

In the end, Starr was the humble leader of a dynasty, of Lombardi-coached Packers teams that won five NFL titles in seven years. Along the way, Green Bay captured an unprecedented three championships in a row from 1965 to 1967, and the first two Super Bowls.

Starr was the most valuable player of those historic first meetings of the NFL and AFL champions, and his bust resides in the Pro Football Hall of Fame in Canton, Ohio.

Starr is one of the winningest quarterbacks in league history and his name ranks among the all-time greats: Otto Graham, Johnny Unitas, Terry Bradshaw, Joe Montana, John Elway, Dan Marino, Brett Favre, Peyton Manning, and Tom Brady.

Starr was not blessed with physical attributes such as a rocket arm or blazing speed. It was his determination, intelligence, work ethic, and preparation that set him apart.

Quarterbacks are ultimately defined by championships, the final measuring stick in a game littered with statistics. And no one can match Starr's success from 1961–67.

"Bart was rarely the best quarterback in the league on a statistical basis," teammate Jerry Kramer said. "But for three hours each Sunday, he was—almost always—the best quarterback in the game in which he was playing."

Former Chicago Bears tight end and head coach Mike Ditka fully concurred.

"Bart Starr was a winner and a gentleman, period," Ditka said. "It was Lombardi's team, but Bart Starr was the quiet glue that held the whole thing together. He was a great leader."

Starr's leadership style belied his mental and physical toughness, and contrasted that of his fiery head coach.

"You know what he'd say if Bart was mad at you in the huddle?" said Gary Knafelc, a tight end with the Packers from 1954–62. "He'd just say, 'Hush up.' He'd control all the guys with just that. He was the quarterback, our leader, and that was unquestioned."

Bryan Bartlett Starr's journey to the National Football League began in Montgomery, Alabama.

He was born on January 9, 1934, to Ben and Lulu Starr, and was named after his father, whose middle name was Bryan. The baby's middle name was in tribute to the doctor, Haywood Bartlett, who delivered him.

His parents called him "Bart" for short, and nicknamed his younger brother Hilton "Bubba."

Ben Starr was a blacksmith who served in the Army National Guard. When his unit was mobilized with the build-up to World War II, the family moved from coast to coast before Starr departed for the Pacific theatre.

Lulu Starr ran a tight and disciplined household with two young boys living in modest housing on the Fort Ord base in Northern California.

"My parents were strict," Starr said. "I was raised in a military family and moving around helped me to learn to adapt to different environments and situations."

After the war, the family moved back to Montgomery and the elder Starr decided to make the military a career. A tough master sergeant, Ben Starr was a dominant figure who demanded his boys adhere to his rules and standards.

The Starr boys got involved in sports, and the younger but more aggressive Hilton received his father's praise while Bart was encouraged to be "more like your brother."

Tragedy rocked the family when Bubba died from tetanus poisoning in 1947 after stepping on an old dog bone in the dirt while playing tag with neighborhood friends. His foot became infected and he died three days later.

This occurred in an era before vaccinations were required for children. Lulu Starr cleaned the wound as best she could and didn't think her son needed the relatively new tetanus shot.

"It was so hard," Starr said. "It rocked our family to the core."

Losing a brother was difficult for Starr, but guilt ravaged the mourning family. Ben Starr pushed Bart to excel in sports, often bringing up comparisons to Bubba's toughness and aggressiveness.

Starr was determined to show his father that he could succeed.

"Of course I wanted my father's approval," Starr said. "I wanted to prove I could be a good athlete. I didn't know it then, but he challenged me when I needed it. And he prepared me for what was to come. Coach Lombardi was a piece of cake compared to my dad."

In junior high school, Starr played wingback, but was switched to quarterback as he entered Sidney Lanier High School, rich in football tradition. Starr was thrilled to build on his budding passing skills, but was upset when he failed to make the varsity squad.

"I was on the JV team and had thoughts of quitting the team," Starr said. "My father had another idea."

Ben Starr calmly told his son that with the additional free time after school, he could spend his time weeding and cleaning the garden. Starr slept on his decision and attended practice the next day with resolve to work even harder to hone his skills.

"Bart's dad was a real taskmaster and could be tough on Bart at times, like all fathers," said Bill Moseley, the Sidney Lanier Poets' head coach.

The 92-year-old Moseley still lives in Montgomery and is always happy to discuss the best player he ever coached.

"When I first saw Bart he was a skinny junior high player," Moseley said with a laugh. "He was kind of quiet, but listened and absorbed everything he was taught. As a coach, I really liked that. And Bart caught on very quickly and tended to the details."

Starr's work ethic was second to none, which is a huge reason he became one of the NFL's ultimate underdog stories.

"He just kept working at it," Moseley said. "He was not some big, strong brute of a player. He'd go home after practice and throw passes through an automobile tire he hung from a tree or practice his moves. He was a student of the game."

Moseley convinced Starr's parents to let him spend a week at the University of Kentucky during the summer before his senior year, learning the mechanics and gaining knowledge from quarterback Babe Parilli.

Young Bart Starr (10) chose the University of Alabama over the University of Kentucky to be closer to his future wife, Cherry, who attended Auburn University.

Starr came to idolize Parilli, plastering his bedroom walls with his pictures. Little did Starr know he would one day compete with him for the starting quarterback job in Green Bay.

"I wanted Bart to gain experience and work with Babe to elevate his game," Moseley explained. "They did double workouts for a week and Bart learned so much from Babe about the mechanics of the position. It worked out pretty well."

Football was Starr's first love, but a classmate was also capturing his attention. Cherry Morton would later become his wife, but the shy Starr lacked the courage to ask her out himself in high school.

So he sent his teammate.

"I told his friend that if Bart Starr wanted to ask me out, he would have to do it himself," Cherry said. "He finally did, but he kept looking down at the ground. He was so sweet."

Starr got his chance to fill in during a varsity game when Lanier's starting quarterback was injured against perennial power Tuscaloosa, which featured a 17-game winning streak.

It was a huge stage for Starr, who was just a sophomore at the time. But Starr responded by leading the Poets to a 13–0 victory—and eventually an undefeated season.

A budding star was born.

Starr was a sought-after college prospect, but chose the University of Alabama over Kentucky for one reason: it was closer to Auburn University, where Cherry intended to study interior design.

"It was the best audible I ever called," Starr said. "She's been my teammate for life."

Like his high school, the Crimson Tide had a tradition-rich football program. Starr was not only closer to his girlfriend, but his father was also pleased that he was just a two-hour drive from seeing his son play.

"Bart would visit me a couple times a month at Auburn," Cherry said. "It was a long drive just to see me for an hour. Other times we'd meet at home (Montgomery) for the weekend outside the football season and we'd have more time together."

Starr earned the No. 3 spot on Alabama's varsity roster in 1952, impressing Harold "Red" Drew and his coaching staff with his passing abilities, decision making, competitiveness, and work ethic.

His lack of foot speed was a point of concern, but the positives outweighed the one negative.

By his sophomore season in 1953, Starr had earned the starting job and was doing triple duty. Due to a change in NCAA rules on free substitutions, Starr was also employed as a defensive back and handled the punting duties.

While his speed was a liability on defense, Starr's anticipation, ability to see plays develop, and tackling skills were positives. Starr was also one of the best punters in the country with a 41.4-yard average—second only to Zeke Bratkowski of the University of Georgia, a man who would later become his teammate and close friend in Green Bay.

Starr led Alabama to a 6–2–3 record, a Southeastern Conference championship, and a berth against Rice in the Cotton Bowl.

In one of the most bizarre plays in college bowl history, Alabama's Tommy Lewis came off the team bench and tackled Rice halfback Dicky Moegle (now known as Dicky Maegle) as he was sprinting down the sideline on his way to a sure touchdown.

Rice led 7–6 at the time, and the officials awarded Maegle a 95-yard touchdown, while Lewis returned to the bench and buried his head in his hands. Photographs and television cameras captured the play live, along with its aftermath.

"I never saw anything like that," said Starr, who was blocked on the touchdown run. "Tommy was such a competitor and it got the best of him on that play."

Rice pulled away for a 28–6 victory as the calendar turned to 1954, a year in which Starr would make the biggest decision of his life.

He had twice before asked Cherry to marry him, but the third time was the charm. The couple eloped and got married on May 8, 1954. Starr's high school and college teammate, Nick Germanos, was his best man.

"We were so young, but we got married when we were both 20," Cherry said. "We were so very much in love and just wanted to be together."

Not only did the couple keep the marriage a secret from their parents, but also from the Alabama coaching staff. Starr feared his scholarship might be revoked, as marriage could potentially affect the focus of an athlete.

After keeping their union quiet for three months, the couple informed Cherry's parents and then Bart's. It did not go over well with Ben or Lulu Starr, who at first wanted the marriage annulled.

They agreed to exchange vows at First United Methodist Church in Montgomery and—at his father's urging—informed his head coach.

Starr's junior season was marred by a lower back injury he suffered in a summer punting workout. The injury affected Starr's entire football season and he spent a week in traction at a Tuscaloosa hospital. The Crimson Tide slipped to a disappointing 4–5–2 that season and Drew was fired.

Former Alabama lineman J.B. "Ears" Whitworth was hired to take the program to the next level. Unfortunately, the team went the other direction.

Whitworth preferred to run the ball, and he also wanted to build for the future with young prospects, which relegated Starr, a passer, to ride the bench. Alabama did not win a single game in 1955 and Starr played sparingly, usually with the game's outcome long decided.

His confidence took a direct hit.

Giving Back

One of Bart Starr's favorite quotes reflects why he has spent a lifetime giving back.

"It's from Winston Churchill and it's so powerful," Starr said. 'We make a living of what we get. We make a life of what we give.'"

The message of giving back was learned at home as a youth and grew into a passion and priority with his wife, Cherry, through his NFL and business careers and into retirement.

"My dad was a military man—a tough master sergeant," Starr said. "I learned about assisting others from my father and mother. I backed off from my health care real estate business (in 2007) to spend more time with Cherry and devote more time to our charitable work."

While Starr has assisted thousands of charities and causes over the past six decades, one remains close to the Starrs' hearts: Rawhide Boys Ranch in rural New London, Wisconsin.

Lives are transformed on the 575-acre ranch along the scenic Wolf River, as at-risk boys from 13 to 19 years old learn to become responsible citizens.

It all started with a phone call from John Gillespie, who founded the non-profit, faith-based residential care center with his wife, Jan, in 1965. Rawhide was struggling in its infancy, and Gillespie turned to the star Green Bay quarterback for help.

The Packers were the toast of Wisconsin and the country after winning their third consecutive NFL championship and second Super Bowl title.

Starr earned a shiny red 1968 Corvette for being named the MVP in Green Bay's decisive 33–14 triumph over the Oakland Raiders in Super Bowl II.

"Rawhide was in tough shape financially in the early years," Gillespie said. "Bart donated that Corvette for our raffle, which took in $40,000 and kept us going."

The mint-condition Corvette has changed hands over the years, but a Hortonville man owns it today and still brings the vehicle back to the ranch for special events.

Gillespie estimated that thousands of boys were helped because of the generosity and support of Bart and Cherry Starr over the past five decades. And it all started with a nudge from Jan Gillespie, who urged her husband to contact the Packers quarterback.

"My wife said, 'Why don't you just call him,'" Gillespie said. "So I called information and got his number—which I thought would be unlisted."

Gillespie called and was flabbergasted when Starr answered the phone.

"I asked if I could speak to Mr. Starr," Gillespie said. "He said, 'No, but Bart's here.' And I said, 'Can I talk to him?' He said, 'You are talking to him.'"

The goal was to set up an appointment with Starr to discuss his vision for the boys' ranch. But he got much more: an invitation to Starr's home that evening.

"When we got there, Cherry was in the kitchen making supper," he said. "And Bart said, 'You're eating with us.'"

After dinner, the couples went into the living room to discuss Rawhide.

"I sat down on their couch with my three-ring binder and presented the concepts," Gillespie said. "Bart and Cherry believed in the same things as we did."

Their common goal was to help troubled teens through a faith-based program that stressed high standards and promoted a strong work ethic.

For decades, the Starrs appeared in television commercials for Rawhide that ran throughout Wisconsin, promoting the donation of vehicles and boats to benefit the ranch.

"It's a fabulous organization, and you'd see if you made a trip out there and met the Rawhide staff and these youngsters," Starr said.

Starr's patience and generosity with fans are legendary, from his days as a player to his last public appearance before his health issues in the fall of 2014.

After a grueling training camp practice in 1963, the weary Packers boarded a bus to head back to St. Norbert College for a few hours of rest. As Starr walked to the bus, he was engulfed by a sea of children eager for an autograph, in an era before cell phones, selfies, and digital cameras.

"Bart signed something for every single kid," former teammate Fuzzy Thurston once said. "While we waited on the bus. Like all of us, he was dog-tired, but he stayed to sign for all those young fans. That's Bart Starr."

Remy Rickert, a Green Bay native, was thrilled to draw Starr as the celebrity Packer in his foursome at the Vince Lombardi Classic, a celebrity charity golf tournament held annually near Milwaukee in the late 1990s.

"It was so thrilling to be able to golf with Bart," Rickert said. "But he told us right up front: I know you may have been celebrating last night when you learned of your selection, but I'm apologizing in advance because this will be the longest round of golf in your life.'"

The reason was logical.

"Bart said he will never walk away from an opportunity to sign an autograph for a fan," Rickert said."And in return for your patience, I will be happy to sign and personalize anything you'd like at the end of our round."

Starr took the time to warmly greet every fan that approached him on the course, stopping his play to sign an autograph or pose for a picture.

"Bart was right, it was the longest round of golf in my life," Rickert said. "It took like seven and a half hours. But it was so cool—he was the consummate gentleman, so humble and genuine and straightforward. Instead of spending five hours with Bart we got extra time. We all loved it."

A prestigious league award bears Bart Starr's name for his lifelong commitment to serving as a positive role model.

The Athletes in Action/Bart Starr award is given annually to the NFL player who best exemplifies outstanding character and leadership in the home, on the field, and in the community.

"It's been a joy because you're bringing attention to people who are committed to God, family,

(continued)

11

Giving Back *(continued)*

and community," Starr said. "I was particularly pleased to present the award to Aaron Rodgers (in 2014)."

Former Packers tight end Gary Knafelc, Starr's close friend and teammate for seven seasons, said it's hard to quantify the impact of his generosity and community service.

"In his lifetime, Bart has helped so many causes—big and small—and raised millions of dollars," Knafelc said. "I've never known anyone give back like Bart.

"It wasn't an obligation, it was a way of life. Bart and Cherry are just good people, who enjoyed helping others. It just comes down to that."

"It was such a difficult season for Bart," Cherry Starr said. "He was so frustrated after working so hard to get back and then not playing. He thought his football career was over."

While Whitworth did not believe in him, assistant coach Johnny Dee did. Dee also coached the Alabama basketball team and pulled some strings to get Starr an invite to the Blue-Gray Football Classic.

The annual game featured some of the nation's best college seniors, serving as a must see for National Football League scouts. It was played on Starr's high school field and provided a storybook opportunity to prove he could compete at the next level despite his disappointing senior season.

With family and friends watching, Starr received just a few snaps near the end of the game. Disillusioned, he again turned to Dee when the second semester began.

Dee said he'd call a friend in the NFL on Starr's behalf. That friend was Jack Vainisi, the Green Bay Packers' director of player personnel.

"I really never thought about Bart playing professional football," said Cherry, who expected him to pursue a military career. "But he wanted the opportunity."

In January 1956, a Packers assistant coach flew into Tuscaloosa to meet Starr and put him through a light workout. Later that month, Starr was the 200th selection in the NFL draft, taken by Green Bay in Round 17.

Interestingly, 44 years later, New England's Tom Brady was the 199th pick of the 2000 draft.

Cherry Starr and her mother had to consult a map to pinpoint Green Bay's location in Wisconsin.

"I grew up in Rome, Georgia, and we moved to Montgomery when I was 14," Cherry said with a chuckle. "I had no idea where Green Bay was."

Starr was a long shot to even make the Packers roster in 1956. He inked a modest $6,500 contract and was given jersey No. 42 in training camp, a number usually reserved for running backs and receivers.

"Fans will ask me to sign my rookie card," Starr once said. "But I tell them the first card has me with No. 42 and in a blue-and-gold uniform."

The writing was on the wall: this 17th-round draft choice was expected to be no more than a training-camp body.

Before reporting to camp, Starr embarked on a rigorous workout schedule with three footballs supplied by Dee to restore his confidence as a passer.

Living with his wife, Cherry, at his in-laws' home in Jackson, Mississippi, Starr threw footballs through a tire erected on a wooden frame in the backyard for several hours each day for a month.

"Cherry was there with me, chasing balls and giving me encouragement," Starr said. "She's been the greatest teammate of my life."

At the University of Alabama, Starr was accustomed to playing before large crowds in a modern stadium and working out in first-rate facilities. That was not the case in Green Bay, with aging City Stadium and its cramped locker room and training room.

"Conditions were quite different in Green Bay at the time compared to what I was used to at Alabama," Starr said. "The franchise was struggling financially at the time and the facilities reflected that."

Starr attended Packers training camp, which was held in Stevens Point, Wisconsin, at that time, and tried proving he belonged.

Starr lacked the skills of the NFL's great quarterbacks at the time: the rocket arm of Baltimore's Unitas or the scrambling ability of Detroit's Bobby Layne.

Instead, Starr relied on his mind, heart, and desire to set himself apart.

He beat out two other players and won the No. 2 job behind Green Bay starter Tobin Rote. Rote took Starr under his wing and also urged him to increase his arm strength.

The Packers were a team headed nowhere fast in Starr's early years. Green Bay went a combined 7–17 in the 1956–57 seasons under head coach Lisle Blackbourn.

Starr was still a work in progress. During his rookie season, he completed 24 of 44 passes for 325 yards with two touchdowns and three interceptions.

In 1957, Starr started several games and completed 117-of-215 passes for 1,489 yards, eight touchdowns and 10 interceptions.

Starr still had doubts about his ability.

"I dwelled on my mistakes and interceptions back then," he said. "I was inexperienced."

The franchise hit rock bottom in 1958 with a 1–10–1 record under Ray "Scooter" McLean, a lenient coach who tried to befriend his players.

"Scooter should not have been moved up," said Don McIlhenny, a Packer halfback from 1957 to 1959. "I remember in the last week of 1958, we were out on the West Coast and we had just got our butts kicked. We had a team meeting and one guy said, 'I got a problem.'

"Scooter started scratching his bald head and said, 'Take your problems to Jesus son. Scooter's got problems of his own.'"

Jim Temp, a Packers defensive end from 1957 to 1960, agreed.

"He didn't exercise any authority and we just had a disastrous season," Temp said. "The players just didn't have any respect for him."

Starr and Parilli split time at quarterback that season, both throwing 157 passes. The big difference was the touchdown-to-interception ratio. Starr threw three touchdowns and 12 interceptions, while Parilli had 10 touchdowns and 13 interceptions.

The organization was a mess.

"Oh man," Knafelc said of McLean. "Scooter would play poker with the players the night before the game. And what was worse is he wasn't even good at it. (Max) McGee would just take him to the cleaners."

Paul Hornung had plenty of success in those card games himself.

"There was no discipline under Scooter," former halfback Paul Hornung said. "Max and I loved to play cards with Scooter because we walked away with his money.

"But we had no leadership on a team that had a lot of talent. It took Lombardi to bring that."

The Packers—and Starr—were forever changed by Vince Lombardi's hiring.

Lombardi's first impression of Starr left him wondering if the mild-mannered quarterback could be the future leader of his team.

"When I first met him he struck me as so polite and so self-effacing that I wondered if maybe he wasn't too nice a boy to be the authoritarian leader that your quarterback must be," Lombardi was quoted as saying in David Maraniss' biography, *When Pride Still Mattered*. "He is the son of an Army master sergeant. He grew up on Army posts and he still calls me 'Sir.'"

Lombardi had traded for Lamar McHan in one of his early personnel moves, and he chose the former Chicago Cardinals and University of Arkansas star as his starting quarterback.

However, by the eighth game of the 1959 season, Starr had earned the job, leading the Packers to four victories in the last five games of a 7–5 season.

Lombardi returned Green Bay to respectability in the league and a third-place finish in the six-team Western Conference, behind the Baltimore Colts and Chicago Bears.

"In Bart Starr, we're going to have one of the great quarterbacks in football," Lombardi told Frank Gifford on his radio show after the 1959 season.

There were, however, growing pains as Starr fought to earn the confidence and respect of his demanding coach.

A turning point in Starr's relationship with Lombardi occurred after a practice session late in the 1959 season. One of Starr's passes was tipped and intercepted, and Lombardi vehemently chewed out his quarterback in front of his teammates on the field.

Starr took exception.

"I said, 'Coach, may I see you in your office after we come off the field,'" Starr wrote in Paul Hornung's book, *Lombardi and Me*. "So I went in to see him and I said, 'Coach, I can take the chewing out. You know by now that I can handle it. But you're chewing me out and demeaning my ass in front of the team that you're expecting me to lead.

"You'll see that you made a mistake about that tipped ball, but you'll apologize to me here in the office, not in front of the team. So if you want to chew me out, do it in the privacy of this office.'"

That simple declaration to his coach showed his growing confidence in himself and his maturation as a leader.

"I think Coach Lombardi respected me more for speaking up on the matter," Starr said.

Bart Starr and Vince Lombardi had a father-son relationship based on mutual respect. Starr earned Lombardi's esteem early on, after walking into his office and politely but firmly asking him not to chew him out in front of the team and undermine his authority as a leader. (AP Images)

Entering training camp in 1960 with heightened expectations by the Packers' ardent fan base, Starr and McHan battled for the starting role. Lombardi tabbed Starr as his starter for the opener against rival Chicago, but he was mediocre in a 17–14 loss to the Bears.

McHan started the following week and led the team to three consecutive victories, including a 35–21 upset victory over Baltimore, the defending league champions, in Green Bay.

When McHan and the offense struggled in the first half against the Steelers in Pittsburgh, Lombardi inserted Starr. The Packers held on to win 19–13.

Unlike the poised Starr, McHan had a fiery personality and was not pleased about being pulled from the contest. He confronted Lombardi at a postgame meal in Green Bay.

"Not a smart thing to do," Knafelc said.

McHan was benched and later traded to the Baltimore Colts.

Starr's 12-year tenure as the undisputed starting quarterback of the Packers had begun. He had earned the job — and his confidence soared.

"It meant a lot to me and I wanted nothing more to prove Coach Lombardi made the right decision," Starr said.

Later that season, Starr displayed the mental and physical toughness that belied his nice-guy image against the rival Bears. After linebacker Bill George sacked Starr and split his lip, he taunted the Packers quarterback.

Blood spewing forth, Starr got back up and got in George's face. Kramer said the offensive unit was surprised at the outburst. When Kramer told Starr he may need medical attention on the sideline, he got a terse response.

"Bart said to [me], 'Shut up and get back in the huddle,'" Kramer said with a chuckle. "I thought, 'Lookie here, our quarterback has some fire in his belly.'"

The Packers finished the year 8–4 and reached the NFL Championship game in 1960, where Green Bay lost 17–13 to the Philadelphia Eagles.

It was a contest between the aging Eagles and up-and-coming Packers that went down to the wire.

Veteran Norm Van Brocklin made a few more big plays than Starr, and a last-minute drive by the Packers ended with linebacker Chuck Bednarik tackling Jim Taylor inside the 10-yard line.

Lombardi's team had played their hearts out, left it all on the field, but had fallen short. Ever the psychologist, Lombardi had a message for his players in the somber locker room after telling the media that he was proud of his team and their performance.

"I remember vividly what Coach Lombardi said to us in the locker room after that loss in Philadelphia," Starr said. "He didn't yell or scream at us. Coach Lombardi's greatest strength was his ability to appropriately handle the situation.

"What he said was my motivation for the offseason and training camp to prepare for the 1961 season. He said, 'Gentlemen, never again will we fail to win a championship game.' And he was right. We didn't lose another one."

A dynasty was in the making.

"Suffice it to say that we were on a mission," Kramer said. "And we were young and strong and confident."

The Packers were at their prime in 1961 and 1962. Starr was coming into his own and mastering Lombardi's run-oriented offense. The head coach and the quarterback were in total sync.

Starr's meticulous pregame planning and film study during the week allowed him to confidently implement Lombardi's game plan for the next opponent.

He looked for tendencies or weaknesses in the defense to exploit, and used his freedom to call audibles when appropriate.

"He was the perfect guy at the perfect time to lead Lombardi's offense," Ditka said. "He called his own plays and not too much bothered him.

"He was respected by his peers and made people around him better. They were a running team first—everyone was back then. But Bart was just so efficient and smart, he took advantage of anything the defense gave him. He didn't make many mistakes and beat himself."

Packers running back Jim Taylor felt the same way.

"You couldn't find a quarterback better suited for our offense than Bart," Taylor said of Starr. "For my money, he's the best quarterback of all time."

Starr became a master of the play-action fake, especially in third-down and short-yardage situations, when the defense was expecting Taylor to get the handoff and plunge forward.

Instead, Starr executed a fake handoff and then dropped back to pass, most often finding a streaking Boyd Dowler or Max McGee for a big gain.

Green Bay's signature play was the power sweep, the ultimate blend of teamwork and precision that defined Lombardi. The Packers practiced it over and over until the timing was perfect, and then methodically ran it until an opponent proved they could stop it.

"We ran that play to death in practice until we had it down," said Fuzzy Thurston, who along with fellow guard Jerry Kramer pulled on the play to lead either Hornung or Taylor around end.

The 1961 season started with a 17–13 loss to Detroit in Milwaukee. The Packers then went on a tear, though, winning six straight games before falling to host Baltimore 45–21.

Green Bay finished the expanded 14 game-season (up from 12 games in 1960) with five victories in its last six games to claim the Western Conference title with an 11–3 record.

The Packers featured a balanced offense triggered by Starr and the running tandem of Taylor and Hornung, the NFL's leading scorer.

The efficient Green Bay offense averaged nearly 28 points per contest and committed 26 turnovers, while its stingy defense gave up just 16 points per game and forced 46 turnovers.

Future Pro Football Hall of Fame Players Ray Nitschke, Willie Davis, and Willie Wood were standouts on a defensive unit that saved its best performance for the championship game.

The Packers faced the New York Giants, a veteran squad spearheaded by quarterback Y.A. Tittle and linebacker Sam Huff. The Giants—champions of the Eastern Conference—went 10–3–1 that season and featured the NFL's top-rated defense.

The title match-up was much more than just big city versus small town motivation for the Packers and Lombardi. It was personal.

A native of Brooklyn, Lombardi served as an assistant coach for the Giants from 1954 to 1958 and was bypassed for the head coaching job by owner Wellington Mara. A victory would accomplish two goals for the Green Bay head coach: secure his first NFL title and defeat the Giants in the process.

The Packers received a huge boost when Hornung, serving in the Army in Fort Riley, Kansas, had his Christmas leave adjusted, which allowed him to play in the game. Lombardi placed a phone call to President John F. Kennedy for assistance in the matter.

Joe Horrigan of the Pro Football Hall of Fame said it was an unprecedented event in league annals.

"We've had presidents call and offer congratulations to teams and players, but never had a president involved with getting a player home on leave," Horrigan said.

"In the history of the NFL, I can't imagine the president of the United States was presented with a request like Lombardi's before. Remember it was a simpler time. Today, a politician would be highly scrutinized for being involved in a sports matter like that."

The residents of tiny Green Bay were at a fevered pitch on December 31, 1961, ready to celebrate a new year and an NFL championship after a 17-year drought.

"Titletown, USA" banners hung throughout the city and signs were prevalent in the City Stadium crowd of 39,029 on a frigid afternoon.

A then-record 55 million viewers watched the championship game, including NFL Commissioner Pete Rozelle. A record share would be distributed to players with the league's new $9.3 million television contract: $5,195.44 to the winners and $3,339.99 to the losers.

Green Bay started slow before erupting for 24 points in the second quarter. The Packers defense was dominant and the Giants struggled to find any offensive rhythm.

After forcing New York to punt on its first two possessions, the Packers drove 80 yards and took a 7–0 lead on a 6-yard run by Hornung. Nitschke intercepted a Tittle pass and Green Bay doubled the margin on Starr's 13-yard touchdown pass to Boyd Dowler.

The rout was on after Hank Gremminger intercepted another New York pass and the Packers surged to a 24–0 halftime lead. Two second-half field goals by Hornung and Starr's 13-yard touchdown toss to tight end Ron Kramer gave the Packers a dominant 37–0 win.

Green Bay's defense was flawless in the shutout, recording four interceptions, recovering a fumble, and limiting the Giants' prolific offense to just six first downs and 130 total yards.

Dan Currie and Dave Hanner carried Lombardi off the field, while delirious fans tore down the goal posts.

Hornung said the Packers offense could have scored 70 points that day.

"I asked Vince on the sidelines to put the first team back in the fourth quarter, but he told me to sit back down," Hornung said. "He had too much respect for the Mara family and the Giants to rub it in. But we wanted to. That game, that day, we could have scored as many points as we wanted to. I think that was our best football team in 1961."

Hornung was at his best on the biggest stage, scoring 19 total points. He had one touchdown, three field goals, and four extra points to set a new playoff single-game record.

Hornung also rushed for 89 yards on 20 carries and caught three passes for 47 yards to earn the game's outstanding player honor and a new red Corvette.

Starr completed 10 of 17 passes for 164 yards and three touchdowns, and elevated his status to one of the game's premier quarterbacks and leaders. Four completions went to Kramer, who totaled 80 yards and two touchdowns.

Taylor called it a championship performance for the ages, one that was forged in Philadelphia.

"We came so close the year before, but we came back in 1961 with the experience and maturity to get the job done," Taylor said. "Looking back, we wanted redemption. We were just so strong and dominant that day against the Giants. We put it all together, just the way Coach Lombardi wanted."

After the game, Bart Starr met with Cherry and his parents outside City Stadium—and heard something he'd wanted to hear for a long time.

After embracing his wife and mother, Starr saw his father with tears in his eyes. Ben Starr hugged his son, and said, "I was wrong, son."

Starr and the Packers elevated their play to yet another level in 1962. Often termed the greatest team in franchise history, Green Bay went 13–1 in the regular season and again defeated the Giants for the NFL title.

"That probably was the best year we had during the Glory Years," Starr said. "Everything just kind of aligned right that season.

"We avoided injuries that season. It was our fourth year with Vince, so we all knew just what he wanted. And a lot of our core guys were in their prime. It was an incredible season."

Green Bay's domination was reflected in the statistics.

The Packers outscored their opponents 415–148 in the regular season. They averaged 5.8 yards per play. They lost 28 turnovers, but created 50 for a plus-22 differential.

Green Bay played its best football when it mattered most, outscoring the opposition 136–35 in the fourth quarter.

Taylor was named the league MVP and led the NFL in rushing with 1,474 yards and scored 19 touchdowns. Starr was the league's top-rated quarterback, completing 178 of 285 passes (62.5%) for 2,438 yards and 12 touchdowns.

Starr threw nine interceptions and sported a team-record 90.7 quarterback rating. Safety Willie Wood led the league with nine interceptions.

"That was a great football team, probably the best of any we had there," Wood said. "I look back now and it's incredible how close we were to going unbeaten. That was an incredible football team. There won't be many like that one again."

Bud Lea, a former *Milwaukee Sentinel* writer, covered the Packers during that memorable season. Years later, Lea was still amazed what he witnessed in 1962.

"They were a veteran team that was loaded with talent," Lea said. "They were a machine, in the midst of a dynasty. And Bart Starr was the man at the controls."

Green Bay's only blemish was a 26–14 Thanksgiving Day loss to the Lions in Detroit that was broadcast to a nationwide audience.

However, it was the wake-up call the Packers needed.

Just four days earlier, Green Bay had defeated Baltimore 17–13 at City Stadium. But Lombardi was not pleased as the Colts outgained his team by 266 total yards.

The Packers carried a 10–0 record to Detroit that Thanksgiving and had out-scored their foes by an average of 23.5 points per game. The Lions had played Green Bay tough early in the season, though, and lost just 9–7.

Now, Detroit was anxious to prove it was the equal of the defending league champions.

The relentless Lions pass rush—led by Alex Karras and Roger Brown—over-whelmed the Green Bay offensive line, sacking Starr nine times. Detroit led 26–0 in the fourth quarter before the Packers rallied for two touchdowns to make the score respectable.

Lombardi addressed the media in the Tiger Stadium locker room and beat reporters were braced for a surly coach after the decisive defeat.

"We couldn't believe it," Lea said. "Vince was even laughing."

The perfectionist knew his team wasn't perfect and he did not publicly admon-ish them. Instead, he issued a challenge.

The overconfidence of his players was a reflection of Lombardi, who in the midst of writing a book, *Run to Daylight*, had allowed a television crew to film team meetings for a report on the making of an undefeated team.

"Let it be an example to all of us," Lombardi told his players, as cited in the book *When Pride Still Mattered*. "The Green Bay Packers are no better than anyone else when they aren't ready, when they play as individuals and not as one....Our greatest glory is not in never falling, but in rising every time we fall."

The Packers did not fall again, winning their next four games to repeat as NFL champions. They earned it the hard way, defeating the determined Giants in New York 16–7, a year after blowing them out 37–0 in Green Bay.

"We won every game but one, from preseason to the NFL championship," said former offensive tackle and head coach Forrest Gregg. "When I got home, my friends in Texas didn't say congratulations on winning another championship. They wanted to know what the hell happened on Thanksgiving Day against the Lions."

Starr, ever the gentleman, didn't want to call the 1962 team the best ever. But he knew just how special that group was.

"Thirteen-and-one and league champions," Starr said deliberately. "It's hard to compare teams from different eras. We were blessed with a great team that understood the teamwork concept—that together everyone accomplishes more. I was just fortunate to be part of such a tremendous group of players and coached by a great coach in Vince Lombardi. We put it all together in 1962."

Former tight end Ron Kramer, who played seven seasons in Green Bay, certainly agreed with Starr.

"That team was incredible," said Kramer. "Everybody was in their prime, everybody had a great year."

Starr said he's come to appreciate how Lombardi motivated that team—and Starr himself— after the Thanksgiving Day defeat.

"We rebounded quickly from that Lions loss," Starr said. "I keenly appreciate how he handled situations and circumstances. He took the pressure off us a little bit.

"Personally, he told me to step up after that game—which was one of my worst performances—and lead this team forward. And that's what I tried to do."

Starr had already stepped up in that 1962 season. He battled a torn abdominal muscle most of that season and hid the injury from his head coach.

Willie Davis said Lombardi knew exactly what buttons to push to motivate his players.

"Now Coach Lombardi had some great locker-room speeches," Davis said. "But that year he talked about the will to win, the will to succeed.

"He eased up after the Detroit loss, but he'd get pretty emotional when he talked and you could look at the faces of your teammates—like Forrest Gregg and Jerry Kramer—and they were getting emotional too. His words resonated with us.

"Of all the teams I was on, that '62 team handled adversity—injuries, distractions, the weather, whatever—the best. Nothing was going to stop us. We found a way to win the championship. We simply wouldn't be denied."

Afterward, Lombardi sent every player a letter. The legendary coach thanked his team for their mental toughness, applauded their character, and reminded them that there is no substitute for winning.

Then, in conclusion, Lombardi wrote that he was sending every player a color television.

"A color TV was big-time back in those days," said Norm Masters, an offensive tackle with the Packers from 1957 to 1964. "But really, that letter has meant a lot to me. I've used it many times in my life and I used so much of what coach Lombardi taught us.

"I'm one of the few guys who saved that letter. Even Vince Lombardi Jr. asked me once where I got it and I said, 'Your dad sent it out to the team.' It's really special to me."

Lombardi and the Packers were dealt a severe blow, though, before the 1963 season—and their quest for a third consecutive NFL title—even began.

Hornung and Detroit defensive lineman Alex Karras were suspended indefinitely by NFL commissioner Pete Rozelle for betting on NFL games.

Losing the versatile Hornung was a blow to the organization and Lombardi, who viewed the "Golden Boy" as a son. More bad news was to come.

After stumbling out of the gate with a 10–3 loss to visiting Chicago, the Packers won four straight. But in Green Bay's sixth game that season, it lost Starr to a broken hand during a blowout road win in St. Louis.

With their star quarterback sidelined for a month, Lombardi turned to backup John Roach for four games and picked up Zeke Bratkowski from the Los Angeles Rams on waivers.

When Bratkowski arrived at his Green Bay hotel after practice, Starr called him and invited him to come to his house and review game film. A bond was formed for life.

Bratkowski could have been a starter for many teams, but he knew his role in Green Bay: back up the franchise quarterback. And unlike his contentious relationship with the volatile McHan, Starr had both a mentor and a pupil.

Together, Starr and Bratkowski would take copious notes in meetings with Lombardi, absorbing all they could from the mind of the master. While there was a friendship, the relationship on the job was all business: they pushed each other in a positive manner in the best interests of the team.

"There was no ego involved," Bratkowski said. "It was all about the team. And that philosophy started with the head coach."

Roach was still the starter when Green Bay faced Chicago in a pivotal rematch for

Bart and Bratkowski

Theirs is a bond that transcends the sport of football.

Bart Starr and Zeke Bratkowski could have been rivals, both striving to be the starting quarterback of the Green Bay Packers. Instead, they became close teammates and lifelong friends, pushing each other to be prepared to implement head coach Vince Lombardi's meticulous game plan.

"The rings tarnish, the money has long been spent, but the relationships are everlasting," Bratkowski said. "You have these individual friendships. It's hard to explain to people.

"When I see my old teammates at golf outings or Packer functions we pick up just where we left off. Everyone still teases and gets on each other and has fun."

Bratkowski and his wife, Mary Elizabeth, have been best friends with Bart and Cherry Starr for more than five decades. The couples get together regularly at their respective homes or on vacation.

"Bart and Zeke are like brothers and Cherry and I are like sisters," Mary Elizabeth said. "It's been that way for all these years."

The Bratkowskis have visited the Starrs frequently as Bart has rehabilitated from health issues that began in the fall of 2014.

"It's not easy, but I see Bart progressing," Zeke said. "I treat him the same as always. I push him a little bit and I know progress comes slow. Like Coach Lombardi said, it's all about the team. And Bart's teammates are here for him now."

Starr and Bratkowski shared a singular focus after Bratkowski arrived in Green Bay during the middle of the 1963 season.

For a bargain waiver-wire price, Lombardi acquired Bratkowski from the Los Angeles Rams in one of the best personnel moves of his illustrious career.

For a $100 investment, Lombardi secured the experience and insurance policy at the team's most critical position for its unprecedented championship run from 1965 to 1967.

Bratkowski was never a full-time starter or league star in his seven-year career in Green Bay from 1963 to 1968, along with an emergency role in 1971.

The former University of Georgia All-American—who edged Starr out as the nation's top punter—was the designated backup to Starr, a future Pro Football Hall of Famer.

After the initial shock of being waived, Bratkowski was thrilled to depart the West Coast for the league's smallest city.

"The Rams were 2–5 and the Packers were 6–1," he said. "I couldn't wait to get packed. It changed my career."

A fresh start waited with the best team in the NFL.

"I knew my role on the team and I was Bart's backup," Bratkowski said. "I was excited to learn from Coach Lombardi and was a student of the game. Our quarterback meetings with him were all football, football, football."

(continued)

Bart and Bratkowski *(continued)*

Bratkowski's mental preparation and work ethic endeared him to Starr and quickly gained the respect of Lombardi.

"Part of my attention to detail was learned in flying school," Bratkowski said. "I was qualified in five airplanes and flying is all about procedures and backups and emergencies.

"I took a lot of notes in our meetings with Coach Lombardi and Bart and I studied together to go into each game based on what Coach Lombardi told us. We were well prepared and understood exactly what he wanted, which helped make us very successful."

Starr credited Bratkowski with helping him develop as a quarterback, as the teammates spent countless hours studying film.

"Zeke was more experienced than me and I learned a lot from him in those meetings," Starr said. "He was the consummate professional and we took a great deal of pride in working together."

Bratkowski's finest moment in his Green Bay tenure came in the 1965 Western Conference championship showdown against the Baltimore Colts at Lambeau Field. The rivals had finished the regular season deadlocked with 10–3–1 records, so a playoff game was required to determine a conference champion.

Starr was injured on the first play of the game, as Colts linebacker Don Shinnick scooped up a Bill Anderson fumble and rumbled 25 yards for a touchdown. Starr, in pursuit, was injured on the return.

"I was running across the field to make the tackle and took a shot in the back," said Starr, who broke a rib. "Typical of Zeke, he was uniquely prepared for the game and took over."

Enter Bratkowski, who stepped in and didn't miss a beat. It turned out to be a battle of NFL powerhouses missing their top quarterbacks, as injuries also sidelined Baltimore's Johnny Unitas (knee) and backup Gary Cuozzo (dislocated shoulder).

the Western Conference crown. The Bears won handily 26–7 at Wrigley Field. That loss would later cost Green Bay a chance to win a third straight NFL Championship.

Starr returned to the lineup on November 24 against San Francisco and the Packers rebounded with a 28–10 victory. Four days later, Green Bay tied Detroit 13–13 on Thanksgiving Day and closed out the season with two victories over the Los Angeles Rams and San Francisco on the West Coast.

Despite the Packers' impressive 11–2–1 record, Chicago won the division with an 11–1–2 mark. And back in 1963, only division winners qualified for the playoffs.

Green Bay's bid for a third straight title had ended. Instead, Chicago defeated the New York Giants 14–10 to win the title.

"That was a great Lombardi team, but missing Bart and Paul hurt them,"

Trailing 10–0 at intermission, Green Bay closed within 10–7 on Paul Hornung's 1-yard touchdown run in the third quarter. Bratkowski then engineered a fourth-quarter drive that ended with a game-tying field goal attempt by kicker Don Chandler with 1:58 remaining.

Starr, with his ribs heavily taped, was the holder for the 22-yard attempt. Chandler's boot sailed over the right upright and was ruled good by the officials. Baltimore players and coaches vehemently claimed it was wide right by several feet.

The controversial kick had rule-changing ramifications, as the NFL raised the uprights to 20 feet for the 1966 season.

The 10–10 deadlock went into sudden-death overtime—the first in Green Bay history—and was ended by another Chandler field goal from 25 yards at the 13:39 mark. Bratkowski was one of several Packers standouts that day, completing 22 of 39 passes for 248 yards against a veteran and talented Colts defense.

"We didn't miss a beat with Zeke in there," Starr said. "It was a clutch, clutch performance and Zeke played exceptionally well against a strong Baltimore team."

Bratkowski was lauded as a "Super Sub," and the victory propelled Green Bay to the NFL Championship against the Cleveland Browns and the first of an unprecedented three consecutive titles.

"Winning three straight championships is just so difficult to do—that's something we're very proud of," Bratkowski said. "My responsibility was very clear: to keep up our high level of play when called upon. It wasn't about individuals, everything was about the team.

"That's why Bart and I worked so hard and prepared so diligently. Coach Lombardi always said we didn't have the best players, but we had the best team."

Ditka said. "We won the NFL championship in 1963. If you want to be the best, you have to beat the best. And we beat the Green Bay Packers twice that season."

Hornung returned in 1964, but Green Bay finished a disappointing 8–5–1 and finished a distant second in the Western Division. Baltimore cruised to a 12–2 season and the NFL title game, while the Packers were doomed by a 3–4 start.

The Packers suffered a bevy of narrow defeats that eventually sealed their fate.

Baltimore won in Green Bay 21–20 in Week 2. Minnesota won in Green Bay 24–23 in Week 4. And the Packers lost at Baltimore 24–21 in Week 6.

The Packers, one of football's most dominant home teams in recent seasons, finished with a 4–3 mark on Wisconsin soil (Green Bay/Milwaukee) and were 4–2–1 on the road.

Starr was knocked cold and out of a late-season game in San Francisco. But Starr showed his toughness by returning the following week and directing the Packers to a 28–21 upset of the eventual NFL champion Cleveland Browns in Milwaukee.

Starr showed his savvy and ability to gamble at the perfect time during Green Bay's win over Cleveland.

Starr audibled out of a run play on fourth-and-1 from his own 44-yard line. Instead, Starr faked to Taylor, held the linebackers, and hit Max McGee with a perfect strike over the middle and a 55-yard gain to the 1-yard line that set up Jim Taylor's game-tying touchdown in the third quarter.

Lombardi lauded Starr's gutsy call in the media, and the quarterback explained how the element of surprise worked in his favor.

"I've called it on fourth down before, but never from that far out," Starr said.

The low-key Starr continued to play in the shadow of players like Baltimore's Unitas. But Starr was far more than just a game manager himself.

For the second time in three years, Starr led the NFL in passing percentage, completing 163 of 272 passes (59.9 percent) for 2,144 yards and 15 touchdowns.

Starr also threw just four interceptions, giving him an impressive quarterback rating of 97.1.

"I admired Johnny Unitas," said Starr, who studied film of Unitas to improve his own play. "He was a great player who was my hero, my rival, and then a great friend."

In a frustrating season that ended with a 24–17 loss to St. Louis in the meaningless "Playoff Bowl," Starr finally learned not to dwell on negatives when he threw a crucial interception or the team lost a big game.

"We all make mistakes and you have to move on," Starr said. "It was a turning point in my career."

There is no doubt the Packers were a run-first team in a run-oriented league.

But with Taylor and Hornung beginning to age and their productivity diminishing, Starr was called upon to carry more of the offensive load in 1965.

At the peak of his game mentally and physically, Starr delivered.

The Packers went 10–3–1 that year and eventually won their first of an unprecedented three straight NFL titles in the playoff era. Starr worked his way out of a midyear mini-slump to complete 55.8 percent of his 251 passes for 2,055 yards and 16 touchdowns.

Starr also threw nine interceptions to finish with an 89.0 quarterback rating.

Starr, never known for his scrambling ability, also hurt opponents with his legs in 1965. He rushed 18 times for 169 yards—a 9.4 yard average—with a long burst of 38.

"Many (scrambles) in my career were not very pretty," Starr joked. "I didn't have the running ability of a Brett Favre or Aaron Rodgers."

Green Bay began that season with six straight wins, then dropped consecutive games to Chicago and Detroit. The Packers rebounded with two straight wins and moved to 8–2. But Green Bay's lackluster play in a 21–10 loss to the last-place Los Angeles Rams in late November was too much for Lombardi to bear.

"He went off on us in a team meeting, telling us that we didn't care if we won or lost," Forrest Gregg said. "We wanted to win just as bad as he did."

Gregg jumped up first to challenge Lombardi's statement, then Starr, and others.

"Like everything he did, Coach Lombardi had a purpose," Starr said. "He challenged our very being. He knew we could fall into a slump again and he wasn't going to let that happen."

Green Bay won its next two games, but tied the 49ers in San Francisco in the season finale. That left the Packers and Colts with identical 10–3–1 records.

A playoff game was necessary and the Baltimore Colts traveled to Green Bay the following Sunday for the Western Conference title.

Lombardi's $100 waiver investment in picking up Bratkowski proved to be genius.

Starr was injured on the Packers' first play from scrimmage. Baltimore linebacker Don Shinnick recovered a Bill Anderson fumble and returned it 25 yards for a 7–0 Colts lead. A pursing Starr took a shot to the ribs on the return.

"I was running across the field to make the tackle and took a shot in the back," Starr said. "Typical of Zeke, he was uniquely prepared for the game and took over."

Bratkowski brought the Packers back to tie the game 10–10 in the fourth quarter on Don Chandler's controversial 22-yard field goal. A heavily taped Starr entered the game to hold for the attempt.

The kick flew high above the right upright and Chandler's initial body language indicated he missed the attempt. But referee Jim Tunney, who was standing directly under the goal post, said the kick was good.

"The kick went down the middle, but the wind was blowing," Tunney said years later. "I was the only official standing under the goal post and it went over the crossbar, and then after it crossed, from the kicker's standpoint, the wind blew it past the right post. In those days, the posts were only 10 feet above the crossbar, so I drew an imaginary line up that side."

To this day, the Colts still insist the kick was wide right. But Chandler, who died in 2011, claimed the kick was good for one reason and one alone.

"Bart said it was good and Bart never lied," Chandler said.

After that season, the NFL raised goalposts from 10 feet to 20 feet so officials could make clearer judgments on similar kicks. On this day, though, all that mattered was Tunney called the kick good—and Bratkowski was up to the challenge of replacing Starr.

"We didn't miss a beat with Zeke in there," Starr said. "It was a clutch, clutch performance."

Chandler drilled a 25-yard field goal in overtime to lift the Packers to a 13–10 win. Afterward, Baltimore coach Don Shula and his team were livid about Chandler's kick that forced overtime.

But the Packers were back in the NFL Championship Game and set to face Hall of Fame running back Jim Brown and the Cleveland Browns.

Throughout the week, Starr's status was a hot-button topic. Starr couldn't lift his arm very high and was experiencing extreme pain. His status would be a game-day decision.

Nearly five inches of wet, heavy snow blanketed Green Bay and Lambeau Field on the morning of January 2, 1965. Simply getting to the stadium for the 1:10 PM kickoff proved challenging for fans and some players.

The Browns' team bus took triple the time to travel down Hwy. 41 north from Appleton to newly renamed Lambeau Field, in honor of Green Bay's founder, player, and head coach who had died the past summer.

When Starr arrived at the stadium, his ribs were heavily taped by trainers and he was given shots to numb the pain. Bratkowski was ready to play if called on, but there was no way Starr was missing an NFL Championship Game.

Starr's mental toughness allowed him to overcome the physical pain. Starr knew that his father—in the stands with his mother and wife—would be proud.

The Packers drew first blood on their opening drive when Starr and Carroll Dale connected for a 47-yard touchdown and a 7–0 lead.

"Cleveland's defensive backs were playing snug," Dale recalled. "I told Bart in the huddle, 'They're playing me tight.'

"He called a deep pass. It was one of those underthrown balls, and I was able to come back and get the pass, while the (defensive) back fell down in the mud, and I got in the end zone. The conditions had something to do with everything that day."

Starr, who drew postgame praise from Cleveland coaches and players for his play-calling and intelligence, gave an honest assessment of the play.

"I didn't throw it like that on purpose," said Starr, who completed 10 of 18 passes for 147 yards with one interception that day. "I didn't have a Brett Favre–type arm. The football was wet and underthrown, and Carroll made a great adjustment to the ball and took it in for a touchdown."

Cleveland responded by taking a 9–7 advantage entering the second quarter after a 17-yard touchdown pass from quarterback Frank Ryan to Gary Collins (the PAT failed) and a 24-yard field goal by Lou Groza.

"The game was tight in the first half," said Dale, whose team led 13–12 at halftime. "With Groza kicking and Jim Brown running, they were always close."

Green Bay's tandem of Hornung and Taylor made the difference in the second half.

The duo combined for 201 yards for the game, with Taylor pounding the middle of the Browns' line for 96 hard-earned yards on 27 carries, while Hornung amassed 105 yards on 18 attempts.

Green Bay's defense did what no other team could in the 1965 season, limiting the sensational Brown to just 50 yards on 12 carries.

Hornung's 13-yard touchdown run in the third quarter was the epitome of the Lombardi sweep and increased Green Bay's lead to 20–12.

Hornung perfectly followed the lead blocks of guards Kramer and Thurston and ran nearly untouched into the end zone as a light rain and snow turned the Lambeau Field turf into a quagmire.

"It was Lombardi/Packer football at its best," former team historian Lee Remmel said. "Basic, fundamental, mistake-free. From a performance and execution standpoint, it was the kind of football he preached here.

"Bart Starr was always at his best in the big games and the weather was perfect for Hornung and Taylor. They're 'mudders.' The Packers came from behind, and as the game wore on, they controlled the line of scrimmage, which carried the day."

The Packers defense, which held the high-powered Browns offense scoreless in the second half and to 161 yards and eight first downs in the game, made two big stops in the third quarter.

Chandler added a 29-yard field goal in the fourth quarter to account for the 23–12 final margin and Herb Adderley intercepted Ryan's pass on the first play of Cleveland's last drive.

As the final gun sounded, Hornung and Taylor carried Lombardi off the field. Hundreds of Packer fans tore down the goal posts, reveling in the franchise's return to championship glory.

"Vince was obsessed with winning three in a row," Lea said. "The Packers didn't do it in '63 with Hornung being suspended. Winning the championship in 1965 was the first of the three."

Starr said winning the championship in adverse conditions was an extra challenge.

"That's what makes this game so great," he said. "It's the ultimate team sport, played outdoors in all weather. It tests you. You have to have the physical prowess to play the game, but also the mental toughness to win. That's what makes the difference."

For veterans like Kramer, in his eighth season, the victory was especially sweet.

"It was a sloppy, muddy day—a lineman's kind of day, my kind of day," Kramer said. "And it was very satisfying, as it had been a couple of years to get the championship crown back on our heads."

The crown was Green Bay's third in five years—the first time that had been accomplished since the Bears did it from 1940 to 1943.

Lombardi paid his newest championship team a high compliment.

"This team has more character than any other team I've had," he said. "This may not be the best team I've had, but it has the most character."

In 1966, Bart Starr was named the Most Valuable Player of the National Football League. It had taken 10 years, but Starr had finally earned national recognition as an elite quarterback, the top player in professional football.

Always the consummate team player, Starr thought the MVP award reflected the quality of the team and should be shared by every member.

"It's not about the individual, it's about the team," Starr said. "I'm honored, but it's about the Green Bay Packers."

Starr led the NFL in passer rating (105.0), completion percentage (62.2), and fewest interceptions thrown (three) that year. He also completed 156 of 251 passes for 2,257 yards and 14 touchdowns, and averaged an amazing 9.0 yards per pass.

On the ground, Starr ran 21 times for 104 yards (5.0 average) with two touchdowns.

Quarterbacks such as Sonny Jurgensen of Washington threw for more yards and Frank Ryan of Cleveland tossed 29 touchdowns. But Starr took home the league's most coveted individual honor.

"I thought Bart was a very crisp passer and could get out of trouble quite well," said former Packers general manager Ron Wolf, who was a scout for the Oakland Raiders during the second half of Starr's career. "I don't think he threw the ball that much or as much as he could have. But I thought Bart was outstanding at what he was asked to do."

Starr's efficiency, leadership, toughness, and cerebral approach helped the Packers go 12–2 in 1966.

In the week leading up to the 1966 NFL Championship game against the Dallas Cowboys, Lombardi was remarkably uptight.

The pressures of the impending title contest—and what loomed beyond—had the veteran Green Bay head coach ornery and impatient.

For the first time, the winner of the NFL championship contest would face the American Football League champion to determine the world champion of professional football.

To escape the cold and snow of Wisconsin, Lombardi took his team to Tulsa, Oklahoma, to practice and prepare for the showdown with the Cowboys. Unfortunately, the same weather greeted the Packers in Oklahoma, forcing the team to practice once in the city's expo center with a low roof and slippery floor.

Another unexpected distraction occurred when a *Dallas Times Herald* reporter said Lombardi told him after a practice session in Tulsa that he was pondering retirement.

The eighth-year Packers coach and general manager had to assure the national media he had "no intention of quitting" as his team prepared for a possible fourth NFL championship in six seasons.

Lombardi's veteran Green Bay squad was favored to defeat a young and hungry Dallas team. The Cowboys were coached by Tom Landry, who had been an assistant with Lombardi on the New York Giants staff one decade earlier.

It wasn't until the Friday evening before the game in a Dallas hotel room at his traditional "Five O'Clock Club" that Lombardi finally lightened up. And it took a crisp afternoon practice at a local high school field for Lombardi to finally feel good.

The Five O'Clock Club was a Lombardi ritual during training camp and road trips, where friends and the media gathered in his hotel suite to share a drink and conversation.

"Lombardi was a nervous wreck all week with the pressure to win," Lea said. "The Tulsa trip didn't work out at all like he planned and he wasn't too happy about it. But Vince was smiling and loose at the happy hour party, but he was extremely nervous matching wits with Tom Landry.

"Lombardi said, 'The hay is in the barn. The team is ready, and if they play their best and lose, there's nothing I can do now to change anything.'"

The championship game would be an entertaining and dramatic matchup that came down to one final play. And the Cotton Bowl crowd of 74,152 on that sunny New Year's Day afternoon witnessed a classic.

Green Bay built a 14–0 lead during a 12-second span in the first five minutes of the contest.

Starr, who would have one of his finest games as a professional with a 304-yard, four-touchdown performance, opened the scoring with a 17-yard pass to halfback Elijah Pitts.

On the ensuing kickoff, returner Mel Renfro fumbled and promising rookie fullback Jim Grabowski picked up the ball and ran 18 yards for the score.

After Don Chandler's second extra point, the rest of the first period belonged to the Cowboys.

Don Meredith, Dallas' talented young quarterback, led two scoring drives to tie the game 14–14.

"We had immense respect for the Dallas Cowboys," Starr said. "They were an excellent team.

"A perfect example was how quickly they regrouped and tied up the game after falling behind. However, we were also confident in our abilities. Coach Lombardi had an excellent game plan and we felt we could be successful in the passing game and by running out of different formations against their flex defense."

Carroll Dale caught a 51-yard pass from Starr to break the tie and Green Bay had a 21–17 lead going into halftime.

The Cowboys closed within 21–20 early in the third quarter, but Starr methodically began to pick apart the Dallas secondary. Starr threw touchdown passes of 16 yards to Boyd Dowler in the third quarter and 28 yards to Max McGee in the fourth to give Green Bay a 34–20 lead and some breathing room.

But Chandler's final extra point was blocked, keeping Green Bay's lead at two scores in an era before two-point conversions. And that seemed to give the Cowboys new life.

Meredith burned the Green Bay defense on third-and-20 with a 68-yard scoring pass to tight end Frank Clarke, a Beloit, Wisconsin, native. Dallas had closed within 34–27 and the boisterous sellout crowd was now back into the game.

The Cowboys defense held and forced a 16-yard punt by Chandler that gave Dallas excellent field position at the Green Bay 47-yard line with 2:50 left.

Meredith drove the team down the field and an interference penalty on safety Tom Brown gave the Cowboys a first down at the Packers' 2-yard line.

On first down, Reeves gained one yard. On second down, though, left tackle Jim Boeke was penalized for a false start, pushing the ball back to the Green Bay 6-yard line.

"When we were leading 34–27 and Dallas had a first down on the 2-yard line, we were terrified," McGee said in Lea's book, *The Magnificent Seven*.

"There was nothing we could do but pray. We hadn't stopped the Cowboys all afternoon…Dallas had the momentum and we were emotionally exhausted. Then somebody in the Cowboys line jumped offside and we were saved."

Meredith's screen pass fell incomplete on second down, and a third-down throw to tight end Pettis Norman gained four yards.

It was do or die. Fourth-and-goal from the 2-yard line with less than one minute remaining.

"Like everyone else, I was very tense on the sidelines as the Cowboys were about to run that play," Starr said. "The blocked extra point, you don't think that thing came into play? Holy cow, if we had made that extra point, we'd have a whole different perspective on that last drive."

Meredith rolled out to his right, but linebacker Dave Robinson broke through and had the Dallas quarterback in his grasp. Meredith's only hope was to throw a desperation pass into the end zone towards Bob "Bullet" Hayes.

It never had a chance, though, and was easily intercepted by Brown, who redeemed himself and preserved the Green Bay win.

"That's probably the play I'll always be best known for…and that's great," Brown said. "We had so many big plays and so many great players. But that was probably my shining moment."

A second straight title was accomplished, but a new challenge remained: the NFL-AFL World Championship Game, better known as Super Bowl I.

Tickets that afternoon for Green Bay's game against AFL champion Kansas City went for $12. More than one-third of Los Angeles' Memorial Coliseum sat empty. And both CBS and NBC carried television rights to the game.

"We had no idea how big of a game that would become," former Packer Willie Davis said. "None whatsoever. Who could have ever predicted it?"

The pressure on Lombardi and his team was immense to uphold the reputation of the established NFL against the upstart AFL. Through the intense media hype, Lombardi did his best to keep his team focused, sequestering his team in Santa Barbara, away from the trappings of Los Angeles.

"Vince made it very clear from our first day out there that we had to win that game," Red Cochran, Lombardi's offensive assistant, said in the best-selling book *When Pride Still Mattered*. "And he didn't want to make a squeaker out of it."

Starr again showed why he will go down as one of the greatest performers in big games, earning MVP honors in the Packers' 35–10 triumph.

Starr threw two touchdown passes to McGee, who came off the bench to replace an injured Dowler and into Super Bowl lore after a night on the town. Starr ran into McGee in the team lobby as he returned to the hotel about 7:30 on game day morning.

Starr was his efficient self, completing 16 of 23 passes for 250 yards and averaging 10.9 yards per pass as Green Bay pulled away from a 14–10 halftime lead.

When presented with the keys to his MVP Corvette convertible, Starr humbly received the award on behalf of his team.

"I accept this on behalf of the other 39 members of the Green Bay Packers," Starr said. "It may sound corny to some, and I don't care if it does. At Green Bay we eat, cry, and live as 40 people. Any award or acclaim for an individual comes from the effort of all 40 players plus the coaches and it's in that spirit that I receive this honor."

While Starr won the MVP, McGee certainly made greater headlines.

McGee, an aging and little-used wide receiver, had just four receptions all season. But when Dowler went down on the Packers' first series, McGee stepped up and caught seven passes for 138 yards and two touchdowns.

What made McGee's heroics even more impressive was that he was operating on virtually no sleep. The night before the game, McGee risked the $15,000 fine and sneaked out of his hotel room to meet up with two stewardesses he'd met earlier that day.

"I was rooming with Hornung and Hornung didn't want to risk going out because the fine was the same as our game check was going to be," McGee said during an interview shortly before his death in 2007. "But when (bed checker Dave Hanner) stuck his head in, I said, 'Are you going to be checking late?' He screamed, 'You damned right I am.' Then he stuck his head back in and shook it no. Well, I almost ran him over trying to get out."

The Chiefs had to be wishing McGee would have never come back. His 37-yard touchdown from Starr in the first quarter was a brilliant one-handed grab that gave Green Bay an early 7–0 lead.

"I was so surprised that I expected to open my other hand and find a silver dollar," McGee told reporters after the game.

Then, late in the third quarter, McGee hauled in a 13-yard touchdown strike to give Green Bay a commanding 28–10 lead. McGee did most of his damage on Kansas City cornerback Willie Mitchell, whom the Packers planned to attack from the get-go.

"It was our plan to throw a lot to the receiver on the weak side," McGee said after the game. "I just happened to be the one."

McGee and Starr weren't the only heroes.

Green Bay led just 14–10 at halftime and Lombardi was livid. The Packers had allowed Chiefs quarterback Len Dawson to scramble around and keep his team in the game.

But on Kansas City's first possession of the second half, right linebacker Lee Roy Caffey deflected a Dawson pass that Willie Wood intercepted. The Packers safety rumbled to the Chiefs' 5-yard line and Elijah Pitts scored on the next play.

Green Bay rolled from there, outscoring the Chiefs 21–0 after intermission.

The Packers finished the game with a 358–239 edge in total yards and converted 73.3 percent of their third downs (11-of-15).

"I was disturbed in the first half," Starr said. "We weren't moving the ball at all. Then we settled down and did just what we were supposed to do—get out there and win the ballgame."

The victory was a relief to Lombardi, who certainly wanted to prove his league was the best. And afterward, he could boast that it was.

"Kansas City has a real top team," Lombardi said. "But I don't think it compares with the top teams in the National Football League."

Kansas City owner Lamar Hunt, a major force in the merger of the two leagues, said: "I'm disappointed. I told somebody they didn't keep the time right. The first half didn't run long enough and the second half ran too long."

For McGee and the Packers, though, things ran just right.

"After I had scored those two touchdowns, Hornung came over to me and said, 'You're going to be the MVP,'" McGee said. "Well I wasn't. But it was a heck of a game."

With the Super Bowl television audience and ensuing coverage, Starr became a national hero to a generation of football fans outside Wisconsin borders. There was one blemish.

Starr was named to his fourth and final Pro Bowl that season. But Rams head coach George Allen—who was also leading the Western Conference All-Stars—named Unitas as his starting quarterback.

The slight understandably irked and hurt Starr, but he handled it like a professional throughout the week.

Cherry Starr ran into Allen in the lobby of the team hotel as she was checking out on the morning of the game. Allen assured her that he was starting Unitas because of Starr's extended season.

"I told him that Bart or I don't hold a grudge and we liked him very much," Cherry said with a laugh. "But I want you to know, Bart has a memory like an elephant."

Starr and the Packers headed to the 1967 season with a giant target firmly affixed to their backs.

Green Bay was aiming for NFL immortality. The rest of the league was hell-bent on making sure that didn't happen.

"It was a very challenging season for us," said Starr, who suffered thumb and rib injuries in the preseason and did not throw his first touchdown pass until Week 6. "We faced a lot of adversity throughout the year with injuries. Every opponent wanted a little extra piece of us as the defending champions."

Hornung and Taylor were gone, as the Packers had elected to go younger at the running back position. But replacements Jim Grabowski (knee) and Elijah Pitts (Achilles tendon) both suffered major injuries.

Lombardi was forced to pick up Chuck Mercein and Ben Wilson to fill the void at fullback. And the Packers offense struggled throughout the season.

Making it to Miami to defend their Super Bowl championship was an arduous task for Lombardi and his aging Green Bay squad.

Green Bay went 9–4–1 during the regular season and won the newly created NFL Central Division—comprised of Green Bay, Chicago, Detroit, and Minnesota. Still, the Packers entered the postseason with consecutive losses to Los Angeles and Pittsburgh, casting doubt if they could complete their mission.

But the veteran Packers put it together in postseason play, when it mattered most.

The Packers defeated the 11–1–2 Rams in Milwaukee with relative ease 28–7 in its first playoff game. Green Bay advanced to the NFL Championship Game against Dallas, a contest that would stamp a dynasty and go down as arguably the greatest game in NFL history.

The temperature at kickoff was 13 degrees below zero and minus-46 with the wind chill. The game was played on a sheet of ice after the field's $80,000 heating system broke—or was turned off by Packers coach Vince Lombardi, as some believe.

The referees' whistles froze. One fan died due to exposure and several others were treated for frostbite.

Making it even worse, Lombardi wouldn't allow anyone except linemen to wear gloves.

Immediately afterward, the game was dubbed "The Ice Bowl."

"The Ice Bowl was just incredible," said former linebacker Jim Flanigan, a rookie that season. "Lombardi wouldn't let you wear gloves, and we had cut-off longjohns and just regular shirts and T-shirts.

"But once you're cold, you're cold. We'd come back to the sidelines and warm up by the space heaters. But I've never been through anything like it."

No one who competed that day was ever part of something like it again. Yet the league had no intention of ever halting the game, which appeared to be a good thing for Green Bay early on.

Dowler, an unsung hero in the contest with four catches for 77 yards, caught touchdown passes of 8 and 46 yards for an early 14–0 Packers lead.

"My first touchdown was an audible by Bart," Dowler said. "He won't tell you all that stuff, but I will. He was the main reason we won the game."

The talented Dallas team, still stinging from a bitter loss to Green Bay on the final play of the title contest a year earlier, fought its way back into the game.

The Cowboys defense ignited the comeback, forcing a Starr fumble that was returned seven yards by lineman George Andrie for a touchdown in the second quarter. Danny Villanueva drilled a 21-yard field goal just before intermission to trim the Packers' lead to 14–10.

After a scoreless third quarter, Dallas took the lead early in the fourth quarter on a halfback option that completely fooled the Green Bay secondary, which had come up to defend the run.

Halfback Dan Reeves fired an option pass to a wide-open Lance Rentzel on a 50-yard play for a 17–14 Cowboys lead. Green Bay was stymied on its first two possessions of the final quarter, but made the last one count.

The all-or-nothing drive began at the Packers' 32-yard line with 4:54 left in the game.

"We believed in Bart," Forrest Gregg said. "And I never saw him perform better than on that drive, when it counted the most."

Dowler added: "Looking back, every call Bart made was perfect. It's not like today when coaches call the plays in a headset. We just took that kind of (performance) from Bart for granted."

In nine plays, Green Bay was poised at the doorstep of the Dallas end zone. First and goal at the 1-yard line. Two rushes by halfback Donny Anderson on the icy turf gained nothing.

Starr called the Packers' final time out and conferred with Lombardi. There was no talk of a game-tying field goal. They were going for the win.

A wedge play was called, but Starr kept the ball himself instead of handing off to Chuck Mercein.

Starr snuck through an alley created by the blocks of guard Jerry Kramer and center Ken Bowman. That duo teamed to push back 6'6", 260-pound defensive tackle Jethro Pugh several yards into the end zone.

Starr crossed the goal line.

Green Bay prevailed 21–17.

"I looked around and saw Bart tumbling into the end zone," Kramer said.

"There wasn't any wild celebration. It was like, 'Whew, we got the job done.' It was a sense of relief.

"I felt a great responsibility because I had suggested that wedge play on Jethro during our film session on the Thursday before the game. I said to Coach Lombardi, 'I think we can wedge Pugh if we have to, he's a little high (coming out of his stance near the goal line).'

"Red Cochran ran the film back a couple times, and Lombardi put it on the short-yardage list. I certainly didn't think the play would come up in the situation it did."

The touchdown triggered a wild celebration at Lambeau Field. Delirious and frozen fans stormed the field and once again tore down the goal posts.

Dallas head coach Tom Landry said the risky quarterback sneak call surprised him.

"If it had failed, they were lost," the Dallas head coach said. "There's no way they could have gotten off another play."

Former defensive end Willie Davis could not bring himself to watch.

"I never saw Bart's sneak until later on television," Davis said. "I was looking up in the stands. I thought if this was going to be the end of the run, I didn't want to see it. What made me realize something pretty great had happened was when I saw the fans go up in arms.

"It was an experience, a game I'll never forget. I still feel the effects of the frostbite on the three fingers on my right hand that I put on that frozen ground in my stance."

The Drive

The greatest game in Green Bay Packers history was decided and defined by a final dramatic drive. A drive that culminated with arguably the most memorable play in NFL history: Bart Starr's quarterback sneak into Lambeau Field's south end zone.

The touchdown with 13 seconds remaining lifted the Packers to a 21–17 win over the Dallas Cowboys for the 1967 NFL Championship. When the Packers won Super Bowl II two weeks later, Green Bay achieved NFL immortality with its third consecutive title.

The game-time temperature was 13 degrees below zero that afternoon and a ridiculous minus-46 with the wind chill.

Steve Sabol, former president of NFL Films, had a sideline view of the historic contest, filming the game with his father, Ed.

(continued)

The Drive *(continued)*

"I think it's the greatest football game of all time," Sabol said in a 2008 interview. "The game conditions, the back and forth, the competitiveness, the high level of play, the dramatic ending, a third straight championship…and that final drive. It was something to witness."

Former guard Jerry Kramer called it a flawless drive, a 68-yard march in 12 plays that perfectly illustrated the teamwork and precision of the team under head coach Vince Lombardi.

"We weren't moving the ball too well in the second half," Kramer said. "But we knew what we had to do on that last drive. And Bart was calling the plays."

The game-winning march engineered by Starr was even more impressive considering the Packers offense had been stymied in the second half—by both the Dallas defense and the bitter cold.

In the third quarter, Green Bay had three possessions that resulted in minus-1, 13, and minus-2 yards. The Packers did no better in the fourth quarter, losing five yards in four plays on their first possession before gaining 20 yards in four plays on their next attempt.

Green Bay trailed 17–14 as it huddled at its own 32-yard line with 4:54 remaining. Starr did not have to utter a syllable to motivate his teammates. He knew.

"It was not necessary for me to say a word," Starr said. "When I looked in their eyes, there was a look of confidence and, 'Let's call the plays and go get this done.'"

On the first play, Starr threw for six yards to Donny Anderson in the right flat. Fullback Chuck Mercein then bolted seven yards around right end for a first down at the 45.

Starr went back to the air to keep the Cowboys off balance, targeting Boyd Dowler for 13 yards over the middle as the drive gained momentum. The march was halted momentarily as defensive end Willie Townes burst through the line to tackle Donny Anderson for a 9-yard loss on the next play.

Facing second-and-19 from the Green Bay 49-yard line, Starr hit Anderson with passes of 12 and 9 yards—both in the right flat—for a crucial first down.

Thirty-nine yards now separated the Packers from the Cowboys' end zone and their mission for championship trifecta. One minute, 35 seconds remained.

Mercein turned a short pass into a 19-yard gain, down to the Dallas 11.

Then came what Starr termed "the best call of my career." The Packer quarterback had been saving this play for right situation—and the time was now.

Mercein shot up the middle for 8 yards on a trap play that took the Packers to the Dallas 3-yard line with 54 seconds left. The play worked because Cowboys defensive tackle Bob Lilly pursued down the line of scrimmage to stop the Packer sweep he had anticipated.

Lilly's greatest strengths were his quickness and pursuit. But thanks to intense film study, Starr used those skills against Lilly.

"We called it a 'Give' play because Coach Lombardi didn't like to call it a 'sucker' play," Starr said.

"Our left guard, Gale Gillingham, pulled and followed him wide. (Defensive end) George Andrie slid down to close the hole, but Bob Skoronski made a great block on him and Chuck had a big hole."

Mercein, a former New York Giants castoff signed by Lombardi late in the season, accounted for 34 yards on the drive. While Mercein lacked speed, his plodding and no-frills running style was ideally suited to the slippery field.

"There were many heroes on that last drive," former team historian Lee Remmel once stated. "Chuck Mercein was one of them. He was a very big factor on that drive and in that game. Bart had confidence in him and used him effectively."

Anderson had the next three attempts at the end zone, but was denied by the icy surface and a stiff Cowboys defense.

On Anderson's first attempt, he gained two yards to the 1 for a first down. On the second, the Dallas defenders stuffed Anderson for no gain. On the third, he slipped after receiving the handoff from Starr, nearly fumbling the football.

It was now third and goal. Sixteen seconds remained. Starr then called Green Bay's final timeout.

"When I called the final timeout, I asked the linemen if they could get their footing for a wedge play, which was our main short-yardage play," Starr said. "That play had worked well for us twice, for a minimum of two yards, earlier in the game."

Starr jogged to the sideline and spoke to Lombardi.

"There was nothing wrong with the play," Starr said. "But the backs are slipping and can't get to the line of scrimmage. I said, 'I'm upright and can just shuffle my feet and lunge in there.'"

Lombardi had a blunt response—and no thoughts of kicking a game-tying field goal to extend the contest any longer. It was all or nothing.

"All he said was, 'Then run it and let's get the hell out of here,'" Starr said. "It was just so typical of this man. It's so bitter cold and it's down to our last play. He was blunt and right to the point."

Starr was chuckling as he ran back to the huddle and called the play: "Brown Right 31 Wedge."

The offensive unit thought Mercein would be carrying the ball. No one was more surprised than the Packer fullback when he did not receive it.

"I knew the play was for me, so I was pretty excited," Mercein said. "I had a few big runs and a pass reception on the drive, and they gave it to Donny twice down by the goal line. So I thought it was my turn to put that cherry on top of the sundae.'"

Another plan was in place, and Mercein only cared that it resulted in a touchdown.

"It just goes to show you how smart Bart Starr is," Mercein said. "The prudent thing to do was not take a chance that I would slip. He took all those potentially disastrous things out of the equation. There was no need to tell me I wasn't going to get the ball."

Starr improvised and the gamble paid off. The rest is history.

Without question, the Ice Bowl is the greatest game in franchise history. Many also consider it the greatest game in NFL history.

And Starr's touchdown remains one of the signature plays in NFL history.

"It's become the trademark of the Green Bay Packers, kind of a franchise play," said former center Ken Bowman. "The funny part is, we were just young football players playing a game we loved to play. No one knew how historic this game, and that play, would become."

After Green Bay's dramatic victory over Dallas, it entered Super Bowl II as a heavy favorite. But a distraction awaited.

Rumors swirled throughout the NFL that this game would be Lombardi's last on the Packers' sideline. The media asked Lombardi all week about his coaching future, and it reached a peak at the press conference on Friday.

"I'm not sure I have the answer myself," Lombardi told reporters. "This is not the proper time to make such a decision. I've got a game to play. I'm exhausted. I'm tired. It's the wrong time to make any decision."

Starr observed: "At the time, none of us knew for certain it would be his last game. There may have been an underneath feeling, but our focus was on the Raiders."

The Orange Bowl in Miami was filled to capacity for Super Bowl II, a stark contrast to half-empty Los Angeles Coliseum in Super Bowl I.

A similar script unfolded in this contest.

Green Bay led 6–0 early in the second quarter when Starr and Boyd Dowler hooked up on a 62-yard touchdown. Dowler beat the initial jam of cornerback Kent McCloughan, caught Starr's pass 20 yards downfield, then outran safety Rodger Bird to the end zone to make it 13–0.

The Raiders answered with a 78-yard scoring drive and pulled within 13–7 after Daryle Lamonica's 23-yard touchdown pass to Bill Miller. Then came the turning point.

The Oakland defense forced a Green Bay punt, but the Raiders' Bird fumbled the fair catch of Donny Anderson's left-footed spiral and the Packers recovered at the Oakland 45-yard line.

Green Bay capitalized as Chandler nailed his third field goal of the half, a 43-yarder with just six seconds remaining before halftime.

From Oakland's perspective, a 16–7 deficit at intermission was acceptable.

"The first half was pretty even—we were in the game," said Wolf, who was working for the Raiders during that game. "We got that huge stop and forced them to punt. We should have had great field position, but Bird fumbled and then Chandler kicks a field goal to put them up 16–7. That was huge, because it was all downhill after that."

The second half belonged to Green Bay, and a major source of motivation for the Packers was Lombardi.

"We decided to play the final 30 minutes for the old man," Kramer said. "We loved him and didn't want to let him down."

The Packers performed like the champions they were, with precision and purpose, and blew the game open in the third quarter.

Starr executed one of his patented third-and-1 passes to McGee, who was playing in his career finale. The play went for 35 yards and Anderson capped the drive off with a 2-yard touchdown run.

Green Bay led 23–7 but received a fortunate bounce to make it 26–7 late in the third quarter as Chandler's fourth field goal from 31 yards hit the crossbar and bounced over.

Green Bay's defense added the finishing blow in the fourth quarter, as cornerback Herb Adderley intercepted a Lamonica pass and raced 60 yards for a touchdown.

"You can't get better than that," Adderley said years later of his Super Bowl interception. "That was such a great time and a great group of men. But that game was kind of the end of our run."

When it was over, the Packers had prevailed 33–14 and captured a remarkable third straight World Championship.

"Not everything came as easy that year as maybe it did in some past years," Dowler said. "I think we had to work a lot harder that season than we did in the past. But when you look back now, it sure was worth it. That was a great ride for all of us."

Green Bay didn't have a single turnover that day and had just one penalty. Starr had a 96.2 passer rating, threw for 202 yards and a touchdown, and was named the game's MVP for the second straight year.

"We've played several games that were better than that one," Starr said. "But we were very good that day. If that game marks the end of our dynasty, that's not a bad game to go out with."

Lombardi's last game as Green Bay's head coach ended like his first one: with a victory ride. Gregg and Kramer hoisted the veteran coach on their shoulders and carried him off the field to the locker room.

"Coach Lombardi was very emotional a couple times with us during the week," Starr said. "Not many people realize how easily this man could laugh or cry."

Two weeks later, at the Oneida Golf and Riding Club in Green Bay, tears were shed as Lombardi announced he was stepping down as head coach of the Packers. Lombardi remained general manager, and then introduced his hand-picked successor: assistant Phil Bengtson.

The Lombardi era in Green Bay was officially over.

"Guys who were at their peak kind of started on their downside when Bengtson took over," said former linebacker Jim Flanigan. "And it was kind of a no-win for Phil.

"Had he won, people would have said he was winning with Lombardi's guys. When he didn't win, he was cast as the villain. Lombardi definitely got out at the right time."

Starr played three mediocre seasons under Bengtson and one under Dan Devine in 1971. Injuries took their toll on Starr, and he retired due to chronic shoulder problems.

Starr returned to Green Bay as quarterbacks coach in 1972 under Devine, and became head coach in 1975. Some his former teammates tried to deter Starr from taking the job, insisting the expectations would be too high based on his success as a player.

Starr could not return his former team to past glory, going 52–76–3 in nine seasons before he was released.

"Going back to coach in Green Bay was the biggest mistake I ever made in my life," Starr said. "I was approached by the organization and it turned out to be an enormous mistake. I was extremely disappointed. I disappointed the Packers and their fans.

"I accept all responsibility. I just didn't get it done. I haven't ever really sat down and analyzed what went wrong. Early on, my inexperience hurt us, but in the later years, we had some good draft choices and we were beginning to make progress. But I don't want it to sound like I'm making excuses. I just didn't get it done."

Bart Starr by the Numbers

4× Pro Bowl selection (1960, 1961, 1962, 1966)
Associated Press First-Team All-Pro (1966)
2× AP Second-Team All-Pro (1962, 1964)
1966 NFL MVP (AP, Newspaper Enterprise Association, *Sporting News*,
    United Press International)
"Whizzer" White NFL Man of the Year (1966)
5× NFL champion (1961, 1962, 1965, 1966, 1967)
2× Super Bowl champion (I, II)
2× Super Bowl MVP (I, II)
NFL 1960s All-Decade Team
Packers Hall of Fame inductee
Pro Football Hall of Fame inductee (1977)
Green Bay Packers #15 retired
Rated #51 NFL Player of all time by NFL.com

Career Stats

Pass attempts: 3,149
Pass completions: 1,808
Percentage: 57.4
TD-INT: 152–138
Passing yards: 24,718
Passer rating: 80.5

Dowler, himself a longtime NFL assistant after his playing days ended, said Starr would have benefited from first serving as an assistant.

"It's a tough thing to do, basically go from player to head coach," Dowler said. "Everything Bart did, he did for the first time. He learned on the job. Bart said to me by the time he figured out how to be a head coach they fired him."

The highlight of Starr's coaching tenure was the 1982 strike season, when the Packers finished 5–3–1 and defeated St. Louis in the first round of the playoffs at Lambeau Field before losing at Dallas.

"In hindsight, it was a mistake on my part as I didn't have the training for the head coaching job," Starr said. "From an emotional standpoint, I wanted to help the franchise. It was my biggest regret, but we make mistakes in life and move on."

Many Packers players of the 1960s often mention a special bond between teammates of the Lombardi era.

Former center Bill Curry's best example came at one of the toughest junctures of his coaching career, when he was dismissed from his position at Kentucky.

A dejected Curry was alone in his office when his secretary knocked on the door.

"I had just been unceremoniously discharged and she said I had a visitor," Curry said. "I said, 'I don't need a visitor right now, but she insisted.'"

Waiting to see Curry was Bart Starr.

"I said to Bart, 'Why are you here?'" Curry said. "Bart said, 'I came to see you.' How many people make a special trip from Birmingham, Alabama., to Lexington, Kentucky, to see a friend who just got fired?"

But that was always Starr.

Classy. Caring. Compassionate.

On top of it, he was one heck of a football player.

"The reason we had success is because that was a great football team," Starr said. "I was just one part of a great team.

"You look at the quality players and look at the leadership we had, and it's easy to understand why we won. I was just so blessed to be in Green Bay when I was and to be led by a gentleman (Lombardi) that's difficult to describe."

The same could be said of Starr. Packer Nation was lucky to see the show.

★ ★ ★

Brett Favre

The man crush was intense.

It had lasted nearly a year. And a tumultuous 1991 season had done nothing to slow the love affair.

Yes, Ron Wolf had it bad for Brett Favre. And it's a good thing for the Green Bay Packers that Wolf's taste in quarterbacks was on par with Derek Jeter's taste in women.

Favre was like that intimidating girl from your high school, that striking blonde who smoked Marlboros and dressed in mostly leather. The one packed with potential, but who scared off most suitors.

But Wolf wasn't afraid of anything. Not rocky pasts. Not reputations of wild behavior. Not a thing.

And on February 11, 1992, Wolf made sure the apple of his eye—his man crush—came to Green Bay.

Wolf, the Packers' general manager for just 2½ months, sent a first-round draft pick—the 17th overall selection—for the highly unproven Favre. Considering Favre had been a second-round pick in 1991, Wolf took enormous criticism throughout the state.

"I got letters that said, 'You completely destroyed the franchise,' and things like that," Wolf said. "But it worked. It worked out and I'm very thankful it did."

When Wolf arrived in Green Bay, his quarterbacking options were an oft-injured Don Majkowski, mediocre Mike Tomczak, and third-stringer Blair Kiel.

Wolf, a former Oakland Raiders employee and somewhat of a daredevil himself, knew something needed to be done.

"There's one thing about this league that's pretty simple: if you don't have a quarterback, you don't have much of a chance," Wolf said. "Well, we didn't have a quarterback and we had to go and get one. I had to do something."

He did, and the rest is history.

When Wolf—and shortly thereafter Favre—arrived, Green Bay was the NFL's version of Siberia. In a few short years, these two men helped turn the NFL's smallest city into a destination spot.

Favre did the unthinkable and won three straight MVP awards. He led the Packers to a championship in Super Bowl XXXI and a runner-up finish the following year.

Favre set virtually every NFL passing record there was during his 20-year career that included 16 in Green Bay. To this day, Favre remains the game's all-time leader in wins.

Favre never missed a start, and he played in more games than any other Packer (277, including playoffs). Favre also led the rebirth of an organization that had gone through more than two decades of despair.

"I think certainly in his era he'd be in the top five (players)," Wolf said of Favre. "When you think of somebody now, you think of the great tradition...that great tradition of the Green Bay Packers. So for Brett Favre to be now said to be the greatest player ever to play for the Green Bay Packers, that's rare air, rarefied air."

Today, the Packers are among the healthiest franchises in sports. But it wasn't like that nearly a quarter century ago, when Wolf had the guts to trade for Favre.

Now, the Favre trade is viewed by most as one of the five most lopsided in NFL history. At the time, though, most thought Wolf was getting the short end of the deal.

"Hey, everyone's got an opinion," Wolf said. "I knew most people probably thought we were getting robbed because they didn't know anything about the guy. But Brett was the guy I thought we had to have."

So Wolf was passionate in his pursuit of Favre.

Wolf first fell in love with Favre while working as the New York Jets' personnel director. Wolf was preparing for the 1991 draft, and both he and Jets general manager Dick Steinberg agreed that Favre was the No. 1 player in that year's draft.

The Jets didn't have a first-round draft choice. When Favre fell out of the first round, though, the Jets tried trading up ahead of Atlanta—which was known to covet Favre.

Steinberg thought he had a deal worked out with Phoenix, one slot ahead of Atlanta. But the Cardinals pulled out at the last moment, and the Falcons took Favre with the 33rd overall pick.

That move was a blow to the Jets, who selected quarterback Browning Nagle—an all-time bust—one pick later. Then-Jets coach Bruce Coslet lobbied hard for Nagle, and Steinberg eventually made Nagle his pick.

In the end, that was a huge break for Wolf and the Packers.

"From my standpoint in the long run, it worked out perfectly for me," Wolf said. "If Brett wasn't in Atlanta, he would have been in New York and I wouldn't have been able to get him."

Wolf was hired as Green Bay's general manager on November 27, 1991. And as fate would have it, the Packers were in Atlanta to play the Falcons four days later.

Wolf had kept close tabs on Favre. And before the game, Wolf told Packers president Bob Harlan he was going down to the field to scout Atlanta's backup quarterback.

Wolf told Harlan that if he liked what he saw, he was going to trade for that player. Just one thing: Harlan wasn't sure who the Falcons' backup quarterback was.

"Ron left and I started looking at the roster to see who the backup quarterback is," Harlan chuckled. "And Ron came back shortly before kickoff and said, 'Bob, we're going to make a trade for Brett Favre. Are you OK with that?' And I told him, 'I promised you it was your team to run, there would be no interference, I'm fine with it.'"

Favre's career statistics read 0-for-4 with two interceptions at the time. Favre had fallen out of favor with Falcons coach Jerry Glanville due to his hard-partying ways, and he'd plummeted to third string on the depth chart.

Glanville wanted Favre out, and Wolf was happy to oblige.

"I had to get him out of Atlanta," Glanville said in a 2010 radio interview. "I could not sober him up. I sent him to a city where at 9:00 PM at night the only thing that's open is Chili [John's]. You can get it two ways, with or without onions.

"And that's what made Brett Favre make a comeback, was going to a town that closed down. If I would have traded him to New York, nobody to this day would have known who Brett Favre ever was."

To this day, both Favre and Wolf disagree strongly with Glanville.

"I think he's covering his rear end. I mean, what a mistake, huh?" Wolf said. "I mean, you're talking about a first-ballot Hall of Fame Player. Every time you go out scouting, this is the one guy you look for. Someone you can hang your franchise on. And they had him in the building and they kept Billy Joe Tolliver over him. And no matter what you do or what you say you made a huge error there."

Added Favre: "I disagree with Jerry because I think if I went somewhere else, where I knew I was going to be playing, I would have cared a lot more. Whether that was New York or Chicago, I just would have cared more. That's human nature."

When Wolf watched Favre throw that day in Atlanta, he saw a player whose arm strength matched anyone in football. He saw a player with remarkable upside. And Wolf knew it was time to play "Let's Make a Deal."

"We came back and at some point we had an executive committee meeting," Wolf said. "I told the people that we were going to make a commitment for this quarterback, told them all about this quarterback, Brett Favre, and how we were going to go work to get him. They had no idea who I was talking about. But they were all for it."

Wolf and Falcons vice president of player personnel Ken Herock—one of Wolf's closest friends—talked four to five times a week for approximately 10 weeks.

Wolf offered a second-round pick. The Falcons demanded a No. 1.

Wolf said if he'd give them a first rounder, he had to get something back. The Falcons balked.

"Finally the call came that said, 'It's got to be a first or we're not going to make the trade,'" Wolf said. "I knew that they wanted to get rid of him. It was just a matter of getting it done. I knew we were going to get this deal done because I didn't think anyone was going to pay what they were asking for other than me."

Wolf figured it didn't pay to play hardball any longer, and just 74 days into his tenure as Packers general manager, he made the deal.

"I looked at it like this: if I was going to be successful, I was going to be successful because of Brett Favre," Wolf said. "And if he wasn't good enough, then I wasn't going to be successful. So I put everything on him and it worked out."

Favre was stunned when he first heard the news. Then he realized this could be the break he needed.

"There were a couple different ways I looked at it," Favre said. "Basically I went through the emotions. And first of all there was this initial shock that you were traded. Your first impulse is that's not a good thing.

"But the second thing is you're traded for a first-round pick, and that's basically better than being drafted in the first round because someone thinks highly enough of you to go through all this. So it was exciting for me.

"I felt like this was a great opportunity. I didn't know a whole lot about the Packers at the time. But I knew a lot about the history of the franchise in general and I knew the franchise was struggling. So I knew this was an opportunity I was lucky to get."

The Packers were definitely the lucky ones.

In 2006, then-Packers team historian Lee Remmel helped Triumph Books put together a list for my book *100 Things Packers Fans Should Know & Do Before They Die*. Remmel labeled Favre as the No. 1 player in team history.

"I was fortunate I got to play with Brett Favre for nine years," said former Packers guard Marco Rivera. "His presence in the huddle, his leadership, it forced everybody to play better. You had to bring your 'A' game when you're going to be in Brett Favre's huddle."

Favre played 16 seasons in Green Bay, was traded to the New York Jets in the summer of 2008, then played one year with the Jets and two more with the Minnesota Vikings.

In that time, Favre set several NFL records, including:

- Most passing yards (71,838)
- Most completions (6,300)
- Most pass attempts (10,169)
- Most wins (186)
- Most starts (298)
- Most interceptions (336)

"Brett Favre is one of the greatest quarterbacks in the history of professional football," said former Denver head coach Mike Shanahan, who led the Broncos past Favre's Packers in Super Bowl XXXII. "You're judged by winning, and he's won more games than any other quarterback who has ever played. He was the face of the Packers and a great credit to our game."

Beyond the numbers, three things about Favre stood out more than any others. His passion, his leadership, and his toughness.

Year by year, the NFL becomes more corporate, more of a business. But Favre played with the boyish enthusiasm you see from fifth graders on local playgrounds.

Every Packers fan that watched Super Bowl XXXI will remember Favre throwing a 54-yard touchdown pass to Andre Rison on just Green Bay's second offensive play of the game. Favre took off his helmet and ran around the Louisiana Superdome like he'd just won the lottery.

This was common behavior for Favre. He rejoiced like it was Christmas morning after scoring the winning touchdown against Atlanta in a critical late-season game in 1994. He'd tackle teammates in the end zone after touchdowns. He threw snowballs at teammates during a playoff win over Seattle in 2007.

It didn't matter how old Favre was. At times, he was like a giant child playing a man's game.

"The one thing I always heard people say and they still say it today is: I never saw someone play football and have more fun than Brett," Favre said. "And that's true. It was fun. It was a lot of fun. And I know my teammates would feed on that and the fans fed on it, too. It was fun. That's how it was. I would have done anything for my team."

No matter how many years he was in the league or how old he was, Favre always seemed to have more fun than anybody else on the field. To the 'Average Joe' who punched a clock all week, Favre's passion resonated.

"People have asked me what's my favorite moment of Brett Favre's career," said former Packers president Bob Harlan. "I really think it was the first touchdown in Super Bowl XXXI when he threw to Rison and he ran off the field with his helmet off. He looked like a kid running home to mom with his first great report card.

"I was so nervous that morning, so nervous about us being in the Super Bowl, and it gave me confidence to see him throw the ball like that and then run off the field like that. That gave me a great feeling.

"I've always told people he plays with a sandlot enthusiasm for the game, and you don't see that very often. He was a fun-loving guy who played very well and showed delight in playing. Sometimes your fans say 'I like college football because of the enthusiasm.' I think Brett put that same enthusiasm on the field on Sundays, and I thought that was enormous for the game."

Favre's leadership was also vital to everything he did.

Irvin Favre—Brett's father—was the head football coach at Hancock North Central High School in Kiln, Mississippi. Brett quarterbacked the Hawks for three seasons when he reached high school. But well before that, Favre followed his father to football practice many days, and unbeknownst to him at the time, began learning leadership lessons that would help him later in life.

"Being around football from a young age, I was around black guys, I was around white guys, I was around football talk and some of the things that are said in the locker room," Favre said. "And there were things said in there that you would never say at home. That was kind of a sacred ground in the locker room.

"So I just kind of learned the ropes at an early age, being around my dad. And you don't know it at the time, but you're learning how to fit in with everyone. And I think I learned a lot of the qualities a good teammate should have."

In a melting-pot sport, Favre understood how vital it was to have a relationship with each and every one of his teammates. He was the glue—and he took that role seriously.

Those around him certainly noticed.

"Here's why there will never be another Brett Favre," former Packers safety LeRoy Butler said. "When Brett Favre got there, you had black guys playing a game of spades, white guys playing backgammon, the younger guys playing video games, the older guys playing hearts. And Brett fit in with every culture.

"He'd go over to the brothers and listen to hip-hop. He'd go over to the white guys and listen to country. He'd go hang out with the hunters, he'd go hang with the young guys. There was no guy that ever did that. Hell, I never did that.

"It's nice when organically, someone can fit in with everybody else and Brett did that. When he came in the locker room, he didn't wait for people to come over to him. He went over to people. And that wasn't publicized. He didn't want the publicity of that.

"But he was an unbelievable teammate. I'm telling you, no quarterback has ever done that, to realize there's so many different cultures in the locker room and he could fit in with all of them. And he fit in.

"He didn't even know how to play spades, but he'd be yelling, 'I got next.' He didn't even like hip-hop, but he would dance to it. He didn't want to get up at 4:00 in the morning to go hunting before practice at 9, but he did it. He didn't want to go to some of these functions with us, but he did it because he loved his teammates.

"I don't think there was ever a guy that loved his teammates more than Brett. It's impossible to think that someone could love his teammates more. I don't think anybody ever put more energy into loving his teammates than Brett did.

"You felt like if you were in a foxhole with somebody, I want a son-of-a-bitch that when I'm asleep won't put his gun down and will give his life for me. That's Brett Favre. That's Brett Favre. I want him in my foxhole.

"He used to give rookies his truck. Brand-new truck to run around in and he'd say, 'I can get another ride.' I mean, who does that? He got along with all the races, all the cultures. I mean they broke the mold on Brett Favre."

They certainly broke the mold when it came to toughness.

Favre started an NFL-record 321 consecutive games (including playoffs) over an 18½-year period in Green Bay, New York, and Minnesota. Of those, 275 starts came in Green Bay.

"I think that streak means more today than it ever has," Favre said. "I knew it was important. I knew it was tough to do week in and week out. It's so tough each week just to get yourself prepared mentally. That really is tough and can be a grind. But then the physical element is even harder.

"None of the things I accomplished are possible unless you're playing—and to play for a long time. And to play all those years and to fight through a lot of things and keep going, I really have to tip my hat to myself on that one."

With good reason. Along the way, Favre had a bevy of injuries that would have sidelined most mere mortals.

Favre suffered a first-degree left shoulder separation in 1992, but played through the injury and led Green Bay to a midseason win over Philadelphia. Favre's toughness certainly impressed Eagles defensive end Reggie White, who signed a free-agent contract in Green Bay that offseason and mentioned Favre as a major reason why.

In 1995, Favre had a severely sprained left ankle and took just six snaps in practice that week. He then went and threw five touchdowns in a critical 35–28 win over Chicago.

Favre had the wind knocked out of him twice and coughed up blood in a 1995 game against Pittsburgh. But Favre stayed in the game and led the Packers to their first divisional title since 1972.

Favre suffered a sprained right thumb during the 1999 preseason, but played the entire year with the injury. Favre had a sprained lateral collateral ligament in his left knee in 2002. But he returned after a bye week and powered the Packers past Miami on Monday Night Football, despite playing with a brace on the knee.

Favre broke his right thumb on his throwing hand early in the 2003 season and played with a splint for nearly three months. Still, Favre didn't miss a game.

"Here's a quarterback with a broken thumb that everybody's really taking for granted," Rivera said of Favre late in that 2003 season. "And we expect him to go out there and have a Brett Favre kind of day. I don't know if I could even throw the ball with a broken thumb and he's doing it. He's unbelievable."

Favre said the broken thumb was the worst injury he ever had to deal with. Amazingly, one week after breaking his thumb in St. Louis, Favre threw three touchdowns and led the Packers to a rare win in Minnesota.

"I think the one game in my mind that comes up the most was the Minnesota game after I broke my thumb the previous week against St. Louis," Favre said. "To go and do that in a dome where we had no success in…that was pretty special.

"It was so hard to grip the ball and throw it like you want to. And then I went and played one of the best games of my life. That was pretty amazing. It felt a lot different when I left the stadium that day than other seasons, because we always seemed to lose in Minnesota."

Favre suffered a concussion against the New York Giants in 2004, then famously returned to throw a touchdown pass before the team forced him to sit. Favre also had right elbow tendinitis in both 2000 and 2010, yet played through both injuries.

"It's beyond reason. It's ridiculous," said Matt Hasselbeck, who backed Favre up in Green Bay. "He's just the toughest guy in the world."

Wolf didn't know he was getting all of that when he made the trade back in 1992. But he did think he was getting something special.

And it didn't take Favre long to begin paying dividends.

Favre immediately showed in his first training camp that he had something few others did: a rocket arm.

The Packers were used to Majkowski's underwhelming arm strength. Instead, the veteran Majkowski succeeded on timing, precision, and accuracy.

Favre was quite different.

Brett Favre was thrown into the fire on September 20, 1992, after Don Majkowski suffered an ankle injury. After a rough early start with four fumbles, the Favre-led Packers defeated the Cincinnati Bengals 24–23 on a Favre touchdown pass in the fourth quarter.

"He was like a wild stallion," former Packers left tackle Ken Ruettgers said. "He tried to throw the ball through anything and everything."

First-year coach Mike Holmgren and Wolf knew it was only a matter of time before they handed Favre the keys to the offense. But when the 1992 campaign began, Holmgren felt more comfortable with the 28-year-old Majkowski.

Green Bay lost its first two games by a combined score of 54–23. And Majkowski was knocked out of a Week 2 loss in Tampa Bay.

Favre replaced Majkowski during that loss in Tampa. And amazingly, his first career completion was to…himself.

Favre rolled right and had his pass tipped up into the air. Favre then instinctively caught the batted ball, but was tackled for a 7-yard loss.

"Is that a trivia question or what?" Wolf said. "That's pretty amazing is what it is."

Several truly astonishing plays happened the following week during a home game against Cincinnati. Majkowski was again knocked out, this time suffering ligament damage in his left ankle.

Favre entered on just the Packers' second series and seemed lost at times.

"When I became a starter, I had no clue what was going on," Favre said. "Maybe that was good. If I told you (back then) I knew what was going on, I was feeding you a line of B.S."

But Favre certainly appeared to know what he was doing by the end of that Bengals game.

Green Bay trailed 20–10 in the fourth quarter when Favre engineered an 88-yard touchdown drive. Favre capped the march with a five-yard touchdown to Sterling Sharpe, the first of 41 touchdowns that duo would connect on.

Then with the Packers in a 23–17 hole in the final minute, Favre somehow led Green Bay on a 92-yard, game-winning march. The clincher came when Favre hit wideout Kitrick Taylor for a 35-yard touchdown with just 13 seconds left.

Amazingly, it was the only receiving touchdown of Taylor's NFL career. And for Favre, it was the first of his 30 fourth-quarter comebacks and 45 game-winning drives.

"It's probably a game that will be talked about forever," Favre said. "And a big reason for that is it's the one that kickstarted everything, it's the one that got it going."

It sure was. Favre took over from that point, but still the somewhat talent-starved Packers were just 3–6 midway through the year.

Green Bay got hot, though, and rolled off six straight wins to improve to 9–6. Amazingly, that was the Packers' longest regular season winning streak since the NFL Champion 1965 squad.

One week later, though, in a win-or-go-home game, the Packers were sent packing. Minnesota rolled past Green Bay 27–7 and clinched the NFC Central division.

Still, the season was a huge success for Green Bay. Favre was perhaps better than even Wolf had hoped. The Packers had found their quarterback of the future. And Green Bay was clearly one of the NFL's up-and-coming teams.

Favre's First Win

September 20, 1992, seemed like just another day when Brett Lorenzo Favre rolled out of bed.

Favre drove to Lambeau Field for his third game as a Green Bay Packer. He expected to spend his day watching Don Majkowski quarterback the team. And maybe, Favre would get in for some mop-up duty in Green Bay's game with Cincinnati.

Instead, Favre's day was the exact opposite of what he imagined.

On that gorgeous afternoon, the fortunes of a downtrodden franchise changed for good. On that day, an organization that had become loveable losers found hope.

On that day, Brett Favre had his coming-out party.

"I'll never forget that day," Packers president Bob Harlan said.

Nor should he.

On that remarkable day, Favre replaced an injured Majkowski and engineered one of the greatest comebacks in team history. In the final four minutes, Favre led scoring drives of 88 and 92 yards as Green Bay rallied past Cincinnati 24–23 for coach Mike Holmgren's first NFL victory.

Favre capped the dramatics with a 35-yard bullet score to Kitrick Taylor with just 13 seconds left.

Between that moment and January 20, 2008, Favre was the starting quarterback in every game the Green Bay Packers played. That remarkable string consisted of 253 consecutive regular season games, and 275 total games including playoffs.

Favre won three Most Valuable Player Awards in that time, led the Packers to the 1996 season Super Bowl title, and became the winningest quarterback (160) in NFL history. Favre also set virtually every meaningful NFL passing record and guided the Packers to non-losing seasons in 15 of his 16 years in Green Bay.

"I'll put it like this, in 38 active years and then I had three years as a consultant, the best player I have ever been around—and I've been around a few—was Brett Favre," said former Packers general manager Ron Wolf, who engineered a trade to acquire Favre. "Here's what he did. He came into the franchise that had the poorest record in the National Football League and years later that franchise had the best record in the National Football League. That's something else."

Indeed it is. But back on September 20, 1992, Favre was nothing more than a mystery to most.

"If there's anything I remember about that day it was just like, 'Wow! Where did this guy come from?'" said former Green Bay linebacker Brian Noble, a teammate of Favre's in 1992–93. "I hadnt seen much of him in training camp and all I knew was he was a young kid with a little bit of baggage. But after that day, people knew about Brett."

Did they ever.

Up until that point, Favre was Johnny Manziel—before there was a Johnny Manziel.

Favre was known more for bar-hopping and carousing than anything on the football field. And after just one season in Atlanta, Falcons coach Jerry Glanville desperately wanted him out of town.

Wolf, who had wanted to select Favre in the 1991 draft when he was with the New York Jets, was happy to oblige.

On February 11, 1992, Wolf sent a No. 1 draft choice to Atlanta for a player who had career passing statistics of zero completions in four attempts and two interceptions. While critics balked at the move, they'd likely agree with Wolf now that acquiring Favre was one of the five most lop-sided trades in NFL history.

"I knew right away we had something special," Wolf said. "The question was how were we going to get him to play?

"You could tell it was just a matter of time as soon as training camp started. And during camp, Holmgren and I had a long talk about how to get him on the field."

Turns out, their dilemma took care of itself. With the Packers coming off a 31–3 drubbing in Tampa Bay in Week 2, Holmgren had contemplated making a quarterback switch before the Cincinnati game. But Holmgren stuck with the veteran Majkowski, fearing Favre wasn't quite ready.

"Mike and I sat down and talked and he asked me if I was OK if we went with Brett," Wolf said. "And I said absolutely. But I don't think Mike felt he was quite ready yet."

Ready or not, it was time.

On Green Bay's second series of that game, Majkowski was sacked by Bengals defensive tackle Tim Krumrie and suffered ligament damage to his left ankle. As he was being helped off the field, NBC announcer Jim Lampley asked: "Will it ever be 1989 for the Majik Man, Don Majkowski, again? It does not appear likely."

Little did Lampley know how prophetic those words would be. And little did people know the type of magic Favre would begin creating.

The early returns in the Cincinnati game certainly weren't encouraging. It was apparent that Favre and the No. 1 offense had spent little time together.

On his 11th play from scrimmage, Favre fumbled a snap from center James Campen and Krumrie recovered for Cincinnati.

Favre's overeagerness was evident as he overshot wide-open receivers Sterling Sharpe and Sanjay Beach in the second quarter. And Favre's frustration was beginning to build after he fumbled on back-to-back plays late in the third quarter.

"I knew as much as I could have possibly known," Favre said. "Basically, the experience I had up until then was very limited. I had studied the plays and basically had not run those plays. But I was able to bail myself out for the most part."

Indeed he was. Green Bay headed to the fourth quarter trailing 17–3 and hadn't scored a touchdown in seven quarters.

But the light seemed to go on for Favre and the entire offense in the fourth quarter. Terrell

(continued)

Favre's First Win *(continued)*

Buckley, playing his first game as a Packer, gave the team a jump-start when he returned a punt 58 yards for a touchdown with 12:43 remaining to trim the Bengals' lead to 17–10.

After a Jim Breech field goal gave Cincinnati a 20–10 lead, Green Bay began its ensuing possession from its own 12. And Favre began to look like he had been playing in Holmgren's West Coast offense for years, not weeks.

Favre guided an eight-play, 88-yard drive in which he made a handful of standout plays. On a third-and-6, he eluded the rush and ran for 19 yards. Favre then fired a 15-yard completion to Harry Sydney and lofted a gorgeous 33-yard completion to a wide-open Sharpe that brought Green Bay to the Bengals' 17.

After a 10-yard bullet to Ed West and an Edgar Bennett run, Favre found Sharpe for a 5-yard score over the middle to pull the Packers within 20–17. The touchdown pass was the first of Favre's career and would be the first of 41 on which he and Sharpe would connect.

"We knew he was going to be a good player just from watching him in training camp," former Packers running back Vince Workman said of Favre. "Most of his passes were just rocket passes.

"You noticed his arm strength right away, especially because Majkowski was more of a finesse passer. But he stepped in that day and took control right away. He had the respect of everybody right away."

If he didn't then, he certainly did by the time the game ended.

Another Breech field goal with 1:07 left made it 23–17. Rookie wide receiver Robert Brooks then dug the Packers an even bigger hole when he caught the ensuing kickoff on the left sidelines and stepped out of bounds at the 8.

All Favre needed to do now was lead Green Bay 92 yards in 1:07 without the benefit of a timeout. No problem, right?

"Brett had a swagger to him, even back then," said left tackle Ken Ruettgers, who played with Favre from 1992–96. "Even though he was 23 or whatever, it was like nothing could faze him."

The improbable odds certainly didn't slow him down on this day, either.

On first down, Favre couldn't find an open man and settled on a check-down to Sydney, who was smart enough to run out of bounds after gaining 4 yards. On second down, Favre stepped up in the pocket to avoid the rush, then found Sharpe wide open down the right sideline.

Sharpe had run past cornerback Rod Jones and help was late arriving from safety Fernandus Vinson. Sharpe reached up high to haul in the 41-yard bullet from Favre, but in doing so, he re-aggravated a rib injury.

With the clock running, Favre raced to the line of scrimmage, then dumped a 12-yard completion to Workman over the middle that brought the Packers to the Bengals' 35. Again, Favre sprinted to the line and spiked the ball with just 19 ticks left.

With Sharpe on the sideline because of his rib injury, things looked dicey for Green Bay. The Packers lined up with Brooks in the left slot, Beach wide left and Taylor wide right. Favre again looked right, where just three plays earlier he had found a wide-open Sharpe.

Favre pump-faked in Taylor's direction and got Jones to bite. Taylor streaked by Jones and had a good three yards of separation.

Favre then fired a laser beam to Taylor that didn't get more than 12 feet off the ground. It was a good thing, too. Vinson was closing fast, and had there been more air under Favre's pass, the Bengals' safety would have likely broken the play up.

Instead, Favre's bullet threaded the needle between the two Cincinnati defenders and landed right on Taylor's hands with 13 seconds showing.

The memorable touchdown pass would be the only one on which Favre and Taylor would ever connect. In fact, it was the only touchdown catch of Taylor's NFL career.

"On that play, I was blocking on a guy and he just kind of stopped,' Ruettgers said. "That usually means he's given up because the ball is in the air.

"So I looked up and saw the ball just zipping down the field to Kitrick Taylor. I mean, it was an NFL Films moment. It was one of the few great moments that as a lineman you not only played, but got to witness at the same time. It was incredible."

In typical Favre fashion, he showed his boyish enthusiasm, ripped off his helmet, and danced around Lambeau Field. The rest of the Packers and the sellout crowd went ballistic, as well.

"I was standing on about the 40 when he threw it," Noble said. "And I remember thinking, 'I'm glad I'm not on the field, because that ball would have hit me in the head.' There was no elevation to it. It was an incredible throw."

Workman marveled at that play—and at Favre, as well.

"I'm just really proud to say I was part of that game and proud to say I played with Brett when he was starting out," said Workman, who was Green Bay's leading rusher that game. "That day and that play really gave us an extra boost of confidence. It was our first victory and it helped us start to believe in ourselves."

That it did. Favre would lead Green Bay on a six-game winning streak later that year and to a 9–7 record for just its second winning season since 1982.

More than that, though, Favre showed the poise, leadership, and ability that made him one of the greatest to ever play the position.

"Brett's career accomplishments will be measured among the greats of the game for the balance of time," Holmgren said. "He truly was as gifted a player as I have ever seen."

Which is something the NFL first began to witness on that memorable day.

Favre finished that first season completing 64.1 percent of his passes, the highest mark ever by a Packers starter. Favre's passer rating of 85.3 was Green Bay's best in eight seasons. And he threw for more than 3,200 yards in just 13 starts.

Not bad for a guy that wasn't always sure what he was doing.

"You could see we were a team on the rise," Butler said. "You could feel it because we finally had a quarterback. We lost that game in Minnesota, but we still felt like we made huge strides. You could tell, things were about to get a whole lot better."

Things certainly improved that offseason.

Reggie White—arguably the most dynamic defensive player in football—signed a four-year, $17 million free-agent contract to leave Philadelphia and come to Green Bay.

White, known as "The Minister of Defense," was arguably the most attractive player to ever reach the free agent market. And when White signed with Green Bay—a team that hadn't reached the postseason since 1982—eyebrows were raised throughout the league.

"The Bible says God is not of confusion, but of peace and a sound mind," said White, an ordained minister from the time he was 17. "That's what I was looking for and I've gotten peace about being here and a sound mind about being here."

The previous season, White's Eagles had lost to Favre and the Packers 27–24. Favre took a beating that day, but threw for two touchdowns and led Green Bay—an 8.5-point underdog—to a stunning win.

That game went a long ways toward White eventually choosing Green Bay. And on the day of White's introductory press conference, he predicted Favre would be better than Philadelphia quarterback Randall Cunningham.

Suddenly, the Packers management was in fantastic shape with steady team president Bob Harlan, a dynamic general manager in Wolf, and an offensive mastermind in Holmgren running the team.

The quarterback was in place. And now, so was White.

"That's what changed the football fortunes of this franchise. It was huge," Harlan said of signing White. "Everyone thought the last place he would sign was Green Bay and it was monumental because not only did he sign, but he recruited for Green Bay and got guys [such as] Sean Jones to come here. He sent a message to the rest of the NFL that Green Bay was a great place to play."

Wolf agreed.

"You can argue all day about what the biggest move was," Wolf said. "But in some order, it's Mike, Brett, and Reggie. Just make your pick."

The Packers seemed ready to make a move as the 1993 season began. Green Bay struggled early, though, and was just 1–3 at the quarter pole.

A huge Sunday-night win over Denver—a game in which White had three sacks—sparked a three-game winning streak. Still, the Packers failed to find a branch of consistency to grab hold of throughout the season.

Despite a loss at Detroit in the regular season finale, the Packers earned the NFC's final playoff spot and qualified for the postseason with a 9–7 record. It was Green Bay's first trip to the playoffs since the strike-shortened 1982 campaign, and the Packers were heading back to Detroit for the Wild Card round.

Green Bay trailed 24–21 in the final minute. The Packers reached the Lions' 40-yard line and were hoping for a potential game-tying field goal. But they got far more than that.

When the ensuing play broke down, Favre scrambled to his left looking for tight end Ed West, who wasn't open. While scrambling, Favre scanned the field and saw Sharpe break free in the back right corner of the end zone.

Favre, who had almost reached the far left sideline, threw back across his body—a pass that carried approximately 75 yards. Sharpe was waiting for the miraculous throw, and the 40-yard touchdown with just 55 ticks left gave Green Bay a 28–24 win.

"It was the play of the year," Holmgren said afterward. "It's just a wonderful, wonderful feeling. We worked so hard to get this one."

Afterward, the Lions couldn't believe what had just happened to them.

"That feeling, when the ball was in the air, and you see the guy wide open in the end zone—it was one of the lowest feelings in the world," Detroit linebacker Chris Spielman said. "Your heart sinks. It's the closest thing there is to being told someone you love has died. I know people won't think it's right to compare those things, but when you live and die for football, it is."

The Packers notched their first playoff win in 11 seasons. It was also the first of Favre's 12 postseason wins in Green Bay, which remains a team record.

Green Bay's journey ended one week later with a humbling 27–17 loss in Dallas. The defending Super Bowl–champion Cowboys rolled off 24 unanswered points, took a 24–3 lead, and coasted home.

Favre finished the game with 331 passing yards, just one shy of the team playoff record. He also threw two touchdowns, but was also intercepted twice.

The season was finished, but Green Bay certainly seemed headed in the right direction.

Favre was up and down throughout the 1993 campaign, throwing more interceptions (24) than touchdowns (19). His completion percentage (60.9 percent) and passer rating (72.2) also went in reverse and several fans called for his benching.

But Holmgren stayed the course with his young, gifted, and at times highly unpredictable quarterback. The playoff win in Detroit gave everyone inside 1265 Lombardi Ave. a good feeling. The future seemed bright.

The 1994 season was a struggle, though.

Just 24 hours before the season began, star wideout Sterling Sharpe tried holding the organization hostage and said he wouldn't play against archrival Minnesota in the opener unless the Packers renegotiated his contract.

Without a doubt, Sharpe's antics cast a black cloud over his standout Packers career, which saw him finish as Green Bay's all-time leading receiver with 595 receptions (a record since broken by Donald Driver).

"In all my years, I've never been through anything like that," Harlan said. "What I remember most vividly is meeting in the draft room with (general manager) Ron Wolf and (coach) Mike Holmgren.

"And it was a shock to all of us. It was unbelievable. But Mike talked about how we'd go and play without him and not miss a beat. It was a real positive attitude."

Green Bay was in the third year of the Wolf-Holmgren regime and was considered a team on the rise. But the Packers had lost four straight games to Minnesota, which was still considered the team to beat in the NFC Central.

Then, on the eve of the Packers' biggest regular season game in more than a decade, Sharpe bailed. This didn't come as a great surprise to anyone, as Sharpe had threatened such a move throughout camp.

Favre, for one, didn't blink.

"Every one of our receivers is faster than Sterling," Favre said. "Now, it's just a matter if they catch the ball and make a play after it. I can't fold the tent. I'm excited."

The Packers' excitement level went up a notch about 8:00 PM that Saturday when the team and Sharpe reached an agreement on some adjustments in his contract. The next day, Sharpe lined up and caught seven passes for 53 yards and a touchdown, and Green Bay defeated the hated Vikings 16–10.

"Please. I'm not going to say a word," Sharpe, who didn't talk to the state media, said after the game. "Nothing has changed."

That wasn't true, though.

Up until that point, Sharpe had been seen by most as the Packers' leader. After the fiasco before the Minnesota game, though, the majority of the team gravitated towards Favre—and never left.

"Up until that point in time, Sterling was 'The Man,'" former Packers linebacker Brian Noble said. "You'd get him the ball as many times as possible and there'd be no argument with that. But people began to think the Packers were only going to go as far as Brett would take us."

Throughout much of the 1994 campaign, though, many began wondering how far that could be.

Green Bay was just 6–7 late in the season. And Favre had struggled so badly, at times, that the coaching staff discussed playing backup Mark Brunell instead of Favre.

"Absolutely, I took that very seriously," Favre said. "It crossed my mind at times. And I placed a lot upon myself to right the ship, if you will. But there are also times when you can put too much pressure on yourself and that's a really bad thing. But there were times when I wondered if every play could be my last."

Green Bay rallied down the stretch, won its final three games to finish 9–7, and earned the top wild-card spot. The highlight came in a 21–17 win over Atlanta in the final game ever played at Milwaukee's County Stadium.

Trailing 17–14, the Packers drove to the Falcons' 9-yard line with 19 seconds left. Green Bay was out of timeouts as Favre came to the line for a third-and-two play.

When no one was open, Favre took off on a mad scramble for the right corner of the end zone. Favre stumbled at the 6, regained his footing at the 3, and lunged for the end zone.

Had Favre been tackled short of the goal line, the game likely would have ended. Instead, Favre narrowly beat rookie cornerback Anthony Phillips to the end zone for a dramatic victory.

"I'll never forget this," Holmgren said that day. "It was a very special moment. Just a wonderful game."

Sharpe was knocked out of Green Bay's final two regular season games, though, with what the team initially described as "stingers." Instead, it was later discovered Sharpe had suffered a spinal cord injury that ended his career.

Green Bay was off to the playoffs, but had to go to battle without their All-Pro wide receiver.

The Packers met Detroit in the Wild Card round for a second straight season, and this time, their defense ruled the day. Green Bay held Lions Hall of Fame running back Barry Sanders to minus-1 yards rushing and powered the Packers to a memorable 16–12 win.

"To hold Barry Sanders, in my opinion the greatest running back ever to play, to hold him for negative yards, I shouldn't even have to say anything," Favre said that day. "That was remarkable. It was really awesome."

Eight days later, though, the Packers were far from awesome.

Dallas, which had quickly become a hurdle Green Bay couldn't clear, routed the visiting Packers 35–9 in the divisional playoffs. Favre had a rough day, going just 18-of-35 for 211 yards, no touchdowns, and one interception.

Green Bay's defense also had no answers for Dallas, which piled up 450 total yards and 28 first half-points.

The Packers' season ended in exactly the same spot it had 12 months earlier: Texas Stadium in Dallas.

On paper, it didn't appear as though much progress was made. Green Bay was 10–8 for a second straight season. The Packers also lost in the divisional playoffs for a second consecutive year.

But one thing that gave Green Bay great hope was the dramatic improvement Favre made. In the first seven games of the 1994 campaign, Favre threw nine touchdowns and seven interceptions, and his job was being threatened. Over the next nine games, Favre threw 24 touchdowns, seven interceptions, and powered the Packers back into the playoffs.

Favre's 33 touchdown passes ranked second in the NFL to San Francisco's Steve Young (35). Favre's quarterback rating of 90.7 was second to Young's (112.8). Favre also ranked fifth in total passing yards (3,882) and sixth in completion percentage (62.4).

No longer was there any mention of Brunell. The Packers were now certain they had their best quarterback since Bart Starr.

"Brett really turned a corner that year," Wolf said. "The second half of that season he was as good as anybody in football."

The following year, Favre was simply the best.

Favre won his first MVP award in 1995. Favre led the NFL in touchdown passes (38) and passing yards (4,413) and led the NFC in quarterback rating (99.5). Favre also threw just 13 interceptions and completed 63.0 percent of his passes.

Making Favre's exploits even more impressive was the fact that he did it without Sharpe. Instead, Favre turned Robert Brooks into a star, after the fourth-year wideout posted 102 receptions, 1,497 yards, and 13 touchdowns. Favre also leaned far more heavily on tight end Mark Chmura, while running backs Edgar Bennett and Dorsey Levens were more heavily utilized in the passing game.

The result was an offense that averaged 25.3 points per game, the Packers' highest total since the 1983 season. The game had slowed down for Favre. He was in total control of Holmgren's sophisticated West Coast offense. And the Packers had become a force in the NFC.

"I didn't think I could (win MVP)…especially without Sterling and a couple of changes with our offensive line," Favre said. "It's hard to go out and throw 38 touchdowns. You've got to start from scratch on offense.

"We had a new flanker, a new X receiver, a new tight end. That's tough. Each year I'll say that. It's going to be tough, but if we stay healthy and we continue to be productive and each guy makes the plays that we've made this year, it won't be quite as hard as I think."

Favre's rise to greatness helped the Packers produce a memorable 1995 season.

Green Bay went 11–5 and won the NFC Central for the first time in 23 years. The Packers' 11 wins were also their most since 1966.

Green Bay was 5–4 just past the midway point of the season, but rallied to win six of its final seven games. The highlight came in the regular season finale, with a division title hanging in the balance.

Green Bay led Pittsburgh 24–19 with just 16 seconds left. The visiting Steelers had driven to the Packers' 6-yard line and faced a fourth-and goal.

Steelers quarterback Neil O'Donnell threw a perfect pass to Pro Bowl wide receiver Yancey Thigpen, who was all alone in the left corner of the end zone. Amazingly, though, Thigpen dropped the ball.

The Packers prevailed and were divisional champs for the first time in nearly a quarter century.

"About time we got a break," Packers linebacker George Koonce said. "I think the whole state of Wisconsin and Packers fans across the nation just opened their Christmas presents early."

Added Holmgren: "When a play like that happens you don't try to figure it out. You just go, 'Thank you.'"

The fun was just getting started.

The following week, Green Bay routed Atlanta—and Favre's former pals—37–20 in the Wild Card round. Favre threw three touchdowns and no interceptions, and had a passer rating of 111.5 that day.

Green Bay then headed to San Francisco to face the defending Super Bowl–champion 49ers in the divisional playoffs.

Every great team has a breakthrough moment. A time they went from being an up-and-comer to a legitimate contender.

For the Green Bay Packers of the 1990s, that time was January 6, 1996.

The Packers were a 10½-point underdog in San Francisco. But Green Bay dominated the 49ers from start to finish and exited with a 27–17 win, the franchise's biggest victory in nearly three decades.

"No one gave us a chance," Butler said. "Everything we read they said we didn't have a chance. If no one is going to give you respect than you have nothing to lose."

Added Wolf: "This is the culmination of a lot of work by an entire team that completely believed in itself. We had to show this, that we are indeed a real football team. By God, I think we've done that."

They certainly did.

On a gorgeous afternoon at 3Com Park, the Packers dominated the 49ers physically. Favre stayed red hot, throwing for 299 yards and two touchdowns.

And when the game ended, there had been a changing of the guard in the NFC.

"It's not like a regular season game," Favre said. "It's a playoff game against the defending Super Bowl champions. It's hard to explain, it's hard to imagine what we've just done."

On San Francisco's first offensive play, quarterback Steve Young threw a swing pass to fullback Adam Walker. Linebacker Wayne Simmons—who had one of the more memorable games by a Packers defender in years—forced a fumble and cornerback Craig Newsome returned it 31 yards for a touchdown.

Before the first quarter was over, Favre led a 62-yard touchdown drive in which he hit tight end Keith Jackson for a 3-yard score. And early in the second quarter, the capacity crowd was completely silenced after Favre's 13-yard touchdown to Mark Chmura made it 21–0.

"The way we started out playing, that set the tempo for the game," said White. "This is the biggest game of my career. It's the farthest I've ever been."

Once the Packers got the lead, the 49ers became one-dimensional and had to throw. And that played right into the hands of Green Bay defensive coordinator Fritz Shurmur.

The Packers sacked Young three times and knocked him to the ground several others. Green Bay's cornerbacks—Doug Evans and Newsome—were terrific against San Francisco star wideouts Jerry Rice and John Taylor.

But the defensive star undoubtedly was Simmons, who battered tight end Brent Jones throughout the game and set the physical tone the Packers wanted to play with.

"He was very physical, and he's an outstanding player," Jones said of Simmons. "You can take any couple of plays and make what you want out of it. I think they made it a point to be physical."

Afterward, the Packers were elated. They had reached the conference championship game for the first time since 1967. And they were headed back to Dallas to battle their No. 1 nemesis with a Super Bowl berth awaiting the winner.

Unfortunately for the Packers, they experienced heartbreak once again, dropping a gut-wrenching 38–27 game to the host Cowboys. Two weeks later, Dallas won its third Super Bowl in four years.

Favre threw a pair of first-half touchdowns—a 73-yarder to Brooks and a 24-yarder to Jackson—as well as a short touchdown to Brooks in the third quarter as Green Bay took a 27–24 lead to the fourth quarter. But Favre had a costly interception in the final period and Dallas outscored the Packers 14–0 down the stretch.

"That '95 season was frustrating, disappointing," Favre said. "But we were right there and I thought it was a matter of time for us. I really did.

"I always felt like, 'We'll be back next year.' It was a matter of time. I thought we went a long ways in a short amount of time and we were a season away from busting loose."

Favre was right. But getting from the 1995 season to the 1996 campaign wasn't easy for the 26-year-old gunslinger.

In February, 1996, Favre had surgery to have bone chips removed from his left ankle. Afterward, Favre suffered a seizure that proved to be his wake-up call.

Favre was addicted to the painkiller Vicodin. And later that summer, he completed an NFL-ordered 46-day stay at the Menninger Clinic in Topeka, Kansas.

Favre married his longtime girlfriend Deanna Tynes that summer. And before training camp, Favre said: "I'm going to the Super Bowl. All I can tell people is if they don't believe me, just bet against me."

If anyone did, they lost big.

Packer Nation had been starving for a champion for nearly three decades. The 1967 Packers were the last team to win a title in Green Bay, and until the Wolf-Holmgren-Favre-White quartet arrived, this tiny city had experienced almost exclusively bad football.

But the 1996 Packers changed all that.

Wolf knew his team was close to a title after the crushing loss to Dallas in the 1995 NFC Championship. So instead of simply waiting for his younger players to grow up, Wolf used free agency to sign defensive tackle Santana Dotson, kick returner Desmond Howard, wideout Don Beebe, left tackle Bruce Wilkerson, and linebacker Ron Cox. He also traded for safety Eugene Robinson.

Wolf made it clear. The 1996 Packers were going for broke.

"I remember in the locker room after the Dallas game, a lot of us were crying," said Brooks, a wideout with Green Bay from 1992 to 1998. "I was crying, Reggie (White) was crying, Leroy (Butler) was crying. Just a whole bunch of us because we knew how close we were and we almost felt shameful that we hadn't got it done.

"But then that offseason, Ron Wolf did a lot of great things. We had a lot of the pieces in place already, and then he went and filled in all the gaps. And when we returned for training camp, we knew. We knew were about to have a special year."

Boy, did they ever.

Green Bay led the NFL in total points (456) and allowed the fewest points, as well (210). No team has accomplished that feat since.

The Packers went 13–3—their best winning percentage since the 1966 team went 12-2—and won the NFC Central by a whopping four games. Green Bay also posted a pair of five-game winning streaks during the season and earned the NFC's No. 1 seed.

Green Bay then dominated throughout the postseason, winning its three playoff games by an average score of 33.3–16.0. The Packers capped off their memorable year with a 35–21 win over New England in Super Bowl XXXI and the franchise's first title in 29 years.

"I kind of felt like the '95, '96, '97 teams were all really the same team," Favre said. "I think more than anything with those teams, there was a belief we could do it. Finally in '96, we broke through. We got it done…and that was a really special group."

It was—largely due to its resolve.

Green Bay won its first three games that season by an average of 29.7 points. But injuries began taking a toll, especially to Favre's favorite pass catchers.

Brooks, who had blossomed into a Pro Bowl player in 1995, suffered a torn ACL and torn patellar tendon during a critical Week 7 game against mighty San Francisco. Two weeks later, second-year wideout Antonio Freeman—a budding star—broke his left forearm. Tight end Mark Chmura was also in and out of the lineup for a stretch.

Suddenly, Green Bay's high-powered offense now featured a receiving corps of Don Beebe, Desmond Howard, and rookie Derrick Mayes. All three were in their first year in the offense.

"We are now a little bit inexperienced at the wideout position," Holmgren said after losing Freeman. "The thing is, you have the MVP in the league playing quarterback, so you don't want to take the ball out of his hands too much."

Holmgren didn't. But the offense still struggled to stay the course.

The Packers prevailed 23–20 in a memorable overtime thriller against San Francisco. That game proved enormous later in the season, when Green Bay edged the 49ers and Panthers by one game for the NFC's top seed.

Following a bye week, though, the Packers—without Brooks and Freeman—struggled mightily on offense in a 13–7 home win over Tampa Bay. Favre, who entered the game with a league-high 21 touchdown passes, didn't throw for a score for the first time in nearly a year.

"Right now it just seems like a bunch of bad luck," running back Dorsey

Levens said. "But you can't sit around and complain about guys going down. You just got to go out and play."

The Packers improved to 8–1 following a 28–18 home win over Detroit. But Green Bay's season hit a crossroads following consecutive road losses to Kansas City and Dallas.

The defeat in Dallas—which came on a Monday night—was one of the most frustrating of the Favre era. Green Bay felt it was ready to leapfrog the Cowboys, and actually would later that season. But playing without legitimate starting wide-outs, Favre and the offense never could get going and the Packers lost 21–6.

Near the end of the contest, tempers boiled over—even from the normally peaceful White. With the game's outcome long decided, Dallas sent kicker Chris Boniol out for an NFL-record-tying seventh field goal.

Afterward, White took exception and got into a verbal altercation with Cowboys star receiver Michael Irvin. Several other Packers were livid, too, and a minor melee ensued.

"If Reggie White needed a sack for a record, I'm sure he'd be on his toes trying to sack our quarterback," Dallas running back Emmitt Smith said. "If they don't understand that, to hell with them."

Green Bay didn't score until just 1:53 remained and was nearly shut out for the first time in five years. And Wolf—never one to sit idly by—knew he had to get Favre another weapon.

So the following day, Wolf signed wideout Andre Rison—who had recently been cut by Jacksonville—off the street.

The ultra-talented Rison had once ranked among the NFL's more gifted pass catchers. But by November, 1996, four teams had already moved on from Rison due to off-the-field issues and personality clashes internally. And when Rison was on the street the previous summer, the Packers wanted nothing to do with him.

"We saved a lot of money, and a lot of heartache because he was a problem internally," Favre said of Rison.

Rison later replied that if he were a defensive player, "I'd try to break his face."

But these were now desperate times in Green Bay. Rison was on the street. And Wolf rolled the dice.

When the troubled wideout tried explaining his past to Holmgren, the no-nonsense coach didn't particularly care to listen.

"I said, 'Stop. We're going to approach this from a different way here. You and I are together for the first time. We start new,'" Holmgren said.

In many ways, the Rison signing breathed new life into the team. Wolf once again showed he was dead serious about winning immediately. There was a renewed energy in the building.

And the Packers picked up where they had started in this once-promising season.

The following week, Green Bay trailed 9–3 at halftime in St. Louis. But Favre was terrific engineering a second-half comeback and an eventual 24–9 win.

Cornerback Doug Evans shook the Packers from their slumber with a 32-yard interception and touchdown early in the third quarter. And Favre threw a pair of second-half touchdowns, including a highlight-reel, 5-yard score to Levens.

Rison, who had been with the Packers just five days, estimated that he knew perhaps 40 plays. But he knew enough to lead Green Bay with five receptions.

Freeman returned the following week and had 10 catches for 156 yards in a 28–17 win over Chicago. And with the Packers once again nearing full health, they averaged 36.7 points over the final three games.

Green Bay closed the year on a five-game winning streak, securing the NFC's No. 1 seed and a bye week.

"Once we started getting our guys back, we really got on a roll," Favre said. "The defense was a constant all year. But then we started picking it up on offense."

That didn't change throughout the postseason. The Packers routed San Francisco 35–14 in the divisional playoffs.

In the first quarter alone, return ace Desmond Howard had a 71-yard punt return for a touchdown and a 46-yard return that set up a second score. The rout was on.

The Packers then hosted Carolina for the NFC Championship, the first time a title game had taken place in Green Bay since the 1967 "Ice Bowl."

The Packers faced two early deficits. But Levens had 205 total yards and Favre threw for 292 yards and two touchdowns.

Green Bay outgained Carolina 479–251 and cruised to a 30–13 win.

"In the second half, once the Packers got things going, they got rolling," said former Carolina head coach Dom Capers, who is Green Bay's defensive coordinator today. "The Packers were the best team and they did something that year that I'm not sure has been done since and that's lead the league in offense and defense.

"Usually a team is very good on offense or very good on defense, but it's hard to get both sides of the ball. And I remember the second half, as the Packers started picking up momentum and the crowd got into the game and we got out of the game, it got really cold out there."

The Super Bowl was next. But for many Packers, the NFC title game was as good as it got.

Green Bay won in front of its loyal followers. Nearly three decades of losing was terminated. And this team on the rise was going places they had never been.

"Out of all our wins, that was the best," free safety Eugene Robinson said of the Carolina victory.

Added Wolf: "That was the game that showed we had arrived. I'll never forget it. Playing in our stadium in front of our fans and going up to the podium to accept that (NFC Championship) trophy. That was some kind of experience."

So was Super Bowl Sunday two weeks later.

Green Bay had some rough patches early. But the Packers settled in, were terrific in all three phases, and rolled past a spunky New England team 35–21. It was the organization's first title in 29 years.

"The biggest thing I remember was holding that trophy up and seeing (Vince) Lombardi's name," Butler said. "It brought a tear to my eye because we said the trophy was coming back home. It was supposed to represent this city and these fans. They named the trophy after a former Green Bay Packer. I mean, it can't get any bigger than that."

Green Bay's heroes that night in New Orleans were abundant:

- Howard, the return ace who was in danger of not making the team in August, set a Super Bowl record with 244 return yards. He also became the first special teams player to ever earn MVP honors. Howard's 99-yard kickoff return for a touchdown in the third quarter broke open a six-point game and was the biggest moment in Green Bay's win.
- Favre, playing less than an hour away from his hometown of Kiln, Mississippi, threw two touchdown passes and no interceptions. His 54-yard strike to Andre Rison came on the Packers' second play of the game, and he later hooked up with Antonio Freeman for an 81-yard touchdown that, at the time, was the longest reception in Super Bowl history.
- White, the greatest free agent in NFL history and the man who made it

chic to play in Green Bay, had three sacks of New England quarterback Drew Bledsoe.

- And Green Bay's defense intercepted Bledsoe four times, with cornerbacks Doug Evans and Craig Newsome, safety Mike Prior, and linebacker Brian Williams all notching picks.

"It's hard to express right now," Packers coach Mike Holmgren said that night. "I look at the faces of my players and my coaches and I see their expressions. And I am humbled by that. I am overwhelmed by it.

"I'm sure it will set in sometime (today). I'm so happy for those guys. They worked very, very hard for this."

Early on, Patriots quarterback Drew Bledsoe was having his way with the Packers defense. After New England fell behind 10–0 Bledsoe threw for a pair of scores, and at the end of the highest-scoring first quarter in Super Bowl history, the Patriots held a 14–10 lead.

But the Packers took control in the second quarter.

Just 56 seconds into the period, Favre and Freeman hooked up on the 81-yard strike that gave Green Bay a 17–14 lead. Freeman got one-on-one coverage with all-rookie safety Lawyer Milloy—a talented player, but one who couldn't run with Freeman.

The Patriots blitzed, but Favre beat it and delivered a strike to Freeman. Green Bay never trailed again.

"I saw (Lawyer Milloy) come up," Freeman said that night. "He was aggressive. There was nobody behind him. I knew all I had to do was beat him at the line and Brett (Favre) would deliver a great ball.

"When I was running, all I could think about was all of those people that doubted me coming out of college. They said I couldn't run across the middle. They said I didn't have 4.3 speed. Now, America, you have to be a believer."

Green Bay's lead grew to 27–14 by halftime, before New England running back Curtis Martin ripped off an 18-yard touchdown run late in the third quarter.

On the ensuing kickoff, Howard fielded Adam Vinatieri's kick at the 1-yard line. The Packers' wedge sprung Howard loose, and 99 yards later he was in the end zone. Favre and tight end Mark Chmura hooked up on a two-point play that gave the Packers a 35–21 lead.

"Desmond's the man," defensive tackle Gilbert Brown said. "If you give him just a little block he's going to take it all the way."

From there, the Packers teed off on Bledsoe, as well as New England's entire offense, and were never challenged.

"You can't replicate what it is we did," Packers guard Aaron Taylor said. "That was an unbelievable team, an unbelievable time, an unbelievable experience."

Favre finished the year with 39 touchdown passes and just 13 interceptions despite operating with a depleted receiving corps. Favre's quarterback rating (95.8) was second to Young's and he ranked fourth in passing yards (3,899).

Favre won his second MVP award, joining Don Hutson as the only other Packer to ever win that honor twice. And Favre fulfilled his early-season dare to "bet against me."

"That was a pretty special year, a pretty special time," Favre said. "Great group of guys. We really were like family. And obviously things were pretty terrific on the field, as well. Those are the kinds of seasons you never forget."

The 1997 campaign had the makings of another memorable one.

Favre was just 27 when the year began, still squarely in his prime and at the peak of his powers. The team was packed with young stars at, or nearing their prime. And there was a nice blend of veterans sprinkled throughout the roster.

That summer, the ever-bombastic Butler predicted the Packers would go undefeated. And with the team Wolf had assembled, most didn't consider that proclamation outrageous.

"I really liked how that team looked going into that season," Wolf said. "We had lost a few players, but we also had the guys ready to step in and replace them."

Things weren't as easy as Butler—or anyone—thought they might be.

The Packers lost 10–9 at Philadelphia in Week 2. Packers rookie kicker Ryan Longwell lined up for a game-winning, 28-yard field goal in the final seconds.

Moments earlier, though, the football Gods smiled on the host Eagles and rain began pouring down. As Longwell approached the ball, his plant foot slipped out from under him. That sent his body slightly out of whack and he missed the kick to the right.

"There were only three rookies that made that team," Longwell recalled. "It was (Ross) Verba, (Darren) Sharper, and myself.

"It was a veteran-laden team, the defending world champs. There was talk of

Brett Favre's characteristic boyish glee was on display during the Packers' 35–21 victory over the New England Patriots in Super Bowl XXXI. (AP Images)

going 16–0 and repeating as Super Bowl champs and as a rookie, we had to fit in. And when you miss that, certainly you didn't want to make a habit of it."

In Week 5, Favre threw three interceptions and Green Bay lost at Detroit 26–15 to fall to 3–2.

The Packers then heated up and won five straight to move to 8–2. But the invincibility that existed in 1996—a season in which many games were finished by halftime—was gone.

While the Packers' overall record was impressive, their average margin of victory was just 5.7 points through 10 games. Week after week, Green Bay's wins were narrow and exhilarating.

In Week 3, the Packers led Miami—a 13-point underdog—just 13–12 heading to the fourth quarter, then escaped with a 23–18 win.

In Week 4, Minnesota had more points (32), total yards (393), rushing yards (185), and first downs (22) than Green Bay had allowed during in any game during its Super Bowl season. But thanks to five Favre touchdown passes and two interceptions by Butler, the Packers hung on for a 38–32 win.

The Packers were dominated by undefeated Tampa Bay in Week 6. But Green Bay prevailed 21–16, thanks in large part to a 77-yard interception return for a touchdown by defensive end Gabe Wilkins.

The Packers defeated winless Chicago 24–23 in Week 7. But it took a game-saving play by safety Eugene Robinson, who diagnosed and denied a two-point conversion pass from Erik Kramer to Raymont Harris.

"Things were a lot tougher that year, for sure," Butler said. "The target on our back was huge."

And even the league's doormats wanted a piece of the Packers. In Week 12, winless Indianapolis hosted the 8–2 Packers. The Colts were led by Lindy Infante, the former Packers coach who was fired just one month after Wolf arrived.

On this day, though, the unthinkable happened. Indianapolis—a 13-point underdog—rolled up 467 total yards and stunned the Packers 41–38.

Favre, though, wasn't deterred.

"We scored 38 points," Favre said that day. "Write what you want. I know we're 8–3 and tied for the lead. We'll be there at the end."

He was right.

Green Bay rebounded with a 45–17 rout of longtime nemesis Dallas. While the Packers had won the Super Bowl the previous season, they didn't get a chance to face the Cowboys on their way to the title.

Now, facing a struggling Dallas team on their own soil, the Packers rolled. Favre threw four touchdowns, Levens had a franchise-record 190 rushing yards, and Green Bay snapped an eight-game losing streak against Dallas, including seven straight at Texas Stadium.

"It feels about like what I thought it would," Favre said. "It's great that we finally beat these guys. It's a shame we had to wait this long. But it's a great win. We finally did it."

That victory jumpstarted the Packers to an outstanding final month of the season.

Green Bay won at Minnesota 27–11 and at Tampa Bay 17–6. Those two wins lifted the Packers to a third straight NFC Central title, making them the first team to achieve that since Chicago had won five in a row in the mid-1980s.

Green Bay finished the regular season with a road win at Carolina and a home victory over Buffalo. Despite some early hiccups, the Packers were 13–3 again. Green Bay had won five straight and 10 of 11. And the Packers were the NFC's No. 2 seed, which meant they received another first-round bye.

"I feel just as good about this team as last year's, if not better," Favre said. "The only unfortunate thing is that we might have to go on the road. But we feel like we're better on the road this season."

After a bye week, Green Bay rolled past Tampa Bay 21–7 in the divisional playoffs. Buccaneers quarterback Trent Dilfer completed just 11-of-36 passes (30.6 percent) for 200 yards as the Packers defense dominated.

Green Bay then cruised past San Francisco 23–10 in the NFC Championship Game held at rainy and muddy 3Com Park.

Favre was patient, took what the defense gave him, and threw for 222 yards and a touchdown. Longwell, who had a sensational rookie season following his rough start, made three field goals. And Green Bay's defense was terrific, limiting the 49ers to just 33 rushing yards and holding Young to a passer rating of just 69.0.

The Packers eliminated the once-dominant 49ers from the postseason for a third straight year. And Green Bay was headed to its second consecutive Super Bowl, this time to meet Denver.

"The road here was quite different," Holmgren said. "I've always preached to enjoy the journey and I mean that. Winning each Sunday is a huge accomplishment and a player and a coach should be allowed to enjoy that regardless of the score. Because you work too hard.

"When you are repeating, some of that glory is taken away from you and it's no one's fault. It's just the way it is. It's harder for your team, coaches, and me to enjoy each win because the expectation level was so high. I battled them and tried to get them to do that."

Green Bay passed virtually every test on its way back to the Super Bowl. But in their quest for history, the Packers fell short.

In Super Bowl XXXII, Green Bay had no answers for Broncos running back Terrell Davis, who ran for 157 yards and three touchdowns despite missing an entire quarter with a migraine headache. The Packers offense also failed to take advantage of several terrific opportunities.

And when it was over, Green Bay suffered a 31–24 defeat that still haunts many—even now.

"That game still drives me nuts," Butler said. "It really does. Did the better team win? I don't believe so. But all that matters, I guess, is the final score."

The Packers of the mid-1990s were in position to be discussed with some of great dynasties in franchise history. They were poised to challenge Dallas as the "Team of the Decade."

Instead, as Green Bay's defensive linemen wilted in the heat and Davis ran roughshod, such hopes vanished. Green Bay had allowed just 61.5 rushing yards per game in the playoffs that season. But Davis and Denver's offensive line dominated the Packers' front four, and the Broncos piled up 179 yards on 39 carries.

"Every time I looked up, this guy Davis is running up and down the field, looking like the best back in the history of professional football," Wolf said. "That was not a great day for us."

Far from it.

Green Bay struck first when Favre hit Freeman with a 22-yard touchdown, one of three TD strikes from Favre that day. But Denver scored 17 unanswered points and took a 17–7 lead with 12:21 left in the second quarter.

With Davis sitting, though, for the rest of the second quarter, the Packers were able to forge a 17-all tie early in the third quarter.

That momentum vanished when the Broncos marched 92 yards in 13 plays for the go-ahead touchdown. Davis capped the drive with a 1-yard touchdown to make it 24–17 with just 34 seconds left in the third quarter.

"It really was unheard of what they were doing to us on the ground," nose tackle Gilbert Brown said years later. "That still bothers people."

Favre responded with a 13-yard touchdown strike to Antonio Freeman that tied the game 24–24. That capped a four-play drive, in which Favre and Freeman hooked up three times and connected for their second touchdown that day.

After each team punted twice, Denver delivered the knockout blow. The Broncos drove from the Packers' 49 to the 1-yard line in just four plays.

On second down, Holmgren ordered his team to allow Davis to score, so his offense would have enough time to answer. The problem is Holmgren thought it was first down.

Had he known which down it was, perhaps his strategy would have changed. As it was, Denver took a 31–24 lead and Green Bay had just 1:45 to pull even.

"There are some people that say Mike Holmgren did not have a good day," Wolf said. "I really don't remember enough.

"But let me ask you this: what are the odds that (Broncos defensive coordinator) Greg Robinson would get the better of Mike Holmgren? They couldn't have been good."

Favre drove the Packers to Denver's 31, where on a fourth-and-6 the Broncos brought seven rushers. Favre tried forcing a ball to Chmura, but the pass was knocked away by linebacker John Mobley and Denver prevailed.

Afterward, an extremely frustrated Wolf said: "We're just a fart in the wind. This ought to take care of all that silly dynasty talk."

Favre saw it a little differently.

"Denver was for real, and I think a lot of people didn't completely find that out until the next year," Favre said of a Broncos team that repeated in 1998. "They proved it against us in the Super Bowl."

Unfortunately for Favre, he never played in another Super Bowl. And while Favre set a bevy of passing records during his glorious career, having just one title keeps him out of most discussions about the best quarterbacks ever.

"Another Super Bowl would have put him in that conversation," Wolf said. "Unfortunately, he couldn't get that done."

Favre won a third straight MVP in 1997, sharing honors this time with Detroit running back Barry Sanders. But when the season ended, that trophy offered little consolation for the one Favre and the Packers truly wanted.

"That was a tough loss, stays with you your whole career," Favre said. "You don't get very many chances at Super Bowls…and it's tough when you let those opportunities go by."

From 1995–97, the Packers went a blistering 37–11. Green Bay was 23–1 at home. The Packers played in three straight NFC Championship games and two Super Bowls, and passed longtime powers Dallas and San Francisco as the conference bully.

But to most, the fact those Packers didn't win more than one Super Bowl will always be somewhat bothersome.

"Dallas was probably the lowest locker room I've ever sat in, because we had them (in 1995)," Butler said. "We were better than them. But (Denver) was the second lowest.

"I think it's human nature to get a little bit complacent. You just dominated an entire season (in 1996) with the No. 1 defense, the No. 1 offense, had a great special teams guy that was MVP of the Super Bowl. Then we had the majority of our team coming back.

"Overall that was a great year, we just didn't get it done. We should have won back-to-back. That will always bother me that we didn't win two straight. We had three or four years in there, from 1995–98, where I thought we were the best team in the NFL. And we should have won more than one Super Bowl."

The 1998 season was an up-and-down affair.

Green Bay opened the year with four straight wins and appeared on its way to big things again. But a changing of the guard took place on a Monday night in early October.

Minnesota came to Lambeau Field, and Vikings rookie wide receiver Randy Moss stole the show. Moss had five catches for 190 yards and two touchdowns that night.

Veteran cornerbacks Craig Newsome and Tyrone Williams were no match for Moss, a 6'4" speedster who immediately changed the entire landscape of the NFC Central. In fact, the following year, Wolf used his first three draft picks on cornerbacks in an attempt to match up with Moss.

That didn't help Green Bay in 1998, though, and the Vikings left town with a 37–24 win. In the process, Minnesota snapped the Packers' 25-game home winning streak, and showed there was a new sheriff in town.

That game threw the Packers into a tailspin, and they dropped five of nine overall. But with a postseason berth slipping away, Green Bay rallied to win its last three games, finish the year 11–5, and claim a wild-card spot.

The Packers appeared to be heating up at the right time. Dorsey Levens, who had missed nine games in the middle of the season with a broken leg, was back. The defense was beginning to find its sea legs. And Green Bay was headed back to San Francisco, a team it had defeated five straight times overall.

"I thought we had all the momentum going into those playoffs," Wolf said. "We were coming around at the right time and we had pretty much had our way with San Francisco."

What followed was one of the greatest wild-card games of all time.

The Packers led the 49ers 27–23 with just eight seconds left. The 49ers had a third down at Green Bay's 25-yard line.

San Francisco quarterback Steve Young dropped back and nearly fell to the ground when he tripped over the foot of a teammate. Young regained his balance, then fired a dart down the seam that wideout Terrell Owens caught to give the 49ers a stunning 30–27 win.

It was a remarkable ending for Owens, who dropped four passes and had a fumble that day. It was also a surreal conclusion for the Packers, who appeared poised to knock the 49ers out of the postseason for a fourth straight year.

On the fateful play—one called "Three Jet Go"—the Packers rushed just three and played zone with eight. Safety Darren Sharper was the primary culprit for the gaffe after dropping too deep in his portion of the zone. Linebacker Bernardo Harris also didn't drop deep enough and safety Pat Terrell was late to arrive.

Owens took a lick when Sharper and Terrell drilled him one yard deep in the end zone. But when Owens held on, Green Bay's five-game winning streak over the 49ers had ended.

"The way this one ended was startling,'" Holmgren said. "When the ball goes down the middle like that, you don't think the ball's going to be caught, ever. I think it was a marvelous catch. It was the perfect throw and he (Owens) made the play."

Favre was brilliant in defeat, throwing for 292 yards and two touchdowns. Favre also engineered an 89-yard scoring drive late—one he capped with a 15-yard touchdown strike to Antonio Freeman—that gave the Packers a 27–23 lead with 1:56 remaining.

On the 49ers' ensuing drive, Packers rookie safety Scott McGarrahan stripped wideout Jerry Rice of the ball and Harris recovered. Officials ruled Rice down, though, and the drive continued.

Replays showed that call was incorrect. But because instant replay didn't begin until the following season, the 49ers kept the ball.

Sixteen years later, Wolf still wasn't happy.

"I'm still mad about that fumble," Wolf said. "I mean, come on. Rice fumbled the ball, Bernardo Harris recovered, and we should have won the game."

That wasn't all that Packer Nation was fired up about. Just five days later, Holmgren was hired as Seattle's head coach, general manager, and executive vice president of football operations.

Things were about to change in Green Bay. And to this day, the major players from those teams wish things could have simply stayed the same.

"Do I think we could have more Super Bowls with Mike (Holmgren)? Absolutely," Favre said. "I think because what we had wasn't broken. If we could have maintained our consistency, I really think we could have won again. And even though a lot of things were the same after he left, a lot of things weren't."

Added Wolf: "I would think we could have won another Super Bowl. For sure. There would have certainly been a chance because of the quarterback. I could see that, yeah. It could have been."

But Green Bay never found out. And Wolf made arguably the biggest mistake of his Packers career by hiring Ray Rhodes to replace Holmgren.

Rhodes had been Holmgren's defensive coordinator in 1992–93, then was the Philadelphia Eagles' head coach from 1995 to 1998. In his four years with the Eagles, Rhodes was an unimpressive 29–34–1 (.461), and was fired after going 3–13 in his final season.

Rhodes had been a key defensive assistant coach in San Francisco during the 49ers' five Super Bowl seasons. In Philadelphia, though, Rhodes' teams got worse every year.

Still, Wolf had so much house credit and good will built up, he could have hired Madonna and the fans would have given him the benefit of the doubt.

"The seat is going to be hot. The shoes are going to be big to fill," Rhodes said at his introductory news conference. "The key is to keep the machine running, keep the machine going. Make sure if you need a new tire here, or a new tire there, you put it on. But don't mess with the engine."

Rhodes never could keep the machine going. Far from it.

Things started out all right in 1999 as Favre led remarkable fourth-quarter comeback wins in three of the Packers' first four games. Green Bay rallied for home wins against Oakland, Minnesota, and Tampa Bay, and sitting at 3–1, it seemed the Packers would be fine without Holmgren.

They weren't.

The Packers finished the year just 8–8, tied for third in the NFC Central, and missed the playoffs for the first time since 1992—Holmgren's first season in Green Bay.

The Packers had been dealt a blow that preseason when Brooks couldn't overcome an array of injuries and retired. The passing offense never recovered and Favre struggled through his worst season since his second year in the NFL. Favre threw 22 touchdowns and 23 interceptions, and finished the season with a passer rating of just 74.7.

As Wolf watched this all unfold, the losing drove him mad. The manner in which it was happening, though, made him even more upset.

Rhodes was the ultimate players' coach, the direct opposite of the tougher, stricter Holmgren. Unfortunately for Rhodes, many players took advantage of his more lenient ways.

Cell phones went off in meetings with no repercussions. A few players were allowed to stay in Florida following a post-Christmas loss to Tampa Bay.

Howard, who was back for his second stint in Green Bay in 1999, said Rhodes was more interested in "playing dominoes with the guys in the locker room than managing the clock against Carolina."

The cold reality was the Packers had become soft and undisciplined. And Wolf knew he had to fire Rhodes.

"We underachieved this year," Wolf said. "We have enough talent here to be a successful team. For whatever reason, the players did not respond to this program."

Wolf went off the board again and hired little-known Seattle Seahawks offensive coordinator Mike Sherman to replace Rhodes. Sherman had been the Packers' tight ends coach in 1997–98, then went to Seattle with Holmgren.

Sherman, a former middle-school English teacher, insisted he would be tougher than his predecessor.

"I started out a seventh-grade middle-school teacher and I don't think there's a whole lot of difference dealing with those guys to a certain degree," Sherman said. "You've got to be organized and disciplined for those classrooms. I consider myself a teacher at heart. In order to communicate your thoughts, you have to be a teacher."

By late in the 2000 season, there were signs that Sherman was indeed the right man for the job.

Green Bay was just 5–7 heading to December that season. The playoffs weren't happening. Thoughts could have drifted to offseason vacations.

Instead, the Packers finished the year with four straight wins—all against NFC Central foes—and ended the season 9–7. Down the stretch, Green Bay won at eventual divisional champion Minnesota and bested playoff qualifier Tampa Bay.

Favre played a much more controlled brand of football, throwing for 20 touchdowns and 16 interceptions. Many of the wild chances he was taking under Rhodes and offensive coordinator Sherman Lewis the previous year had been eliminated.

Favre led four fourth-quarter comebacks that season. And when the year ended, optimism was back in the air.

"I really felt like we were going places after that season," Favre said. "We finished strong. Guys seemed to have bought into the way Mike (Sherman) wanted to do things. I think we were all pretty excited the way that year ended."

That excitement was tempered somewhat when Wolf retired five weeks after the season ended. Wolf had turned the Packers into an NFL power. But at 62 years old, Wolf didn't feel like he could do the job with the same vigor he had a decade earlier.

"For me personally, I got out at the right time and I'll tell you why," Wolf said. "I couldn't do what I had to do anymore. I was not happy with myself that I couldn't give as much as I needed to give to get the job done the way that I wanted to get it done. I would have just been stealing money from the Packers and I didn't want to do that."

The Packers' woes grew, though, when they promoted Sherman to the dual role of head coach and general manager. Wolf liked the direction Green Bay was headed, and didn't want to saddle Sherman with a new boss. So Wolf recommended to Harlan that Sherman be given both jobs.

"I was reluctant to bring in someone over Mike who he might not get along with, someone who would probably change a scouting department that I thought was very efficient," Harlan said years later. "Even though I'm not fond of the one-man system, I thought at that particular time it was the best.

It wasn't.

Wolf had brilliantly restocked the roster late in his career and given the Packers a chance to be competitive for years. He traded for young standout running back Ahman Green. He found five starters—tight end Bubba Franks, tackles Chad Clifton and Mark Tauscher, linebacker Na'il Diggs, and defensive end Kabeer Gbaja-Biamila—in the 2000 draft.

The future looked bright and Green Bay played winning football the next several seasons. But the dual role was too much for Sherman, who bungled multiple drafts and struck out repeatedly in free agency.

Green Bay returned to the playoffs from 2001 to 2004, largely due to Favre and the players Wolf left behind. But by January 2005, Harlan admitted the Sherman experiment hadn't worked and took away his general manager duties.

"This move is not meant in any way to criticize any element of Mike," Harlan said the day he named Ted Thompson Green Bay's new general manager. "I think the world of him.

"I'm doing this because I feel it's the best move for the future of the franchise. It's going to free him up to spend more time coaching, not worrying about general manager obligations. It gives him one more accountable person to be there to help him make football decisions. And I think that's important. And I've always felt that we need to do whatever it takes to help the head coach and general manager be successful. And I told Mike, 'This move is being made not to criticize you. It's being made to help you.'"

While Sherman was a disaster as general manager, he was an awfully solid football coach. And the Packers continued to trend upward in 2001.

Favre threw eight touchdown passes in Green Bay's first three games of 2001 and the Packers opened the year 3–0. The Packers played at a high level throughout that campaign, finished the year on another three-game winning streak, and ended the season 12–4.

That was Green Bay's best record since the NFC Championship team in 1997. And the Packers—who finished one game behind Chicago for the division title—earned the top wild-card spot.

The Packers welcomed old playoff foe San Francisco to Lambeau Field for a Wild Card game. And thanks to Favre's brilliance and a terrific defensive effort, Green Bay escaped with a 25–15 win.

Favre had 226 of his 269 passing yards in the second half. He also led Green Bay to scoring drives on four of its first five second-half possessions.

"You take away the interception, I don't think a quarterback could have a better game than that," Sherman said of Favre's performance. "He took total control of that football game. He made something out of nothing on numerous occasions. He just played a Brett Favre–type game."

In some ways, the NFC Divisional playoffs the following week were just as much a Brett Favre-game.

No player in NFL history threw more career interceptions than Favre, who finished with 336 picks over his 19-year career. Favre was never afraid to take chances. And when his team was down, he'd often throw caution to the wind and fire into double and triple coverage.

While several quarterbacks continue to play it safe when trailing—knowing their statistics can be negatively affected by taking chances—Favre didn't care. If he was going down, he was going down swinging.

Never was that more evident than in St. Louis the following week. The Packers fell behind early and Favre & Co. had to take several chances to get back in the game.

Most failed. Favre finished with six interceptions—which tied an NFL record—and the Packers were routed by St. Louis 45–17.

The Rams returned three of the interceptions for touchdowns. And the Packers had eight turnovers that led to 35 St. Louis points.

"I could have thrown eight had we gotten the ball back," Favre said. "I was going to keep chucking."

Favre had played at an extremely high level once again in 2001. He finished with 32 touchdown passes and 15 interceptions, and posted a quarterback rating of 94.1.

But the ending in St. Louis left a bad taste everywhere. And Green Bay was hell-bent on changing things in 2002.

For most of that season, it appeared the Packers would do exactly that.

Green Bay strung together a seven-game winning streak and was 8–1 just past the midway point in the season. Favre led fourth-quarter, come-from-behind wins against Atlanta and Carolina. And through nine games, Favre had thrown 17 touchdowns and just four interceptions.

Favre had a memorable game that season, playing through a sprained lateral collateral ligament in his left knee and leading the Packers to a 24–10 win over Miami on Monday Night Football.

Favre had been knocked out of the previous game by Washington linebacker LaVar Arrington, and his "Iron Man" streak was in serious doubt. But Favre benefitted from a bye week, then played with a brace in powering the Packers past the Dolphins.

"Nothing surprises me with him," Green said.

Favre was 16-of-25 for 187 yards with one touchdown pass against the Dolphins. And when backup quarterback Doug Pederson replaced Favre late in the game, the crowd serenaded him with chants of "MVP! MVP! MVP!"

"It's not too bad," Favre said afterward of his knee. "It's a little stiff. I survived. The brace hindered me a little bit. I knew it would, but overall it served its purpose."

The Packers were 12–3 late in the season, but injuries had begun to take a toll. Green Bay still had a chance to clinch the No. 1 seed in the NFC, but was routed by the host New York Jets 42–17 in the regular season finale.

That loss dropped Green Bay to the No. 3 seed in the postseason. And the following week, the unthinkable happened. Green Bay lost its first home playoff game in franchise history, falling to Michael Vick and upstart Atlanta 27–7.

Favre took the loss extremely hard, and for the first time ever, skipped his postgame press conference.

"'To say this is disappointing is as big an understatement as I could ever make," Sherman said. "We did a lot of things right this year in the regular season. We didn't do them right in the postseason."

Unfortunately, the same held true in both 2003 and '04.

Nothing came easy for Green Bay in 2003, as it began the year 4–5 and was just 6–6 heading to the final quarter of the season. But the Packers caught fire down the stretch, winning their final four games to capture the NFC North by one game over Minnesota.

The miraculous finish featured some of the more remarkable moments of Favre's Green Bay career.

First, with the Packers sitting at 8–6 and in Oakland for a Monday Night Football game, Favre learned his father, Irvin, had died following a heart attack. Favre contemplated not playing, but instead, he had the performance of his life.

Favre threw four touchdowns and for 399 yards and led the Packers to an unforgettable 41–7 win over Oakland. NFL Network recently voted this the No. 1 game of Favre's magnificent career.

"I knew that my dad would have wanted me to play," Favre said. "I love him so much, and I love this game. It's meant a great deal to me, to my dad, to my family, and I didn't expect this kind of performance. But I know he was watching tonight."

Green Bay remained in the playoff hunt, but needed a minor miracle in the final week of the season. Not only did the Packers need to beat visiting Denver, but Arizona (3–12) also had to win at division-leading Minnesota (9–6).

Amazingly, both results took place.

First, Green Bay destroyed the Broncos 31–3. The Minnesota–Arizona game was unfolding at the same time, and virtually none of the 70,000 inside Lambeau Field knew what was happening.

Back in 2003, the Internet wasn't available on cell phones. And Sherman had ordered that the Vikings score be kept off the Jumbotron so his players wouldn't be distracted.

"We knew (Sherman) took it off the board…but basically you just paid attention to the crowd," Packers running back Tony Fisher said. "And when you saw the crowd erupting, you knew something good was happening."

With Green Bay's game well in hand, though, everyone was searching for ways to follow the Vikings game. Many in club seats had the game on their televisions, and word filtered through the stadium. Green Bay radio announcers Wayne Larrivee and Larry McCarren also began broadcasting the Vikings game to their statewide audience.

And what everyone experienced was a magical moment.

Trailing 17–12, Arizona had time for one final play from Minnesota's 28-yard line. Cardinals quarterback Josh McCown took the final snap with just 4 seconds left on the clock, then avoided trouble by rolling to his right.

Something to Believe In

Even now, more than a decade later, everything remains a blur.

The emotions. His surroundings. The decision. It's all somewhat of a purple haze.

What remains crystal clear is what happened between the white lines.

On December 21, 2003, Irvin Favre had a heart attack and died. He was just 58.

The next day, the Packers—in the middle of a fight to reach the playoffs—were playing in Oakland. Most figured that Brett Favre, who had played in 204 consecutive games, would sit this one out.

But Favre did what he always did: he played. And my, oh my, how he played.

On *Monday Night Football*, in primetime, Favre threw four touchdowns for 399 yards and led the Packers to a 41–7 win over Oakland.

"The previous day when I got the news is all kind of a blur," Favre said. "But the game itself, much like the way I played, is still really clear. The flow of emotions was much like a roller coaster. You throw a touchdown and it's a total high. Then you go back to the sidelines and it hits you again and you start thinking that you have to fly home after the game and your dad is going to be buried. That's tough and this is all going on during the game.

"But when I was playing, when I was in the game, I was really zeroed in on what I had to do as hard as that might be. So it was up and down, up and down, back and forth.

Favre played in 277 games during his 16 years in Green Bay, including the playoffs. But his passer rating of 154.9 that night was the best of his Packers career.

Not only did Favre shine one day after his father's death. He did so in the "Black Hole," where Oakland's boisterous crowd did everything it could to rattle Favre.

By the end of the night, the rambunctious fan base was actually cheering for Favre—knowing they'd witnessed a once-in-a-lifetime event.

"I've never seen a leader or a player like Brett in my career, and I'm pretty sure that nobody else in this locker room has," former Packers tight end Wesley Walls said. "I think we wanted to make him proud. Just getting up in front of the team at such a horrible and difficult time in his life really showed he cared about us. That was something I'll never forget."

Packers wide receiver Antonio Freeman, who caught a franchise-record 57 touchdowns from Favre, couldn't believe what he seeing either.

"What he had to deal with was unmeasurable," Freeman said. "You can't put a price on what he did. I don't know how he did it, but he did it in fine fashion."

Favre gave a performance that night that was truly unforgettable. Favre was razor sharp throughout, but his receivers were equally brilliant.

"We had a meeting with the receiving corps and made a pact that whatever he put up, we were going to come down with," Packers wideout Robert Ferguson said. "We rallied around our leader."

They sure did.

(continued)

Something to Believe In *(continued)*

On just Green Bay's fourth play from scrimmage, Ferguson held up his end of the bargain with a sensational 47-yard grab. Two plays later, Walls snared a 22-yard touchdown pass in the back of the end zone on a play that appeared to have little chance of success.

"That's probably one of the best passes I've ever made," Favre said. "It had to be perfect, and then I still wasn't even sure if Wesley could get there or not.

"But it was like that all night. There were so many balls where I thought, 'There is no way they should have caught that pass. There is no way that should have been caught by our guys.' Then, it was not only caught, a lot of them were caught for touchdowns."

Favre hummed a gorgeous 23-yard touchdown pass to Walker later in the first quarter. Favre also lofted a 43-yard touchdown strike to Walker when the standout receiver outmuscled Raiders defensive backs Phillip Buchanon and Anthony Dorsett for the ball.

Favre hit Walker with another 46-yard completion, then capped that drive with a 6-yard touchdown pass to tight end David Martin shortly before halftime.

Favre completed his first nine passes and threw for a personal-best 311 yards and four touchdowns in the first half alone. He also finished the first half with a perfect passer rating of 158.3.

"It was a magical night," Walker said.

Walls was part of a Super Bowl championship team in San Francisco and played in an endless stream of enormous games. But Green Bay's trip to Oakland in 2003 will always remain among his most memorable.

"He played an amazing game for us, and we all felt we had to do the same for him," Walls said of Favre. "Sometimes in special circumstances, you make special plays. I think it's fair to say we were inspired by Irv. Someone was watching down on us. I fully believe that."

That someone may have been Irvin Favre.

And with a little help from above, Irvin's son—the courageous and indestructible Brett Favre—gave the performance of his lifetime.

"I just know this: my dad wouldn't have wanted me to play. He would have demanded that I play," said Favre, who was coached by his father in high school. "So I didn't know what to do for a while. I wanted to play and I wanted to honor my dad, but I wasn't sure how I'd play. But my prayers were answered."

Green Bay stayed in contention for a playoff berth that night in Oakland. And the Packers qualified for the postseason the following week when Arizona stunned Minnesota in the final seconds to give the Packers the NFC North Division title.

If there was such a thing as divine intervention, Favre was becoming a believer.

"I've been around people who have lost a family member or lost someone close to them and they say that that person's there watching, or angels, or whatever," Favre said. "And I would say that two weeks ago I didn't really believe in that. But I think we'd better start believing in something."

That night in Oakland, Favre gave plenty of people something to believe in.

McCown found little-used wideout Nathan Poole in the right corner of the endzone. Poole made a spectacular grab, got one foot down, then was pushed out of bounds by Minnesota's Denard Walker and Brian Russell.

Poole's touchdown was under review for four minutes, and after much deliberation, it was ruled he was forced out of bounds while making the catch. The play stood.

Green Bay's game ended at virtually the same time, and the Packers knew by watching their fans and via reports from upstairs that they were NFC North champions.

Favre raised his arms to the sky, then teared up. Sherman was doused with a bucket of water. And Lambeau Field became bedlam.

"I had no idea what was going on and it was mad confusion," right guard Marco Rivera said. "Then I saw the crowd react and I thought, 'What the hell's wrong with the crowd? The game's not going on. Is there a fight over there?'

"Then I finally asked (director of football administration) Bruce Warwick and he said, 'Oh my God! Arizona just scored.' It was unbelievable. We were in the playoffs."

Green Bay was in, and was also red hot.

The Packers had won four straight games, and suddenly looked like a fantastically dangerous outfit.

"I've said all along—and I don't know if anybody's bought into it—I think we're a better football team this year," Sherman said. "Record doesn't always dictate how good you are. I think we're a better team this year.

"We're healthier at this point of the season. We limped into the last four ballgames, really we limped all the way through the season last year, and it was a tremendous stress and strain on our football team. Every week we had to patch something up and fix someone up and throw him out there and see if he could go.

"This year, the energy level at this point in the season in practice, in the locker room, in this building, is very high. And they're very excited about the postseason and playing as many more games as they'll let us play."

Green Bay opened with a thrilling 33–27 overtime win over Seattle in a Wild Card game. The game ended when cornerback Al Harris jumped in front of a Matt Hasselbeck pass intended for wideout Alex Bannister on the first possession of overtime. Fifty-two yards later, Harris was in the end zone and Green Bay was celebrating, on its way to the divisional playoffs in Philadelphia.

After his father, Irvin Favre, passed away suddenly the day before, Favre led the Packers to an emotion-fueled win over the Oakland Raiders on Monday, December 22, 2003. His spectacular performance included four touchdowns and 399 yards passing en route to the 41–7 victory with his teammates rallying behind him.

"I jumped a lot of routes," Harris said. "(Hasselbeck) made a lot of good reads because I jumped a lot of routes today and he would look it off and go to the guy that was open.

"I was just praying that he would throw the ball, because I knew I was going to gamble on that play. As a [defensive back], you pray that they will run that route—a hitch or a slant—something you can jump quick and get to where you have to go."

One week later, though, the Packers suffered one of the most frustrating losses in franchise history, one known today as simply "Fourth-and-26."

With just 1:12 left, the Packers led the host Eagles 17–14 and Philadelphia faced a fourth-and-26 at its own 26-yard line. A math professor at the University of Wisconsin-Green Bay later calculated the odds of the Eagles picking up a first down as 1-in-339.

But to the shock and dismay of Packer Nation, this was the Eagles' lucky day. Philadelphia quarterback Donovan McNabb drilled a strike to wideout Freddie Mitchell that was good for 28 yards.

Philadelphia drove for the tying field goal. And after a costly Favre interception in overtime, the Eagles kicked a game-winning field goal and prevailed 20–17.

"Let's not sugarcoat it," said Packers defensive coordinator Ed Donatell, who was fired the following week. "It's part of Packer history. They'll talk about it for a long, long time."

That's for sure.

Green Bay sat in a Cover 2 defense and rushed four. And when the pressure was nonexistent, the middle of the field was wide open.

Nick Barnett, Green Bay's middle linebacker, had failed to get a deep enough drop with Mitchell. Safeties Marques Anderson and Darren Sharper had inexplicably fallen 30 yards deep into coverage.

McNabb fired a laser to Mitchell, and when Bhawoh Jue made a poor play on the ball and both safeties arrived late, Mitchell picked up 28 yards and the most impossible of first downs.

Green Bay seemed disorganized before fourth down, though, which led to second-guessing later.

"Quite frankly, we should have called a timeout," cornerback Michael Hawthorne said. "We should have called timeout to regroup and play the defense that we know will make them catch everything in front of us."

That fast, the season was over. So was all of the momentum and energy that had filled the building the past six weeks.

That loss would be Sherman's last true chance at experiencing greatness in Green Bay. And when presented the golden opportunity, Sherman's team struck out.

When the 2004 season began, there was a definite hangover effect.

Many Packers—especially the offensive linemen—were still angry with Sherman for punting on fourth-and-1 from the Eagles' 41-yard line late in the NFC divisional playoffs. Had the Packers—who were averaging 5.7 yards per carry—converted, the game would have been over. Others were frustrated that Donatell had been made a scapegoat for the late-game collapse.

All of those frustrations were evident as Green Bay began the year just 1–4. But Favre and the Packers eventually found their groove.

Green Bay rolled off six straight wins and notched victories in nine of its final 11 games. The Packers surged to a 10–6 mark, won their third straight divisional title, and seemed to once again have momentum heading toward the postseason.

Favre had a memorable four-touchdown game and led the Packers to a narrow 34–31 win over visiting Minnesota in Week 10. Just six weeks later, the Packers beat Minnesota by that identical score in the Metrodome and captured the divisional title.

Those same teams met for a third time in the Wild Card round, only this time the results were much different as Minnesota rolled to a 31–17 win.

Vikings quarterback Daunte Culpepper was brilliant, completing 19 of 29 passes for 284 yards, four touchdowns and no interceptions, and posted a quarterback rating of 137.1. Favre, meanwhile, had another playoff meltdown, firing four interceptions and just one touchdown and finishing with a 55.4 quarterback rating.

The game is probably best remembered for Vikings wideout Randy Moss pretending to moon the Packers crowd after whipping Harris for a fourth-quarter touchdown. But the bigger issue was Green Bay let another golden opportunity pass.

"I just know that when you get this opportunity that it's special, because you don't get it that often," Favre said of playoff games. "I'm a little bit spoiled because we've gone to the playoffs a lot, and people expect that out of us. I expect it. I expect us every year in the playoffs.

"So to say we wasted an opportunity, I hate to say we wasted it because guys, we could have easily given up after 1–4. And I think that says a lot about the character of this team. We got here, but it's what you do with it after. Some teams are content with just getting to the playoffs, and that's a good thing. But I've been to the top, and I know what it's like. I hope these guys get to do that sometime because it's a special thing."

That offseason, Thompson replaced Sherman as general manager. And Sherman seemed to go into a deep funk.

Sherman, already somewhat of an introvert, kept to himself more than ever. He confided in only a couple of his assistant coaches. And communication, never a strength of Sherman's, became even worse.

"The head coach thought he was the only one with any brains," said Johnny Roland, who spent the 2004 season coaching Green Bay's running backs before taking the same position in New Orleans this offseason. "There was a lot of collective knowledge in the people that have left. And that knowledge wasn't listened to."

Sherman cleaned house on the defensive side of the ball after the 2004 season. But Roland and wide receivers coach Ray Sherman made lateral moves and joined other organizations.

"Why do you think those guys left?" said Jeff Jagodzinski, who coached Green Bay's tight ends from 1999 to 2003. "It wasn't to go to a better team. It's because in Green Bay, your ideas don't get listened to."

The Packers looked like a team in need of fresh ideas in 2005.

Green Bay lost its first four games and was 1–7 at the midway point. The Packers slumped to 2–10 and finished the year 4–12, the worst season since the 1991 team had the identical record.

Lindy Infante was fired after the 1991 train wreck. And Sherman endured the same fate this time around.

"I have no regrets over the last six years," Sherman said at his final press conference. "I gave this job everything that I had and I'm proud of what we accomplished during that time. When we got here in 2000, it was said that this team was in decline after a couple of Super Bowl seasons. I thought we were able to resurrect some things and win some football games and I'm proud of that."

Still, the Packers appeared to be a team in decline.

Favre was coming off the worst season of his career, one in which he threw 20 touchdowns and 29 interceptions. The roster had some talented veterans that Wolf had found, and some gifted youngsters Thompson had plucked in the 2005 draft. But because Sherman's drafts were largely devoid of talent, the Packers were missing elite players who should have been entering their prime years.

In addition, Favre—who had hinted at retirement since the 2002 playoff loss to Atlanta—had not committed to a return in 2006.

It was under this backdrop that Thompson hired Mike McCarthy as the 14th head coach in Packers history. McCarthy was Green Bay's quarterbacks coach in 1999 and had a history with Favre. And McCarthy said he had no problem waiting on Favre to make a decision.

"I'm not into soap operas, daytime or nighttime," McCarthy said. "He's a Hall of Fame quarterback. He deserves the time to sit down with his family and make a decision. And that's where we are. And I'm perfectly comfortable with that."

It took Favre until April 26—three days before the NFL Draft that year—before announcing he would return in 2006.

"People will say, 'he's coming back for money, he's coming back for records, or he wants to make a difference especially since he was a part of a 4–12 team.' None of those are true," Favre said. "I would love to get this team back on track and into the playoffs. That's my, as everyone else in this building, feeling, is that we will be back."

Amazingly, they were.

Thompson and McCarthy were still trying to dig out of the mess Sherman had left behind. The Packers began the 2006 season 1–4 and were 4–8 late in the year.

But Green Bay caught fire and set the course for what would be a memorable 2007 campaign. The Packers won their final four games and finished the 2006 season 8–8.

The most memorable moment came in the regular season finale, a 26–7 win over divisional champion Chicago on *Sunday Night Football*. Favre threw for 285 yards and a touchdown to power the Packers past the Bears. Then when he teared up in a postgame interview, most assumed Favre had played his last game.

"If this is my last game, I want to remember it," Favre said as tears streamed from his face. "It's tough. I love these guys. I love this game. What a great way to go out against a great football team. I couldn't ask for a better way to get out."

But Favre wasn't finished. Far from it.

On February 2, 2007, Favre committed to playing a 16th season with Green Bay. For Favre, it was remarkably early in the offseason to make such a commitment.

What followed was a 2007 season that ranks among Favre's finest ever.

Favre threw 28 touchdowns and just 15 interceptions that season and his passer rating of 95.7 was his best since the 1996 campaign. Favre threw for 4,155 yards, the third-highest total of his Packers career.

And Favre helped Green Bay go 13–3, win the NFC North, and lock down the No. 2 seed in the postseason.

"I've said that this whole year that winning games in general, every time you win one you should feel thankful because there was a time where we won and no big deal. What's so hard about this?" Favre said. "And the last two years were a little bit of a wake-up call, especially 4–12. That hasn't even come close since I've been here. So to win 13 this year is something special."

The majority of the 2007 season was extremely special for Favre and the Packers. Green Bay opened the year 4–0. And in Week 4, Favre broke Dan Marino's record for career touchdown passes when he zipped No. 421 to Greg Jennings.

"I mean his experience, the ability to get the ball out of his hand and the urgency and accuracy that he's throwing the football with, that's what makes Brett Favre Brett Favre," McCarthy said. "He can make the tight throws, and he's just doing an excellent job managing the game, and letting our playmakers make plays."

Favre would also pass Marino later that season and become the NFL's all-time leader in career passing yards, passing attempts, and completions.

"I've said this all along and will continue to say it, I've never considered myself in the same league as Dan Marino," Favre said that season. "What a great passer, maybe the greatest passer ever.

"The way he did it is probably the way you would coach another guy to do it. The way I've done it, I don't know if you would coach guys to do it that way. But it's worked for me, and to be mentioned in the same breath with him is quite an honor."

Favre and his weapons were in sync all season, and records fell in the process.

Favre hit Jennings with an 82-yard touchdown on the first play of overtime to lift Green Bay past Denver 19–13 on a Monday night. Favre led the Packers to three straight wins over Minnesota, Carolina, and Detroit, games in which he had three touchdowns and no interceptions.

And to the amazement of many, Green Bay headed to the postseason as a legitimate Super Bowl contender.

After a bye week, running back Ryan Grant was the star of the NFC divisional playoffs. Grant ran for 201 yards and three touchdowns to lead the Packers to a stirring 42–20 win.

Grant overcame two early fumbles and set a new franchise postseason rushing record. Grant's rushing mark was also the seventh highest in NFL postseason history.

"It's unfortunate what happened," Grant said of the two early fumbles. "But I really appreciate everybody backing me. They backed me the whole time.

"From the training staff to the coaches to the players, everybody just said, 'Stay with it. You know what you've got to do. Let it go.'"

Favre had a big game himself, throwing three touchdown passes and posting a quarterback rating of 137.6. Snow fell throughout the game, and picked up dramatically in the third quarter. And with the game well in hand late, Favre made a snowball and drilled wideout Donald Driver in the back. Driver later retaliated with a snowball to Favre's head.

That scene was a microcosm of just who Favre was, and why Packer Nation loved him so.

"I hit Donald with a snowball. I did," Favre said. "When I kind of packed it up and threw it, it got kind of hard, like a golf ball. So I kind of threw it at his back or his butt or something.

"I'm thinking, 'You don't want to puncture an eye or something.' He turns around, packs one and hits me in the face. Good thing it hit my face mask, it might have hit my tooth or something."

In all, the Packers couldn't have had much more fun in the snow. Unfortunately for Green Bay, that fun would end one week later.

Green Bay hosted the New York Giants in the NFC Championship Game, and entered the contest a 7.5-point favorite. Packer Nation was already making its Super Bowl plans.

But something happened on the way to heaven. In the third-coldest playoff game in NFL history—one with minus-3-degree temperatures and a wind chill of minus-24—the Giants stunned the Packers 23–20 in overtime.

On Green Bay's first possession of overtime, Giants cornerback Corey Webster intercepted Favre. Moments later, New York kicker Lawrence Tynes drilled a 47-yard field goal and the Giants had a stunning win.

Two weeks later, the Giants won Super Bowl XLII.

"In some ways, it was a surprise to a lot of people we were in this game," Favre said. "Unfortunately, the last thing you remember usually is a game like tonight. For me, the last play. But there have been so many great achievements that will stand out."

Amazingly, that final pass for Driver—the one intercepted by Webster—was Favre's last in a Packers uniform.

Most expected Favre to return to Green Bay for the 2008 season. Instead, on March 4, 2008, Favre said he didn't have "anything left to give" and retired.

"I know I can still play, but it's like I told my wife, I'm just tired mentally. I'm just tired," Favre said. "If I felt like coming back...the only way for me to be successful would be to win a Super Bowl. To go to the Super Bowl and lose, would

Favre's Top 10

Brett Favre didn't like the question.

Favre was announcing his retirement from the Green Bay Packers in March 2008—a retirement that, of course, lasted just three months.

A reporter asked Favre to reflect on his favorite games and plays, something the Hall of Fame quarterback was reluctant to do.

"I hate when that question is asked," Favre said. "I don't have one. I really don't. I know if you ask anyone who's covered the Packers or Brett Favre over the years, ask them their top five plays or games, they're going to give you some, as I probably could, too. But it's too hard. They all meant a lot to me."

Perhaps Favre didn't want to list his most memorable performances. But we don't mind.

1. Honor Thy Father

Just one day after his father Irvin died, Favre decided to play on a Monday night in Oakland. He proceeded to give arguably the finest performance of his career.

Favre completed 22 of 30 passes for 399 yards and four touchdowns, including memorable scores of 22 yards to Wesley Walls and 43 yards to Javon Walker. Favre's 311 passing yards in the first half set a new team record and his passer rating of 154.9 that night also set a new team record.

Favre's legendary night added to his legacy as an all-time great. And most importantly, he guided the Packers to a critical 41–7 win.

"I knew that my dad would have wanted me to play," Favre said. "I love him so much, and I love this game. It's meant a great deal to me, to my dad, to my family, and I didn't expect this kind of performance. But I know he was watching tonight."

2. Simply Super

The Green Bay Packers hadn't played in a Super Bowl in 30 years. So when the Packers faced New England in Super Bowl XXXI, there was a mix of excitement and trepidation.

Favre did all he could to eliminate the latter. Playing in the Louisiana Superdome, less than an hour from his hometown of Kiln, Mississippi, Favre hit Andre Rison for a 54-yard touchdown on Green Bay's second play from scrimmage.

"People have asked me what's my favorite moment of Brett Favre's career," Packers president Bob Harlan said. "I really think it was the first touchdown in Super Bowl XXXI when he threw to Rison and he ran off the field with his helmet off. He looked like a kid running home to mom with his first great report card."

Favre later hit Antonio Freeman for a then–Super Bowl record 81-yard touchdown and the Packers leveled the Patriots 35–21. Favre finished the day 14-of-27 for 246 yards and helped bring the Lombardi Trophy back to the NFL's smallest city.

(continued)

Favre's Top 10 *(continued)*

3. The Start of Something Wonderful

Favre was nothing but a backup quarterback when Week 3 of the 1992 season rolled around. By the end of the day, he was Green Bay's quarterback of the present—and future.

Favre replaced an injured Don Majkowski and led the Packers to a dramatic 24–23 win over Cincinnati. Favre capped the come-from-behind victory with a 35-yard touchdown to Kitrick Taylor with just 13 seconds left.

Remarkably, Favre was the Packers' starting quarterback the next 253 games (275 including playoffs).

"I shudder to think where we would have been without (Favre)," former Packers general manager Ron Wolf said.

4. What's He Doing?

It was December 18, 1994, when Favre made the Packers' biggest play of the year. It was one that showed both his guts and his recklessness all at once.

Green Bay needed a win over Atlanta in the final game ever played at Milwaukee's County Stadium to keep its playoff hopes alive, but trailed 17–14 late. Favre and the Packers drove to the Falcons' 9-yard line in the closing moments, and with the Packers out of timeouts, coach Mike Holmgren had a simple demand of Favre.

"Whatever happens, don't scramble," Holmgren told Favre. "Because we don't have any timeouts and if you get tackled in bounds, the game's over. Throw it someplace where we have a chance to score or throw it away. Do not run around!"

Favre was always one for the dramatic, though, and when no one got open, he took off running. Favre dove for the right corner of the end zone and hit pay dirt with just 14 ticks left on the clock. His gutsy, mad scramble gave Green Bay a 21–17 win and helped it clinch a playoff berth the following week.

5. How Sweet It Is

Green Bay hadn't hosted a title game since the legendary 1967 "Ice Bowl" when Carolina came to town for the 1996 NFC Championship game. Favre and the Packers were hell-bent on making up for lost time.

Favre threw for 292 yards with touchdown passes to Dorsey Levens and Antonio Freeman. And the Packers rolled past the Panthers 30–13 to earn a berth in Super Bowl XXXI.

"I remember telling the fans and the media before the season started that we were going to go to the Super Bowl," Favre said afterward. "And in two weeks, we'll be in New Orleans."

6. Record Setter

Favre always said records didn't mean anything to him. But you wouldn't have known that following his 421st touchdown pass—one that gave him the all-time NFL mark.

Favre hit Greg Jennings for the record-setting score during a 23–16 Green Bay win in Minnesota on September 30, 2007. Favre would go on to finish his glorious career with 508 touchdown passes.

"I think Brett will appreciate it when it's all said and done after the fact, when the season is over and his career is over," Packers coach Mike McCarthy said. "It's a milestone that he hit, and he's got a lot more left."

7. Streak Buster

Green Bay hadn't won a playoff game in 11 seasons when it went to Detroit's Silverdome in January 1994. And it looked like that streak of ineptitude would continue late in the game, when the Packers trailed 24–21.

But Favre made one of his all-time-great individual plays, when he eluded trouble and scrambled to the far left side of the field. Favre threw across his body and into the right corner of the end zone, where Sterling Sharpe was waiting to haul in a 40-yard touchdown with just 55 seconds left that gave the Packers a 28–24 win.

"I think when Brett rolled left, the defense was reading his eyes and they drifted to their right," Sharpe said. "Brett looked over and made a great throw."

8. Monday Night Magic

There was something about Favre and Monday nights. Favre threw a 99-yard touchdown pass to Robert Brooks in 1995. He had a brilliant game against San Francisco in 1996 that helped the Packers win in overtime and eventually land the No. 1 seed in the playoffs. Favre completed a miraculous game-winning touchdown pass to Antonio Freeman in 2000 that helped the Packers defeat Minnesota. And he threw for 359 yards and three touchdowns in a win against Chicago in Champaign, Illinois, in 2002.

But one of Favre's all-time magical moments on Monday night came during the 2007 season. The Packers and Denver had just gone to overtime tied at 13. On the first play of overtime, Favre wound up and lofted a bomb into the Mile High Stadium air that landed on the hands of Jennings. Jennings, who whipped cornerback Dré Bly on the play, hauled in the perfect pass and raced home for an 82-yard touchdown that gave the Packers a 19–13 win.

"That was fun," Favre said. "I can't wait to watch the tape."

(continued)

Favre's Top 10 *(continued)*

9. New Sheriff in Town

Perhaps the game that showed the Packers had indeed arrived came during the 1995 divisional playoffs. Favre and the Packers stormed into San Francisco—the defending Super Bowl champs—and knocked off the 49ers 27–17.

Favre was magnificent, completing 21 of 28 passes for 299 yards and two touchdowns. And even though Green Bay fell the following week in Dallas in the NFC Championship game, its win in San Francisco was a springboard to future successes.

"I thought that game was huge in terms of helping us get where we wanted to go," Wolf said. "That was a great, great win."

10. Mr. Tough Guy

Favre had several injuries that nearly put an end to his record-setting streak of consecutive starts. But that streak appeared in great danger in 1995, when Favre missed an entire week of practice with a severely sprained left ankle.

Not only did Favre play on that Sunday against Chicago, he lit the Bears up for five touchdowns and led the Packers to a 35–28 win. That was just the 59th game (including playoffs) of a streak that will be remembered for years to come.

"(Brett's) so important to this team," defensive end Reggie White said that day. "Everybody realizes it."

almost be worse than anything else. Anything less than a Super Bowl win would be unsuccessful.

"I know it shouldn't feel unsuccessful, but the only way to come back and make that be the right decision would be to come back and win a Super Bowl and honestly the odds of that, they're tough. Those are big shoes for me to fill, and I guess it was a challenge I wasn't up for."

During his 16 seasons in Green Bay, Favre set career marks for most passing touchdowns (442), passing yards (61,655), wins by a starting quarterback (160), and consecutive starts by a quarterback (253) in NFL history. He also set records for most completions (5,377), attempts (8,754), and interceptions (286).

"The guy is an all-time great," New York Giants general manager Jerry Reese said of Favre. "I mean, are we ever going to see another guy like Brett Favre? I doubt it."

Brett Favre by the Numbers

Brett Favre not only holds most passing records in Green Bay history, but he finished near the top of the NFL's all-time list in several categories, as well. Here's a look at those:

Consecutive Starts All-Time (by a quarterback)

297	Brett Favre, Green Bay	1992–2010
208	Peyton Manning, Indianapolis	1998–2011
167	Eli Manning	2004–present
144	Philip Rivers	2006–present
116	Ron Jaworski, Philadelphia	1977–84

Career Touchdown Passes

530	Peyton Manning
508	Brett Favre
420	Dan Marino
396	Drew Brees
392	Tom Brady

Career Pass Completions

Brett Favre	6,300
Peyton Manning	5,927
Dan Marino	4,967
Drew Brees	4,937
Tom Brady	4,551

Career Passing Yards

Brett Favre	71,838
Peyton Manning	69,691
Dan Marino	61,361
Drew Brees	56,033
Tom Brady	53,258

Career Passing Attempts

Brett Favre	10,169
Peyton Manning	9,049
Dan Marino	8,358
Drew Brees	7,458
John Elway	7,250

Overall Wins, Starting QB, All Time

Brett Favre, GB–NYJ–MIN	186	112	0	.624
Peyton Manning, IND–-DEN	179	77	0	.699
Tom Brady, NE	160	47	0	.773
John Elway, DEN	148	82	1	.643
Dan Marino, MIA	147	93	0	.613

(continued)

Brett Favre by the Numbers *(continued)*

Other Favre Marks in Packers History:

8,754—Favre holds the franchise record for most passing attempts in his Green Bay career.

55—Favre's number of 300-yard passing games.

16—Most consecutive seasons of 3,000 or more yards passing (1992–2007).

372—Favre's completions in 2005, the most ever by a Packer quarterback in a single season.

4—Most seasons leading the league in touchdown passes (1995–97, 2003).

63—Most games with three or more touchdown passes.

10—Quarterbacks who have backed up Favre and went on to start for other teams. The list, and teams they started for, includes: Don Majkowski (Indianapolis, Detroit), Ty Detmer (Philadelphia, San Francisco, Cleveland, Detroit), Mark Brunell (Jacksonville, Washington), Doug Pederson (Philadelphia, Cleveland), Steve Bono (St. Louis), Rick Mirer (New York Jets, Oakland), Aaron Brooks (New Orleans), Matt Hasselbeck (Seattle), Danny Wuerffel (Washington), and Henry Burris (Chicago).

"He's one-in-a-million," Pittsburgh director of football operations Kevin Colbert said. "Anyone that's had the chance to watch him play all of these years should be thankful for the opportunity."

Of course, Favre was far from done.

In late June 2008, Favre told McCarthy he was interested in returning. The Packers had already committed to 24-year-old Aaron Rodgers, though, and were ready to turn the page.

That set up a soap opera summer, in which was Favre was eventually traded to the New York Jets for a third-round draft choice. Favre played one year with the Jets, then played his final two years with the Minnesota Vikings and posted a 2–2 record against the Packers.

It was a strange end for arguably the greatest Green Bay Packer in team history. But Packers fans who were treated to 16 years of Favre saw one of the NFL's greatest entertainers of all time. They watched a true original at the position. And they experienced a renaissance and winning football after more than two decades of misery.

"As you get older, as we all get older, you learn to appreciate things more," said Favre, who dabbles in a variety of projects today and is a co-owner of Sqor Sports. "And I think experience plays a big part of that, and obviously at 22, 23, 24, I didn't have that. But I was always a historian and really a respectful player. And I knew what the guys had done before and I understood how lucky I was to do it. So I kind of knew I was part of something special even as it was going on.

"And now today, you know it even more. It had been so long since the Packers had any success, and to be part of teams that got things turned around and going in the right direction was really special. That whole period was something special. And I know I appreciate it now more than I did back then. I don't want to say it was easy, but for a lack of a better term, that's what I felt. What's the big deal? We're just winning games and doing what we're supposed to.

"I hope I did my part. I believe I did. I think I was part of something that was very special and returned the franchise back to prominence. And I take a tremendous amount of pride in that.

"By no means do I think I did that alone. I was a part of one of the greatest teams and greatest groups of guys that's played in Green Bay. And I think the thing that means the most is when people tell me, 'I love watching how you play because that's how I'd play.' They always talk about how much fun I was having. That's pretty neat. That's fun. I think people could relate to me and that really means the most. That's what I love to hear."

And that's why Packer Nation loved to watch Favre.

★ ★ ★

Aaron Rodgers

What if?

These days, that very question must send shivers throughout Packer Nation. But back in the early part of 2002, Aaron Rodgers thought long and hard about giving up football—and going to college strictly as a student.

Rodgers, a senior at Pleasant Valley High School in Chico, California, back in January 2002, hadn't received a single Division I scholarship offer. In fact, his only Division I opportunity came from the University of Illinois, which offered him the chance to walk on.

So the prospect of giving up his football dreams was now a stark reality.

"There was a time I thought about that, for sure," Rodgers said. "I had finished my senior year of football, I wasn't playing basketball. It was January and I was working out and stuff and meeting with a couple of coaches.

"The reality was sinking in that, 'Hey, you're not going to get a scholarship.' So now I had some choices to make."

Rodgers, an exceptional student, would have had his pick of universities, and was thinking about a career in law.

But the path that eventually led him to Green Bay was first paved by Craig Rigsbee. And today, Rigsbee should probably receive holiday cards from Packers fans everywhere.

Rigsbee was the head football coach at Butte College, a two-year community college of 12,000 students in northern California. Rigsbee, Butte's athletic director today, had watched Rodgers in a passing league the previous summer and liked what he saw.

Rigsbee's Butte College Roadrunners were a national power, and he thought Rodgers could be his next great quarterback.

There was just one problem: Darla Rodgers.

"I lived one cul-de-sac away from his family, so in January (of Rodgers' senior year) I walked over there one night," Rigsbee said. "Right away his Mom, Darla, said, 'No kid of mine is going to a [junior college.]'"

It's easy to see why Mrs. Rodgers felt that way. Aaron Rodgers' grades and test scores were outstanding, and maybe, just maybe, it was time to give this whole football thing a rest.

The thing is, Rodgers wasn't ready to rest. And if Butte College was the best offer Rodgers was going to get, then convincing Mom became the next step in continuing to pursue his football dreams.

"Initially, my mom didn't want me there," Rodgers said of Butte College. "My dad had gone to a few Butte games and it was a wild bunch. So she didn't think that was a good spot for me.

"But coach Rigsbee is like a big brother still. He's one of the greatest guys I know. He's done so much for so many guys at Butte College. Once he came over, he's a heck of a recruiter. It was a no-brainer. That's where I wanted to go.

"I remember one question that kind of sealed it for me. I said, 'Coach, if I have one good year, would you be willing to allow me to leave?' And he said, 'For sure. I don't want to get in the way of you fulfilling your dreams. But you've got to win the starting job first.' So I went out there and won the job."

The rest, of course, is history.

Today, Rodgers is well on his way to one of the most decorated careers in NFL history and is one of the league's all-time rags-to-riches stories.

After sitting behind incumbent Brett Favre for three seasons, Rodgers has run with his opportunity the last seven years.

Rodgers led the Packers to a win in Super Bowl XLV. Rodgers won the NFL's MVP award in both 2011 and 2014. And he is on pace to produce one of the greatest statistical careers in NFL history.

Consider some of the gaudy numbers Rodgers has put up during his first seven years in the NFL:

- Rodgers' career passer rating of 106.0 is No. 1 in NFL history for players with at least 1,500 passing attempts. Rodgers' rating is more than eight points ahead of second-place Tony Romo of Dallas (97.6).
- Rodgers is the only quarterback in NFL history to record a 100-plus passer rating in six consecutive seasons (2009–14). In fact, no other quarterback has accomplished that in more than four straight seasons.
- Rodgers ranks No. 1 in NFL history in career interception percentage (1.64). He's also first in touchdown-to-interception ratio (226-to–57, 3.96 percent).
- Rodgers ranks No. 3 all-time in completion percentage (65.8) and yards per attempt (8.22).
- Rodgers is one of only three quarterbacks in NFL history to register two seasons with a 110-plus passer rating (2011, 2014). The other two are Peyton Manning (2007, 2013) and Tom Brady (2007, 2010).
- In the Packers record books, Rodgers holds six of the top seven single-season marks for passer rating (2009–14). He also holds three of the top five for passing touchdowns (2011–12, 2014), five of the top six for completion percentage (2010–14), and three of the top five for passing yards (2009, 2011, 2014).
- Rodgers holds five of the top seven streaks in Packers history for most consecutive passing attempts without an interception.
- Rodgers has posted five 4,000-yard passing seasons (2008–09, 2011–12, 2014), which is tied with Brett Favre for the franchise record.
- Rodgers is the only quarterback in NFL history to register three seasons with 500-plus attempts and seven or fewer interceptions (2009, 2011, 2014). No other quarterback has done it more than once. Rodgers is also the only 4,000-yard passer in league history to throw six or fewer interceptions, having done it twice (2011 and 2014).
- At the end of the 2014 season, Rodgers had streaks of 418 consecutive passing attempts and 36 consecutive touchdown passes at home without an interception. Both are NFL records.
- Rodgers has posted the top three single-season passer-rating marks at home in NFL history (minimum 100 attempts), highlighted by his NFL-record 133.2 rating in 2014. Rodgers also posted a 128.5 rating in 2011 and a 126.4 in 2013.

- Rodgers has helped the Packers average 28.5 points per game in his 103 career regular-season starts. That's No. 1 among quarterbacks since 1950 (minimum 100 starts).

Granted, today's NFL looks nothing like the one of previous generations. Every rule that's been added over the last 30 years favors more offense. Quarterbacks are protected like never before. So coaches have wisely turned the NFL into primarily a passing league.

Still, what Rodgers has done is absolutely head turning—no matter what era you're from.

"I've been pretty vocal," Packers left guard Josh Sitton said. "I think he's possibly the best ever."

Those closest to Rodgers certainly agree.

"(Rodgers) is clearly the best decision maker that I've been around probably since my time in Kansas City with Joe Montana," Packers head coach Mike McCarthy said. "(Rodgers) does not get bored throwing an easy completion, and that's a great tribute to have as a quarterback.

"He's clearly in tune taking what the defense gives you. He can throw the tight spots. He has the anticipation and arm strength and accuracy to attack the seams, but he does a great job of staying disciplined and staying within the offense."

ESPN's Trent Dilfer, who won a Super Bowl with Baltimore in 2000, has always been a big Rodgers supporter.

"We've been spoiled as a football-viewing audience the last 20 years where we've gotten to see the greatest quarterbacks who ever lived," Dilfer said. "If you took the best elements of each of those signature quarterbacks—John Elway's arm strength and athleticism; Kurt Warner's anticipatory accuracy; Tom Brady's accuracy and fourth-quarter heroics; Peyton Manning's line-of-scrimmage dominance—Aaron Rodgers is the composite of all the great quarterbacks wrapped into one dude."

But back in 2002, Rodgers was a dude highly uncertain about his football future.

There wasn't a single NCAA Division I school that offered Rodgers a scholarship. And Rodgers' eventual landing spot was a junior college that, in essence, was a last resort.

"Oh yeah, that was always a driving force, feeling like I was overlooked and feeling like I needed to prove myself, whether that was as a backup or as an unknown throughout my high school time," Rodgers said. "I think you can tap into that and get some motivation from that.

"That's what makes you a talented player is you have to have that belief in yourself, even when it's unfounded. It's that confidence that you're better than people say you are and that's how you make people better around you. A strong belief in yourself, which allows other people to believe in you, as well."

It's certainly understandable, though, why so few believed in Rodgers.

When Rodgers entered high school, he was a scrawny 5'2" and 130 pounds. Even at the start of his senior year, Rodgers was just 5'10" and 165 pounds, smaller than most collegiate kickers.

"He was little," said Ron Souza, Rodgers' quarterbacks coach at Pleasant Valley High School. "But he was very gifted for a little guy.

"He had excellent mechanics and he always had a great understanding of football. Watching film, his readiness to learn, the whole mental part he was terrific at. And then he started growing."

Rodgers lit it up his last two years at Pleasant Valley High, throwing for more than 4,400 total yards during his junior and senior seasons combined. He also set school records for touchdown passes in a game (six) and all-purpose yards (440), and twice was an all-section choice.

But Rodgers was far from a household name. And Chico, located 90 miles north of Sacramento, is hidden away in the Northern Sacramento Valley.

"We just don't get a lot of exposure up there because maybe a lot of the coaches and players don't understand how to get the most exposure for your players," Rodgers said. "For me, I didn't go to any Nike camps, didn't get my name out there.

"We're north of Sacramento and we just don't produce a lot of top athletes. You look at my high school team and we had three guys who went on to play football...so it's not like we've got a hotbed of Division I athletes over there. So a lot of times when one does come along they get overlooked."

Which eventually led Rodgers to Rigsbee and Butte.

"Coach Rigsbee really eased any doubts," Rodgers said. "He said you have an opportunity at Butte to compete for a spot. We have a great team around you and we'll get you to the college you want to go to."

Rigsbee certainly did that.

After training camp that summer, the Butte coaching staff had some tough decisions to make.

Third-year quarterback Brian Botts had paid his dues, enjoyed a solid camp, and had the support of every assistant coach on the staff. Except one.

Rigsbee felt that Rodgers was the perfect trigger man for his offense. And even though Rigsbee was severely outnumbered, he pulled rank and let his assistants know this wasn't a democracy.

"Every guy on the staff said they'd go with (Botts)," Rigsbee said. "Finally I said, 'This is why I'm the head coach. We're going with Aaron.'

"The kid had been here two weeks and he was already better than the kid that was here three years. And I said after a game or two, he's going to be 100 times better."

He was.

Rodgers led the Roadrunners to a 10–1 record that season, a No. 2 national ranking, and a NorCal Conference championship. Rodgers also threw for more than 2,400 yards, a school-record 28 touchdowns, and just four interceptions.

Perhaps most importantly, though, Rodgers learned how to lead.

"That was the most important year of my young football career," Rodgers said. "I learned a lot about myself that year, being an 18-year-old playing with guys from all over the country and different countries: Canada, a 25-year-old center, guys who had been to prison, guys who had been bounce-backs from Division I, local guys, and trying to be an 18-year-old and lead those guys and figure out a way to lead them.

"I learned a lot about leadership and a lot about myself and I also got my confidence back because I had a real good season, so that was an important year. Still keep in touch with a lot of those guys and my coach as well."

Rigsbee had also promised Rodgers he would do everything possible to help him land a Division I scholarship after one season. So that October, Rigsbee arranged for University of California coach Jeff Tedford to attend practice.

It's been widely reported that Tedford came to see Butte tight end Garrett Cross that day. And while Cross eventually went to Cal, Tedford was there for a different reason.

"He was there to see Aaron," Rigsbee said. "And it was kind of a wild practice.

"We were throwing on every play and running 7-on-7 drills. I mean, we never ran 7-on-7s on Mondays, so guys were wondering what was going on. At the end of practice, Tedford came over to me and said, 'He's the best junior college quarterback I've ever seen.' And I just said, 'Right on!'"

Right on indeed, as Tedford offered Rodgers a scholarship that day.

"Seeing him in person, he was very impressive," Tedford said. "He was very accurate, threw the ball well and had a tight spiral. It was a very pleasant surprise to find out he was very strong in other categories as well."

That's for sure.

Rodgers didn't win the starting job during fall camp in his first year at Cal, but claimed it in Game 5 of that season. Rodgers led the Golden Bears to a 7–3 mark in their final 10 games, throwing for 2,903 yards and 19 touchdowns.

Rodgers, who's extremely protective of the ball, had streaks of 98 and 105 consecutive passes without an interception. He led the Bears to late-season wins against Washington and Stanford to clinch a berth in the Insight Bowl. Then Rodgers threw for 394 yards and was named MVP in Cal's bowl win over Virginia Tech.

Rodgers was even better the following year, when he guided the second-highest scoring offense in school history. Personally, Rodgers threw for 2,566 yards and 24 touchdowns, with just eight interceptions, and was named first-team all-Pacific 10.

After Rodgers' junior season, NFL scouts gave him a first-round grade and many believed he would be taken extremely early in the draft. So he declared for the NFL Draft with one year of eligibility left.

It was quite a journey for a player who couldn't get a glance from college recruiters just three years earlier.

"Recruiters put so much into height and weight," Rodgers said. "I was a little under what I am now, and my area doesn't get heavily recruited, either. I'll tell you what: I'm a firm believer that everything happens for a reason."

Rodgers has the ability to make that statement now. Back in April 2005, though, he certainly felt differently.

Rodgers headed into the 2005 NFL Draft packed with optimism.

Rodgers was one of the stars of the 2005 NFL Combine. And most "experts" believed he would be selected in, or near the top of, the first round.

One night during the NFL Combine, Rodgers sat down with members of the Green Bay Packers' front office. But with the Packers slated to pick at No. 24, both sides figured they wouldn't see each other again.

"I remember telling them 'Trade up. I'd love to play for you guys,'" Rodgers recalled. "And they were saying, 'Well, you probably won't be available when we want to get you.'"

Amazingly, he was.

Rodgers has become the NFL's poster boy for waiting his turn. And the greatest example of that came on April 23, 2005.

Rodgers woke up that Saturday morning believing there was a solid chance the San Francisco 49ers would take him with the first overall pick. Instead, the 49ers called and said they'd be going in a different direction.

What Rodgers didn't expect is the next 22 teams on the clock would also bypass him.

Rodgers had gone to New York to be part of the draft festivities. He was also one of a handful of players invited into the green room—a spot for potentially high draft picks—at the Jacob K. Javits Convention Center.

One by one, the other players in the room were drafted. Eventually, Rodgers was the only one left—and seeing him sit there uncomfortably was almost hard to watch.

"Well, obviously when you're sitting in the green room, you just want to get out of there," Rodgers said.

The Packers had Rodgers ranked far higher than No. 24 on their draft board. And when Rodgers plummeted, Green Bay's decision makers were almost as shocked as Rodgers himself.

"I got called in a couple picks before our pick into the draft room to ask me once again my opinion and what I thought of him," said Darrell Bevell, who was Green Bay's quarterbacks coach at the time. "I was getting excited from a selfish point of view to get to coach a guy like that and get a guy in the first round and start to groom him. So that was exciting.

"If there was a report that he was going to slip I would have been shocked. I'm still in a little bit of a state of shock that he came down to us."

Shocking for Green Bay, and brutal for Rodgers.

Not only was Rodgers scorned by his beloved 49ers, he lost millions of dollars by sliding down draft boards.

"(Former 49ers safety) Merton Hanks told me, 'You should play your career with a chip on your shoulder regardless and always feel like you've got something to prove,'" Rodgers said the day he was drafted. "And I've got a lot to prove."

No. 24

Aaron Rodgers always wanted to go home.

In the end, it was probably best that he didn't.

Back in April 2005, the San Francisco 49ers held the No. 1 pick in the NFL Draft. Rodgers, who grew up in nearby Chico, California, idolized the 49ers as a child and always dreamed of playing there.

San Francisco general manager Scot McCloughan and head coach Mike Nolan were torn between quarterback Alex Smith of Utah, Rodgers of California, and Michigan wide receiver Braylon Edwards with the No. 1 overall pick that season.

In the end, the 49ers thought Rodgers was too arrogant and settled for too many checkdowns in a programmed offense at Cal. They felt Edwards was too scary in the attitude department (and they were right).

So San Francisco chose Smith.

Twenty-three picks later, with Rodgers stunningly still on the board, Packers general manager Ted Thompson made the overlooked quarterback his first-ever selection. In those few short hours, the futures of both franchises were shaped—even though no one knew it at the time.

"Me and Mike (McCarthy) and Ted are kind of all in this thing together, Rodgers said. "Ted drafted me with his first draft pick and obviously Mike was his coach that he wanted.

"We've had a lot of ups and downs together, mostly ups. But it's a great relationship and there's a lot of trust on both sides and appreciation for how we go about our jobs."

It's fascinating to think how things could have gone differently for Rodgers—and the Packers—if San Francisco had gone with Rodgers over Smith back in 2005.

Smith was given every opportunity to win the starting job in San Francisco, but largely failed. And eight seasons after drafting him, the 49ers traded Smith to the Kansas City Chiefs for two second-round draft choices.

Rodgers, on the other hand, was heartbroken when his hometown 49ers went with Smith. But Rodgers landed in the perfect place, was given a chance to watch and learn, and has taken the NFL by storm since becoming a starter in 2008.

"I think every player, particularly quarterbacks, the path that you're put on has a lot to do with your success," McCarthy said. "There's a lot of factors that go into developing a quarterback. Obviously they both had unique ability to even be considered to be part of the conversation of being the No. 1 pick in the National Football League."

McCarthy was San Francisco's offensive coordinator when it drafted Smith. And McCarthy is the first to admit that was a no-win situation for any rookie quarterback.

Smith was thrown into the fire from day one, and in 2005 was asked to lead a dreadful offense. In his rookie season, Smith threw one touchdown pass and 11 interceptions, and had a miserable passer rating of 40.8.

(continued)

No. 24 *(continued)*

Smith improved gradually over the next two years, suffered a broken bone in his right (passing) shoulder in 2008, then had somewhat of a breakout season in 2009 with 18 touchdowns and 12 interceptions.

Smith and the 49ers went backward in 2010, but eventually made gains and reached the 2011 NFC Championship Game. But by 2012, Smith lost his job to up-and-coming Colin Kaepernick, and was eventually traded.

Rodgers, on the other hand, sat behind Brett Favre for three seasons and was given the chance to develop—something incredibly rare for first-round draft choices these days. And when Rodgers' time finally arrived in 2008, he was ready.

Call it dumb luck if you will, but the Packers were certainly lucky that Rodgers fell in their lap back in April 2005.

When the 49ers decided on Smith, it sent Rodgers into a free fall. Only Cleveland, Tennessee, and Arizona were teams with top 10 picks that had a possible need at quarterback, and when they went in different directions, Rodgers kept spiraling.

"I think the need for a quarterback after the first pick was just not there and a lot of teams need a guy that can come in right away and be successful," Rodgers said. "A lot of teams are set with their quarterback and at the same time a lot of teams didn't need a quarterback at the same slot and they were hoping to get more picks and trade down, and when it came down to it they took a guy who was going to fill an immediate need right away. After the 49ers there weren't many teams who needed a quarterback at that slot, obviously."

There was a possibility Houston would snag Rodgers at No. 16 in that draft, but when the Texans passed, no one between picks 17 and 23 needed a quarterback. And even though Green Bay had more pressing needs on the defensive side of the ball, Rodgers was far and away the highest remaining player on Thompson's board.

Rodgers was in the NFL's green room for 4 hours and 35 minutes that day. And in all, 21 teams passed on him—including two teams that ignored him twice.

While Rodgers was brokenhearted, he was also smart enough to understand there could be some benefits.

Sitting behind the legendary Favre could give Rodgers a chance to develop at his own pace. On the flip side, several young quarterbacks drafted much higher were thrown to the wolves well before they were ready, lost confidence, and were out of the league far too soon.

In Green Bay, where Favre was still going strong, Rodgers had no immediate pressures like so many of his peers.

At the end of that wild Saturday, the Packers were the big winners.

"Did we think he was going to be there when we were watching tape? No," Thompson said. "But over the course of the last week or so there was a couple of, I don't know, websites or ESPN or something that said maybe he might get there. So, I went back and did a little more work just to make sure. But I feel very comfortable that this kid warranted being picked where we were at."

Rodgers certainly benefited from sitting behind Favre for three years. Rodgers also learned from terrific teachers like McCarthy and former offensive coordinator Joe Philbin.

"I think it's about opportunity and it's about performance and production, and he's answered the bell," McCarthy said of Rodgers.

Rodgers certainly did that.

There was a Super Bowl title and Super Bowl MVP in 2010. Rodgers won NFL MVP awards in 2011 and 2014.

And Rodgers has destroyed the Packers—and NFL—record books during his first seven seasons as a starter.

Throughout, Rodgers was always driven by the fact the 49ers—and most teams in the league—passed on him back in April 2005.

"I think there's a lot more in life that drives him than that," McCarthy said. "But that's part of his history. It's always going to be there. It's not going to go away. So I'm very happy the way it worked out. Things happen for a reason.

"Life's about opportunities and it's about what you do with them. I never really worried too much about the opportunities I wasn't given. I always focused on the ones I have been given and he's a great example of that. I think he has fun with it more than anything.

"It's definitely an experience he can use, but also it's an experience to be a great role model with. It's a great story."

One that worked out perfectly for Green Bay, and took years for San Francisco to recover from.

"The more I thought about it the more I realized it could be a great fit for me, being able to learn from one of the best quarterbacks of all time and to not be thrown in the fire right away and to come to a team with a storied franchise and a winning tradition," Rodgers said. "I think it's going to be exciting. It's going to be a great fit."

In some ways, it was. In others, it was tough on everyone involved.

Rodgers was always a Favre fan. Like much of Packer Nation, Rodgers loved watching Favre turn nothing into something and create one highlight-reel play after another.

In fact, when Rodgers arrived at Butte College back in the fall of 2002, he wore Favre's No. 4 after his first two selections were gone.

Rigsbee remembers asking Rodgers why he picked No. 4.

"He told me, 'I just love how Brett Favre plays,'" Rigsbee said. "Pretty ironic." Indeed.

Favre was 35 years old when the Packers drafted Rodgers. He was still playing at a high level, but realized Green Bay had just drafted his likely successor.

Favre was always lauded as a great teammate and leader. In this case, though, Favre wasn't hip on training a player 14 years younger than him to one day take his job.

"Brett and I actually got along well," Rodgers said. "We had a lot better relationship than I think was reported. Obviously, I was drafted to be his successor, and as I get older, you can see how that would be difficult to take if you don't feel like you're ready to move on. I understand that. But him and I got along well.

"We had a couple of good conversations over the years. His personality of being a starting quarterback and being a leader, I don't think he felt it was ever his responsibility to get me ready to play. And I never felt like that either. I had a quarterback coach who I could work with. That wasn't Brett's job. His job was to be the best he could be for the No. 1 offense and my job was to support him, get our defense ready to play, and give him any tips I could come up with and get myself ready to play just in case something happened."

Rodgers discovered quickly, though, that Favre wasn't going to offer up a lot of secrets to his success. So Rodgers tried gleaning every possible nugget by watching and studying everything about Favre's game.

The two men were dramatically different and had largely contrasting styles. But there was still plenty Rodgers pulled from Favre that helped him years down the road.

"I listened a lot," Rodgers said. "I've always felt like whether it was my high school coaches, my junior college coaches, Jeff Tedford and his staff (at Cal). Whoever you're interacting with, you can take something away, even if you don't mesh with them personality-wise or you don't get along with them, you can always take something away from that.

"And I learned a lot about tying footwork to the throws. When you're growing up and watching TV, they'd always talk about how Brett's footwork was crazy. He was throwing from all these platforms and different arm angles. But the genius of it was what he was actually doing is he was always tying his feet to the proper throw and he was throwing off balance so many times that it looked a certain way because no one else was doing it consistently. I think nobody else was working on those types of throws and you could see him doing it in practice.

"We didn't operate in a perfect practice environment, which I think really helps quarterbacking. We're not just dropping back without any pressure in 7-on-7 drills. You're testing yourself, you're extending plays in those drills. You're throwing from awkward angles. You're moving your feet around. You're seeing how your body reacts to hard rolls left and right, move up in the pocket and kind of throw off your wrong foot. And the genius of his footwork is that he practiced those things. So to him, at least, those things really weren't exceptional plays. It's stuff he had ingrained in his muscle memory and that's because of the genius of the footwork he had used.

"Really, that was great. And then the eye control. He had just phenomenal eye control. He would look guys off all the time and throw those passes in practice. I work on all of those things today. You have to work on the awkward body angles that you can get in so that when you're in those in live game situations, you can throw an accurate football."

To this day, Rodgers chuckles when thinking back on that first season in Green Bay.

The Packers had what they called a "Feel Good Saturday." During a light practice before Sunday's game, the scout team offense led by Rodgers was told to throw interceptions to the defense.

The belief was this could get the defense in the right frame of mind for the following day. Rodgers, though, wanted nothing to do with that strategy.

"I knew that those reps on the scout team were going to be invaluable to me in my career, so on the Saturdays, they wanted us to throw interceptions every time and make the defense feel good," Rodgers said. "I kind of rebelled against that because, as you know, I don't like throwing interceptions. Instead, I would throw no-look passes to my guys and work on my eye control and looking one way and throwing another way. And I actually got reprimanded my first year for doing that in a Saturday practice by Mike Sherman.

"But like I always tell the young guys and the new quarterbacks, the only way to develop the habit is to exaggerate it in a practice setting. I always tried to exaggerate those things, and a lot of that I took away from watching Brett."

For the better part of three seasons, though, watching was about all that Rodgers did.

The 2005 campaign was a miserable one in Green Bay. The Packers were ravaged by injury, began the year 0–4, and finished 4–12.

That was Green Bay's worst season since 1991. And afterward, Mike Sherman and his staff were fired.

It was a rough year for Rodgers too. He relieved Favre in three games during his rookie season and went 9-of-16 for 65 yards. Rodgers didn't throw a touchdown, had one interception, and posted a paltry quarterback rating of 39.8.

One season in, Rodgers was still being billed as the heir apparent to Favre. His play, though, didn't exactly win anybody over.

"I think Aaron will be fine when he gets his chance," wideout Donald Driver said that year. "Now hopefully, he doesn't get that chance for a while. The best thing that could happen is for Brett to come back, because that man still has a lot of football in him. Then Aaron could keep learning and be even more prepared when his chance comes along."

Rodgers was certainly doing his part to get ready.

McCarthy ran an offseason quarterback school that has always drawn rave reviews from the participants. Rodgers may have been the star pupil, and used that opportunity to sharpen his mental game and bond with McCarthy.

"The thing that really helped was the offseasons," Rodgers said. "In 2006 and '07, as I went through the quarterback school and learned a lot about offense and defense and blitzes and coverages and how to get the most out of my talent…we really started to get on the same page and jell together. It's a great relationship now and there's a lot of love and respect, on and off the field."

Still, Rodgers was a long ways away from seeing the field. Favre had a bounce back year in 2006, and Rodgers saw precious little time on Sundays.

To Rodgers' credit, though, his day-to-day consistency was a real strength. Rodgers made the most of his limited repetitions in practice, he continued to master the offense through film study, and he became a popular figure in the Packers' locker room.

"He practices like he's ready," Green Bay tight end Bubba Franks said. "You never know until you put him in, but he's practicing like he's the starter which has got to give him a little confidence.

"The coach lets him go with the (No.) 1's and he gets good reps. But right now, no one's sure how he'll do until he gets out there and does it."

Rodgers saw action in just two games that season and struggled. He completed just six of 15 passes for 46 yards, didn't have an interception or touchdown pass, and finished with a quarterback rating of 48.2.

The most frustrating afternoon of Rodgers' season came during a 35–0 home loss to mighty New England in late November. Favre left the game late in the first half with an elbow injury and the Packers trailing 21–0.

Rodgers had a chance to show the fan base what the future might look like. Instead, they had to be longing for the past after Rodgers went just 4-of-12 for 32 yards, took three sacks, and fumbled once.

"I think I put him in a tough situation trying to get out there and throw the ball every time," McCarthy said. "I thought sometimes he got out of the offense, but I thought he made some plays with his feet.

"I think you see his athletic ability. It was a great test for his preparation, how important it is for the backup quarterback to prepare harder and more than the starter....He was put in a tough spot."

Adding injury to insult, Rodgers suffered a broken foot and spent the final six weeks of the regular season on injured reserve.

As Rodgers' second season in Green Bay came to a close, the jury was still out.

"He's got talent, he has ability, he has know-how," McCarthy insisted of Rodgers. "When his opportunity comes, I want to put my foot on the gas and go with him. The only thing you don't know with a quarterback until he gets a chance is if he can lead your offense."

The Packers began getting far more favorable answers in 2007.

Green Bay was the NFL's surprise team that season. The Packers raced to a 10–1 start that year and Favre was in the midst of a renaissance season.

Green Bay went to Dallas in late November to face a Cowboys team that was also 10–1. That marked just the eighth time in NFL history two teams 10–1—or better—had met.

On many fronts, the night was a disaster for the Packers. Favre struggled miserably, threw two early interceptions, then exited with an elbow injury and the Packers in a 27–10 hole.

Over the next two-plus hours, though, Rodgers showed there might indeed be life after Favre.

Green Bay never could get over the hump, and fell 37–27 in a game that eventually gave the Cowboys the NFC's No. 1 seed. But Rodgers won a lot of people over with his performance that night.

Rodgers finished the game 18-of-26 for 201 yards, threw his first NFL touchdown pass, and posted an impressive quarterback rating of 104.8.

"I just can't say enough about his preparation, because I didn't even blink," McCarthy said of Rodgers. "I didn't throw anything out.

"I've been in that position before when you have to go to your backup or go to your third guy or even your fourth guy. I went through it in San Francisco, and you just start crossing plays off the chart, and that wasn't the case. I thought Aaron did an excellent job."

Even Favre sang Rodgers' praises afterward.

"I thought he played great," Favre said that night of Rodgers. "Gave us a chance to win. I thought he was ready to play. I was hoping it would be in different circumstances…but I thought he did a fine job."

Thompson, the man who drafted Rodgers and had yet to receive a return on his investment, was also quite giddy.

"I'm not trying to be glib, but I've liked him all along," Thompson said of Rodgers. "Yeah, he went through some tough times, but preseason games and that sort of thing, and even the (New England) game he played in (2006), I don't think necessarily is the telling tale.

"I think he's a young man that's confident, that's smart, that is physically talented, that believes he can play, and has understood and accepted the role that he's in, even though he still wants to play. I'm proud of the way he carries himself. I think he's going to be a good player, and I'm pleased with the way he's playing now."

The week after the Dallas game, though, Rodgers suffered a hamstring injury in practice and was inactive the final four weeks of the regular season. That marked the second straight season Rodgers missed substantial time, and many wondered if he could stay on the field.

The Packers defeated Seattle 42–20 in the NFC Divisional playoffs that season. But their year ended in heartbreak with a 23–20 overtime loss to the visiting New York Giants in the NFC Championship game.

Favre struggled that night, and his overtime interception led to a game-winning field goal by the Giants' Lawrence Tynes. Still, as the Packers left that offseason, no one expected the 38-year-old Favre to call it quits. He was still playing at an elite level, the Packers were one game from the Super Bowl, and their future was remarkably bright.

"Honestly, I don't think he knows," Packers reserve quarterback Craig Nall said of Favre. "It's one of those things where you don't want to make a hasty decision right after the season's over because you're making that more on emotion than anything.

"Personally, I hope he does come back because I think he's such an advocate for this league and he's meant so much to the town of Green Bay and the NFL in general. I hope he comes back because I like watching him play, I always have. But at the same time, if he decides to retire, he's more than deserving of doing that. I don't think anybody would fault him for making that decision."

Rodgers himself expected Favre back. And when Rodgers left Lambeau Field that frigid January night, he still had no idea what his own future in Green Bay held.

But on March 4, 2008, Rodgers' life got a whole lot crazier.

By 7:00 AM that day, Rodgers had received eight phone calls. There were too many text messages to count. Favre was set to call it quits. The Green Bay Packers were now officially Rodgers' team.

"I'm in a good situation, I've got a great team around me," Rodgers said shortly after news of Favre's retirement broke. "A lot of people have been focusing on what I'm going to do. It's what the team is going to do, really. I'm an important part of that and I know my role. I need to play well, and I'm not really going to have a grace period either.

"The expectations that people are going to have are very high. The expectations I have of myself are very high as well. I've definitely been told there haven't been a lot of guys following a legend that play well. Hopefully I'll have like a Steve Young kind of experience here."

Rodgers, a passionate San Francisco 49ers fan as a child, watched closely when Young replaced the legendary Joe Montana in the early 1990s. Although Young eventually guided the 49ers to a championship in Super Bowl XXIX, not all San Francisco fans were rejoicing.

"I know a lot of friends and family who were Joe Montana fans who it didn't matter how good Steve Young did," Rodgers said. "They weren't going to cheer for him because he wasn't Joe Montana."

Despite little game experience, the Packers were remarkably confident moving forward with Rodgers. In fact, at the 2008 NFL Combine, one Packers assistant coach said he believed Green Bay would have won the Super Bowl in '07 if Rodgers had been the starter.

No one will ever know that answer, but Rodgers had become far more comfortable with the NFL game since arriving, something he showed during that stellar performance in Dallas in 2007. Rodgers had also formed a tight bond with several teammates, earned the respect of the locker room, and tried becoming a leader.

"I like the fact that he has come into a situation that is difficult and he has taken on those responsibilities," Packers general manager Ted Thompson said. "The fans haven't seen him, but he goes out to practice every day, he's very well received by his teammates, he and Brett got along well, he understood his role.

"That's a difficult thing to do for a young man that wants to play. So, I think he's positioned himself as a leader even though he wasn't playing, and I think he's positioned himself to be a leader going forward."

Before Rodgers could lead, though, he had to survive the "Summer from Hell."

On June 20, 2008—the final day of offseason practices—McCarthy took a call from Favre. The quarterback who always struggled to make up his mind told McCarthy he still had an "itch" to play and wanted back in.

"When he picked up the phone again after he dropped it, he said, "Oh, God, Brett. You're putting us in a tight spot,'" Favre said of his conversation with McCarthy. "He said, 'Brett, playing here is not an option.' Those were his exact, exact words."

On July 8, Favre met with McCarthy and Thompson and expressed a strong desire to play. The Packers' brass tried talking Favre out of that decision.

On July 11, Favre asked the Packers for his release so he could return to the NFL with another team. Green Bay, believing that Favre wanted to return to the NFC North with either Minnesota or Chicago, denied his request.

On July 17, the Packers accused the Vikings of tampering, something that was never proved. Favre did not show up for the start of training camp on July 27, but two days later, faxed his official request for reinstatement to the NFL.

Day after day, Rodgers was bombarded with a bevy of questions—and very few were about anything happening on the field. To his credit, Rodgers handled the situation about as well as any 24-year-old could.

"I don't need people to feel sorry for me," Rodgers said. "Playing quarterback is a tough job, and there's a lot of scrutiny that goes along with that. You get too much blame a lot of times, you get too much credit a lot of times. And you just have to stay balanced and stay even-keeled.

"The last three years and this offseason have made me the person I am today, and I wouldn't have changed it for anything."

Finally, on August 6, the Packers traded Favre to the New York Jets for a fourth-round draft pick. Once and for all, the Packers were officially Rodgers' team.

Rodgers had played the role of good soldier through the chaos, saying all the right things and never losing faith that he would keep the starting job the organization handed him months earlier. For that, he won plenty of points.

"I think nationally I earned a lot of respect for that," Rodgers said. "I think I earned a lot of fans nationally, who maybe didn't know me or know a lot about me, by handling things the way I did.

"It was a difficult situation, but I just tried to be as honest and as classy as I possibly could. I realized the situation was way bigger than myself, and I think in doing that, I earned the respect of my teammates, from the organization and from our fans. And I think people that didn't know me nationally took notice, too."

After just 24 career starts, though, people were taking notice—for all the wrong reasons.

The Packers were just 6–10 in Rodgers' first season. Green Bay had suffered through a brutal five-game losing streak that year—its longest since the 1990 season—and finished seven games worse than the previous year.

Rodgers played fairly well, throwing for 4,038 yards, 28 touchdowns, and just 13 interceptions in that 2008 campaign. He completed 63.6 percent of his passes and his passer rating was an impressive 93.8.

Rodgers' accuracy and arm strength were both better than advertised. His decision making and command of the offense were impressive. In addition, he fought through a sprained right shoulder and started all 16 games.

But the Packers went 0–7 in games decided by four points or less that year, which led to the gigantic slippage in the standings.

"Just too inconsistent," Rodgers said of his first year as a starter. "I hold myself to a high level of expectations and I was just way too inconsistent. I had multiple games of over a 100.0 quarterback rating, but two games where I threw three interceptions.

"My goal is to decrease the distance between a very solid game and the inconsistent games. The very best quarterbacks in the NFL are able to do that. Their bad games are never that bad. Overall, I was proud of the fact I played 16 games. I was proud of the way I handled the (Favre) situation, which was a tough situation. But I was disappointed that I played too inconsistently for us."

The 2009 campaign didn't begin much better.

The Packers were 4–2 when Favre—now a member of the Minnesota Vikings—led the hated Vikings to a 38–26 win in Green Bay. The Packers then went to winless Tampa Bay as a 10-point favorite, but suffered an unimaginable 38–28 loss.

As the now 4–4 Packers prepared to host Dallas, the fan base was in a tizzy. Before the game, fans paraded outside Lambeau Field wearing "Fire McCarthy" and "Fire Thompson" buttons.

And with Favre and the Vikings running away with the NFC North, Packer Nation wasn't exactly thrilled to have Rodgers running the show.

"I can tell you that '09 was a tense season for everybody, especially coming off of '08 the way we played," Rodgers said. "That was a pretty tense year. We all kind of felt like we were playing for our jobs."

If that was indeed the case, Rodgers and the Packers began to play lights out. And that night against Dallas was a major turning point.

The Cowboys came to Lambeau Field winners of four straight games and leading the NFC East with a 6–2 mark. The Packers entered as a three-point underdog on their own field, knowing another loss might keep them from the postseason.

Rodgers keyed a pair of huge fourth-quarter touchdown drives, running for one score and throwing for another. Green Bay held Dallas to season lows in rushing yards (61) and total yards (278).

And the Packers exited with a critical 17–7 victory.

"I don't necessarily point to that game, but I know we got on a run there which got us going really good," Rodgers said. "And that was an important win for us. Our defense hit a stretch there where we started playing really good."

The Dallas game started a five-game winning streak in which Green Bay climbed to 9–4, jumped right back into the playoff hunt, and silenced many who doubted Rodgers and the Packers.

Following a 37–36 loss in Pittsburgh, Green Bay posted blowout wins over Seattle and Arizona and earned the top wild-card spot with an 11–5 record.

The fifth-seeded Packers drew fourth-seeded Arizona in the opening round. And the teams produced a playoff game for the ages, one that ended with a heart-breaking 51–45 overtime loss for Green Bay.

Rodgers set a Packers postseason record with 423 passing yards, threw four touchdowns, and ran for one more. But Cardinals old pro Kurt Warner, who would retire at the end of the season, destroyed Green Bay's overmatched secondary and completed a remarkable 29 of 33 passes (87.9 percent) for 379 yards, five touchdowns, and no interceptions.

Unfortunately for Rodgers and the Packers, the game ended when Rodgers held the ball too long and was stripped by Arizona's Michael Adams. Karlos Dansby recovered the fumble and went 17 yards for a touchdown that gave the Cardinals a victory in the highest-scoring postseason game in NFL history.

Despite the disappointing conclusion, there was plenty of good for Rodgers and the Packers in 2009. And in many ways, it set the Packers up for much of their 2010 success.

Rodgers had a breakout year, finishing fourth in the NFL in passer rating (103.2), passing yards (4,434), and touchdowns (30). He also threw just seven interceptions and his interception percentage of 1.29 ranked first in football.

Rodgers also became the first quarterback in league history to eclipse more than 4,000 passing yards in each of his first two years as a starter. And Rodgers' 4,434 passing yards were second in team history, behind only Lynn Dickey's 4,458 in 1984.

More importantly, though, Green Bay won 11 games after winning just six the previous campaign.

"This is just going to make myself and these guys want it that much more," Rodgers said of the loss to Arizona. "It might not look like we came that close, but we still feel like we were close to achieving all the goals we set forth at the beginning of the season."

They most certainly were. And little did anyone know it, but 12 months later those goals would be met.

The Packers, one of the trendy preseason picks to win the Super Bowl in 2010, had an up-and-down regular season.

Green Bay was devastated by injury. The Packers failed for much of the year to find a branch of consistency to grab hold of.

And when Rodgers suffered a concussion late in the season, the Packers suffered a two-game losing streak and dipped to 8–6.

Rodgers returned for a Week 16 game against the visiting New York Giants, a contest that remains one of the most memorable of his stellar career.

In a must-win game, Rodgers had arguably his finest performance. Rodgers threw for a career-high 404 yards, tied a personal-best with four touchdown passes, and posted the third-highest passer rating of his career (139.9).

"He is a great quarterback all around," Giants safety Deon Grant said of Rodgers. "He can run, he has a great arm, and he has one of the fastest releases that you can get so he wasn't allowing our defensive line to get there. He has a great coaching staff and he has weapons. When you have those weapons that you can plug in that is what makes him dangerous all around."

One week later, the Packers and Bears met for the 181st time. And the NFL's oldest rivals produced one of the most memorable games of their 90-year history.

Chicago, which had already clinched the No. 2 seed in the NFC, competed like it was the Super Bowl and showed no mercy. Green Bay, which had to win to reach the postseason, mounted an unforgettable rally and produced a 10–3 victory.

Rodgers and the Packers had clinched the sixth and final playoff spot in the NFC. And even though that meant Green Bay would have to play all of its postseason games on the road, the Packers weren't complaining.

"I'm just proud of them," McCarthy said of his team. "We've had a different road we traveled this year and we've met every challenge. We're at 10 wins and we're one of six teams in the NFC. This is an exciting day for the organization. It's an exciting day for our fans. And we're excited as a football team."

Rodgers then led one of the most improbable postseason runs in NFL history.

Rodgers opened with a big performance at Philadelphia, where the Packers survived a late rally and notched a 21–16 win. Rodgers threw three touchdowns, completed 66.7 percent of his 27 passes, and had a lights-out passer rating of 122.5.

"I'm probably biased, but I think Aaron Rodgers is probably as good [an] in-and-out-of-the-pocket quarterback as there is in football today," McCarthy said that night. "His ability to play in the pocket, trusting his footwork, the time clock, the ability to come out of the pocket to buy time, that's Aaron's strength.

"And on top of that…he has the arm strength to make all of the throws. It gives you a lot of versatility as a play-caller and as an offensive schemer when you have a quarterback right now with his experience, playing as well as he is. He's a special player."

Never was that more evident than the following week.

Green Bay went to top-seeded Atlanta for the divisional playoffs as a two-point underdog. But Rodgers and the Packers blew the lid off the Georgia Dome.

Rodgers, making just his third postseason start, had a game for the ages. He completed 31 of 36 passes for 366 yards, threw three touchdowns and no interceptions and posted a passer rating of 136.8 in Green Bay's stunning 48–21 win.

Rodgers set Packers playoff records for completions (31) and completion percentage (86.1), and had the second most passing yards in team history (366). In 10 possessions, Rodgers led Green Bay to five touchdowns and two field goals, and the Packers never punted.

"This probably was my best performance—the stage we were on, the importance of this game," Rodgers said afterward. "It was a good night."

That's putting it mildly.

"You look at that Atlanta game, which everybody has, and I think that's the best I've seen a quarterback play," said Packers left tackle Chad Clifton, who also played eight years with Brett Favre. "Just the plays he made with his arm and with his legs, he's a special player."

Rodgers wasn't nearly as sharp the following week, when the Packers defeated Chicago 21–14 in the NFC Championship Game. Rodgers had just a 55.4 quarterback rating, but he did have an early rushing touchdown and helped the Packers race to a 14–0 lead and eventually hold on for his biggest win ever.

"I can play a lot better than I did (against Chicago), that's for sure," Rodgers said. "You've got to give credit to Chicago's defense. They had a good plan for us, but I didn't throw the ball as well as I wanted to."

Two weeks later, in the biggest game of his life, Rodgers threw the ball exactly how he wanted. Time and time again.

Rodgers was as crisp as a quarterback could be in leading the Packers to a 31–25 win over Pittsburgh in Super Bowl XLV.

Rodgers' passer rating was 111.5. His 304 passing yards might have been 450 if it hadn't been for a bevy of drops.

Most importantly, though, Rodgers was terrific in taking care of the football. He threw three touchdown passes, didn't have an interception or fumble, and was an easy choice for MVP.

Aaron Rodgers was phenomenal in Super Bowl XLV, with an almost flawless performance that won him MVP honors.

"He played great," McCarthy said. "We put everything on his shoulders. He did a lot at the line of scrimmage for us against a great defense. He did a hell of a job."

Steelers coach Mike Tomlin agreed.

"He made plays," Tomlin said of Rodgers. "We didn't get turnovers. We know that they're capable of getting plays in chunks. We knew that they would throw the football quite a bit and they did. He didn't fold under the pressure.

"I thought we hit him some early, we got to him as the game went on. But he showed his mettle and continued to stand in there and throw the football and throw it accurately. I tip my hat to him for that."

Rodgers had his coming-out party during that memorable 2010 campaign. But the party certainly didn't stop in the years to come.

Rodgers played remarkably well throughout the 2011 campaign. And after 13 games, Rodgers and the Packers were still undefeated.

Dating back to Green Bay's 2010 Super Bowl run, it compiled a 19-game winning streak that began on December 26, 2010, and lasted until December 18, 2011.

"It's a pretty cool accomplishment to not lose in a year," Packers right tackle Bryan Bulaga said. "It is pretty cool. I've never been part of something where you win that many games in a row. Not many guys have."

Sitton, the Packers' best offensive lineman, agreed.

"That's pretty impressive to go a year straight," Sitton said. "I know it's my longest winning streak."

Many players insisted they'd given little thought to the 19-game winning streak. But when most realized it was the longest streak of their lives, that impressive run became even more notable.

"I've told so many people that this is something special," said wideout Donald Driver. "That streak—and what we have a chance to do this year—is something I think the fans will cherish for a long time. And not just the fans, the players too. We'll always cherish it."

The Packers' winning streak finally ended when they dropped a 19–14 decision in Kansas City in Week 15. But "The Streak" was packed with impressive achievements:

- Green Bay didn't trail a single time in the fourth quarter of those 19 games. And only twice—against Chicago in Week 17 of 2010 and vs. the New York Giants in Week 13 of 2011—were the Packers tied in the fourth quarter.
- Green Bay averaged 33.79 points per game during "The Streak." And in seven of the 19 games, the Packers eclipsed 40 points.
- Green Bay was plus-31 in takeaways during its memorable run. And in the 19 games, Green Bay won the turnover battle 14 times, lost just once, and tied four others.

An NFL lockout that took away offseason practices didn't hurt Green Bay or lead to any complacency. Instead, when the Packers came back in 2011, they were focused on building what they had started in 2010.

"I think at the beginning of this season we were so focused and everybody was buckled in like, 'Let's do it.' And that mindset and mentality really helped us," Packers safety Charlie Peprah said. "None of us got complacent. The mindset at the start of the year was we're not defending anything. We're hunting. And I think that mindset really took hold in the locker room."

Added McCarthy: "I personally always viewed the undefeated season as really just gravy. The goal is to get the home-field advantage and win the Super Bowl."

Green Bay stayed on course for that.

The Packers finished the regular season 15–1—the best mark in franchise history. And Rodgers had arguably the finest quaterbacking season in team history.

Rodgers led the NFL in quarterback passer rating (122.5) and yards per attempt (9.25). He also finished No. 2 in touchdowns (45) and completion percentage (68.3) and No. 5 in passing yards (4,643).

Rodgers' 45 passing touchdowns set a single-season franchise record and ranked No. 4 in NFL history at the time. His passing yardage total also ranked No. 1 in team history, and he threw just six interceptions.

"Every Monday, when you watched the game from Sunday, you'd see the things that he did and how accurate he was and how productive he was," said Tom Clements, who was Green Bay's quarterbacks coach in 2011. "Just all along you knew he was having a great year.

"Obviously when you kind of live vicariously through your players, you're happy for them. When someone does well, you're happy for them and it kind of makes you feel great."

Rodgers became just the third Packers quarterback to ever win MVP honors. Starr won the award in 1966, while Favre captured three straight MVPs between 1995 and 1997.

"He's playing as well as anyone ever has," said Edgar Bennett, who played five seasons with Favre and was Green Bay's wide receivers coach in 2011. "All I know is we are extremely blessed and fortunate to have a guy like Aaron Rodgers as our quarterback. This guy is phenomenal. He really is."

Wideout James Jones, who also played with Favre, agreed with Bennett.

"There ain't nobody better right now," Jones said. "I'm not sure if there's ever been anybody better here.

"I'm not saying he's better than Brett, but Aaron's my quarterback and I'm

Total Recall

Brett Goode has watched episodes of *Jeopardy!* with Aaron Rodgers. And Goode, the Green Bay Packers' long snapper, always leaves rather amazed by the quarterback.

"The guy's just smart across the board," Goode said of Rodgers, who became a *Jeopardy!* champion himself in 2015. "His memory is incredible."

Jeff Saturday, Green Bay's starting center in 2012, noticed the same thing immediately after arriving in Green Bay. And Saturday had one overriding thought.

"Aaron's memory is a lot like Peyton Manning's," said Saturday, who spent 12 seasons in Indianapolis snapping the ball to Manning.

"We'd be in center-quarterback meetings early in the week and he'd bring up some blitz that happened against Miami, or whatever, something that's pertinent to this week. He'd say, 'Oh, we got them on this blitz.' He just has a great recall for remembering those plays and he'll adapt and adjust and look for ways to take advantage of that."

Rodgers' physical gifts—the big arm, terrific accuracy, and underrated athleticism—have been well chronicled. But an elephant-like memory might be the most important of Rodgers' talents.

Once Rodgers sees a defense, he locks away all of its strengths, weaknesses, and tendencies. Rodgers studies the pros and cons of players throughout the league and can recite them in the blink of an eye. And while defensive coordinators might bounce from job to job, Rodgers never forgets how they like to attack.

As much as anything, it's Rodgers' mental skills that have helped him win a Super Bowl, two MVP honors, and a Super Bowl MVP award.

"The ability to recall things quickly certainly helps," Rodgers said. "One of the most important things a quarterback can have, I think mental and physical toughness are at the top. Then a good memory is right near, kind of a near second tier. You have to be able to learn from your mistakes, but also recall information you saw during the week or from previous weeks or previous years very quickly.

"What that means to me is when I'm visualizing things, you want to have a feeling after that visualization, a positive feeling or kind of a negative memory and kind of tag it in your brain that way. Then when it pops up again, it immediately hits your brain a certain way. Breaking the huddle and thinking about this play, I immediately recall either a positive or negative feeling from the memory I have associated with that and being able to have a quick recall is important."

Rodgers noticed at a young age that certain things stuck in his head that seemed to escape many others. Especially with sports.

Rodgers loved to play the old Strat-O-Matic baseball game. And to this day, he can still recite statistics from former San Francisco Giants players—which was typically his team of choice.

In casual conversation, Rodgers points out that onetime Giants third baseman Kevin Mitchell had 47 home runs and 125 RBI in 1989. Interestingly, he's exactly right.

Rodgers does the same with heroes from his youth like 49ers quarterback Joe Montana.

(continued)

Total Recall *(continued)*

"The more times you punch 'em on a calculator, the more times they become kind of stuck in your brain, what those averages and those ERAs are," Rodgers said. "I just liked doing quick math like that."

Rodgers certainly studied hard. But he admits learning came relatively easy, and once something was on the board, it was probably embedded in Rodgers' head.

"He's just really damn smart…and he definitely knows how smart he is," Packers right guard Josh Sitton said of Rodgers. "But to be a quarterback in this system, you have to be. He'll talk about a certain play or a certain defense and he'll say something like, 'Oh yeah. That was like the Bears did to us in '09.' The guy has a great memory."

Rodgers skipped a grade in math. He was in a Gifted and Talented Education Program. Rodgers had straight A's his first three semesters of high school. And the only C Rodgers had in high school came in calculus.

"I loved math, as long as it wasn't calculus," Rodgers jokes.

Rodgers loves to crunch numbers in his head or recite odd statistics.

That quick mind and recall ability was a big reason Rodgers had a 3.6 GPA in college and a Wonderlic score of 35.

"I like the mental math," Rodgers said. "Just seeing things quickly can really help."

Especially on the football field.

Rodgers has copious notes from every game he's ever played. He'll review them each time he's set to face an opponent. But many of Rodgers' best notes are the ones deeply embedded in his brain.

"You can be sitting there talking to him and he can go back and remember exactly what happened on a certain play or at different times in games," said Goode, one of Rodgers' best friends. "This game has a lot of mental elements to it. And when you can recall other games and other situations, that's a huge positive. I think that goes with his smartness and being able to recall things."

Saturday watched for years as Manning was the most mentally prepared player on the field each week. And although Saturday played just one season with Rodgers, he notes the parallels between Rodgers and Manning are uncanny.

"I think any time you get around people who excel in the quarterback position, those guys learn so much from seeing things and being involved in things and they can recall what hash they're on, what the down and distance were, all that stuff," Saturday said. "And any time you can recall back to plays or blitzes or even formations where they give away tendencies or tips, any time you can recall back to those it gives you a true advantage."

When Rodgers gets to the line of scrimmage, he goes into total recall mode.

He remembers what the Bears like to do on third-and-8. He knows what the Lions will do with their safeties against three-wide-receiver looks. And he's pretty sure whether or not the Vikings are disguising a blitz or actually dropping into coverage.

"I've been visualizing since I was in junior high playing sports," Rodgers said. "And I think that approach forces you to be able to recall things very quickly. And you add that to an already pretty good memory.

"When you visualize you have to remember those plays that you think about in your mind. So it's stuff that you've seen on tape or plays that you've made in practice.

"When you're into a game, they've played you a certain way…it's not even that you set something up, but you've run some similar type plays and you go over and look at the pictures and make a small adjustment and you're able to cash in on something that you've seen.

"And there's a feeling that you have that you played against these guys for so long and you expect them to react a certain way and they do. And when you come away with the touchdown, those are the fun moments and the ones you really smile about."

Rodgers says he studies foes as much as ever today. But he also does a self-scout now so he's not tipping anything off to foes.

As Rodgers keeps passing mental tests, his performance on the field has come up aces, as well.

"I know my memory is probably not real normal," Rodgers said. "But I think it's important to have that kind of recall as a quarterback because the ability to react quickly and not be bogged down with your thoughts is an important part of playing the position well.

"I always like to have a picture in my mind as we break the huddle once the play comes in, just a quick recall. It could even be a game I didn't play in where I saw something with that player, something I saw in practice, something I saw on film in that situation. The ability to recall has been a big part of my success and I think it's something you really need to work on. It's the visualization and the practice of visualization."

always going to have his back. And I'm saying I'd take him over anybody because I got his back like that. He's my quarterback and I'll take him over anybody that's playing today, yesterday or in the future."

Unfortunately for Rodgers and the Packers, the 2011 season ended with a whimper.

Green Bay was an 8½-point favorite against the New York Giants in the NFC Divisional playoff that season. But the visiting Giants stunned the Packers 37–20, putting an end to Green Bay's hopes of repeating as Super Bowl champs.

Green Bay's preparation was certainly affected following the death of Michael Philbin—the 21-year-old son of Packers offensive coordinator Joe Philbin. But Green Bay was also thoroughly outplayed by a red-hot Giants team that would go on to win Super Bowl XLVI.

"We got beat by a team that played better tonight," Rodgers said afterward. "That's the reality of this league. Been in it for a while and been in the playoffs four times, and three times you lose your last game and you go home, and the one time you have that euphoric feeling that you keep fighting for.

"It's tough. Didn't think it was going to end tonight, felt good about our chances, felt good about our team. Personally, I didn't play as well as I wanted to."

Indeed, Rodgers picked the worst possible time to have his worst game of 2011.

Rodgers had been so good for the preceding year-and-a-half that Packer Nation now expected greatness on a weekly basis. On this night, though, Green Bay's faithful witnessed the type of mediocre quarterbacking that much of the league lives with each week.

Rodgers completed 56.5 percent of his 46 passes and his passer rating of 78.5 was his lowest in a full game since October 31, 2010. The Giants played mostly man coverage with two deep safeties, and when Rodgers refused to take chances, New York's pass rushers sacked him four times.

"Did we rattle him? Maybe a little bit," said Giants cornerback Aaron Ross, whose team had lost to the Packers 38–35 one month earlier. "I just think we did a good job locking on to the receivers and taking away some places he wanted to go."

Even when Rodgers had clean looks, he made some scattershot throws. And it led to an incredibly frustrating ending to a season filled with so much promise.

"It doesn't feel good. It's not where I expected to be standing," McCarthy said afterward. "I have to stand here, obviously, but it's not the way I expected to feel standing here. It's very disappointing. It's a locker room that expected a lot more and rightfully so.

"I wish I would have done a better job tonight. It was an excellent regular season, but we clearly understand in Green Bay it's about winning champion-ships. Just going to the playoffs is not enough. We're disappointed as a football team. We're disappointed for our fans.

"We had a heck of a run in the regular season. I thought we were playing very well down the stretch. I was really anticipating us playing very well today. I have to look at myself and go back and find out why I didn't have the team in that mode because I thought the preparation was very good this week."

While the 2011 ending was rough, Green Bay's future was bright thanks largely to Rodgers.

In Rodgers' first four seasons, he threw 131 touchdowns to 37 interceptions, won a Super Bowl, and captured MVP honors in 2011. In Favre's first four years, he threw 108 touchdowns to 64 interceptions, and won MVP honors in 1995.

The Packers struggled out of the gate in 2012, opening just 2–3. But Green Bay reversed course with a memorable 42–24 win in Houston.

That night, Rodgers tied Matt Flynn's franchise record with six touchdown passes, including three to Jordy Nelson. Rodgers also completed 24 of 37 passes for 338 yards as Green Bay routed the previously undefeated Texans.

"Aaron was on fire," McCarthy said. "He played through some bumps and bruises there in the second half so clearly one of his better performances as a Packer."

Rodgers was taking his share of heat for Green Bay's slow start in 2012. After one of the top performances of his career, Rodgers was asked what message he sent to his critics.

"Shhh," Rodgers said during an NBC interview.

Later, he elaborated.

"Of course I heard (the criticism)," Rodgers said. "I mean it wasn't like I paid a lot of attention to it, but people, whether it's good stuff or bad stuff, friends of mine they like to tell me what's being said out there.

"I'm not someone that watches a lot of TV or puts a whole lot of worth into some of those comments, but I feel like I've always played with a chip on my shoulder and it helps when people give me a reason to have that chip on my shoulder."

Rodgers certainly played with a chip on his shoulder the rest of the 2012 season. Green Bay won five in a row and nine of its last 11 games that year.

Defenses played the Packers differently than past seasons, employing two deep safeties all year and a man underneath, taking away the big play and testing Rodgers' patience. Still, Rodgers stayed within the offense and took what defenses allowed.

That helped the Packers capture the NFC North Division with an 11–5 record, one game better than runners-up Minnesota and Chicago. And Rodgers finished with another huge season.

Rodgers threw for 39 touchdowns and just eight interceptions. Rodgers led the NFL in passer rating (108.0) for a second straight year, becoming the first quarterback to accomplish that since Peyton Manning, who had done it in 2004–06.

Rodgers finished third in the NFL in completion percentage (67.2), the second-best total in team history behind only his 2011 mark. Rodgers also threw for 4,295 yards and led the NFL in touchdown percentage (7.1).

With a big finish, Rodgers vaulted himself back into the MVP discussion again. The award eventually went to Minnesota running back Adrian Peterson, though, who ran for 2,097 yards that season.

"I'm biased," Packers left guard T.J. Lang said. "But the way that he plays, I think he's under a big microscope because of how good he is. An average game for him is a really good game for a lot of other people.

"The way he's had to adjust to how defenses are playing us and still putting up good numbers says a lot about the type of guy he is. I'm always going to say he's the MVP."

Once again, though, the playoffs were a major downer for Green Bay.

The Packers rolled past Minnesota 24–10 in the NFC Wild Card round. The Vikings played without starting quarterback Christian Ponder (triceps) and were forced to turn to backup Joe Webb. And the divide between the two quarterbacks was cavernous.

Rodgers threw for 274 yards and a touchdown, while Webb was just 11-of-30 for 180 yards with one touchdown and one interception.

"I look at it as I'm going against the Minnesota Vikings defense and that's what I've prepared for and that's the film I watched," Rodgers said. "Our defense did a good job today of slowing them down in the passing game and not letting Adrian (Peterson) have the big runs. Joe (Webb) had some good runs early that kept some drives going, but eventually we were able to get ahead and make them have to do some more passing and we did a good job against that."

That set up a homecoming for Rodgers, as the Packers headed to San Francisco for the NFC Divisional playoff. Rodgers, who grew up less than three hours north in Chico, California, was headed back to the Bay Area for the first time in his NFL career.

"It will be fun," Rodgers said. "I went to a few baseball games there growing up, and saw a game there when I was in college. It will be loud, it will be a great environment, and it should be a good show for the fans."

Since the start of the 1995 season, Green Bay was a remarkable 13–2 against the 49ers. The only losses came in the 1998 postseason and the 2012 season opener, in which the 49ers dominated the Packers 30–22 at Lambeau Field.

Rodgers was now presented a chance to leave his mark on a rivalry that was largely one-sided in recent seasons.

"I know Aaron Rodgers clearly understands the importance of quarterback play in a game, and more importantly in playoff games," Packers coach Mike McCarthy said. "I know he'll particularly be excited to go back to San Francisco and play in northern California. That's always exciting for him personally.

"He's steady. He's been through enough now, I don't see him overreacting or trying to put more pressure on himself. He's a big-time preparation player as far as what he puts into each game, and that won't change this week. He'll be clutch for us like he always is."

Rodgers was fine against mighty San Francisco. But Green Bay's defense was miserable.

San Francisco quarterback Colin Kaepernick accounted for 444 total yards—including 181 on the ground—and the 49ers cruised to a 45–31 win. Kaepernick also threw for two touchdowns and ran for two more.

In all, Green Bay's defense gave up the most total yards (579), most yards rushing (323), and second-most points in the playoffs in franchise history.

"We just didn't get it done in the second half," Rodgers said. "I knew we were going to have to score some points. We knew we were going to have to put up at least 38 points."

The 2013 season was a frustrating one for Green Bay.

The Packers were rolling along, had won four straight games, and were sitting at 5–2 in early November. But on Green Bay's first series during a Monday night game against Chicago, Rodgers was sacked by Bears defensive lineman Shea McClellin and broke his collarbone.

The injury bug had hit the Packers harder than any team in football since 2010. But this marked the first time Rodgers missed any significant time.

"Aaron's the one guy we really just couldn't lose," Packers veteran cornerback Jarrett Bush said. "We've had a lot of injuries around here, but never really the quarterback.

"We've been really lucky. But losing Aaron, that's going to be tough."

It was.

The Packers lost that night to Chicago. Rodgers would miss the next seven games, too, and Green Bay went just 2–4–1 in those contests.

Reserves Seneca Wallace, Scott Tolzien, and eventually Matt Flynn did what they could. But the gap between that trio and Rodgers was monumental—and the Packers slipped to 7–7–1 overall.

Amazingly, though, as Green Bay headed to the final week of 2013, it still had a chance to win a third straight NFC North title. That's because Detroit had bottomed out and Chicago couldn't pull away.

And in the nick of time, Rodgers returned for the regular season finale in Chicago.

"I'm excited to be back with the team," Rodgers said on the day he was cleared by Green Bay's medical staff. "I mean this is a fun day for me, but I think the focus needs to be on this game and the opportunity we have to win the division, which is our first goal every year.

"We're in it, you know we have a chance against our rivals and what a better way than to go down there and get some redemption and host a home playoff game."

Late in the game, though, redemption didn't look probable.

Green Bay trailed Chicago 28–27 with 46 seconds left in a showdown for the NFC North title—and the division's only playoff berth. The Packers faced a fourth-and-8 from Chicago's 48-yard line, which in essence meant it was a win-or-go-home play.

The Bears rushed seven and the Packers blocked with just six. Rodgers was nearly leveled by Bears right end Julius Peppers, but fullback John Kuhn got just enough of Peppers and Rodgers escaped to his left.

Downfield, Bears safety Chris Conte let wideout Randall Cobb slip behind him. And when Rodgers delivered a strike to Cobb, the shifty receiver raced home for a remarkable 48-yard touchdown that gave the Packers a stunning 33–28 win.

It was arguably Green Bay's biggest play in the closing moments of a must-win game since Brett Favre hit Sterling Sharpe for a 40-yard touchdown in the 1993 Wild Card playoff.

"Aaron and Randall just made a phenomenal play," McCarthy said. "Those two guys making a great, great play, that will be running on the highlight reel for the rest of my time on this earth. What a great finish."

Packer Nation held its collective breath on November 4, 2013, when Aaron Rodgers was slow to get up following a sack by Chicago Bears linebacker Shea McClellin. Rodgers broke his collarbone and missed seven games.

The play gave Green Bay (8–7–1) a third straight NFC North championship and its seventh divisional title since 2002. It also vaulted the Packers into the postseason for a fifth straight year under Rodgers.

"I was able to get the edge and saw Randall running wide open," Rodgers said. "I knew I had to get a little bit on it just to make sure that I didn't way underthrow him. When that ball came down in the end zone, it was just pandemonium."

The final play capped a memorable 15-play, 87-yard drive that took nearly six minutes. Along the way, the Packers converted three fourth downs.

"To pick up three fourth downs on that last drive. Wow," Packers nose tackle Ryan Pickett said. "What are the odds of that?"

Really, the odds of Green Bay's final offensive play working didn't appear great—at least initially.

Kuhn, who was serving as Rodgers' personal protector, recognized that the Bears were bringing more rushers than Green Bay had blockers. So Kuhn changed the blocking scheme, so the front five in essence made a wall.

Kuhn was then responsible for Peppers, who was coming off the edge. Kuhn was able to get his right shoulder into Peppers' left hip, which did just enough to slow the Bears pass rusher. Ironically, Peppers was an unrestricted free agent after that season and signed with Green Bay.

"The line did a good job sealing everybody off, leaving one for me," Kuhn said. "I just tried to get as much of (Julius) Peppers as I could."

Rodgers had a rough start to this showdown game with two first-half interceptions and a quarterback rating of just 44.7 at halftime. And the Packers were in a 28–20 hole early in the fourth quarter.

Back came Rodgers, though, who entered the day with just five fourth-quarter comebacks in his career. But Rodgers picked the perfect time for No. 6.

First, Rodgers threw for 68 yards during a six-play, 77-yard touchdown march that pulled the Packers within 28–27. Then after the defense came up with its first stop of the second half, Rodgers orchestrated what was arguably the drive of his life.

"It was a special moment," Rodgers said. "There's nothing quite like a road victory and especially on this stage right here. We had to win to get in, otherwise we're going home. And there were a lot of opportunities for us to give up, and we just kept believing in each other.

"So I'm proud of our guys, thankful for the opportunity. I feel very blessed, I appreciate the prayers from all the fans and obviously my friends and family, but this is a great group of guys. We just want to keep this journey going."

Unfortunately for the Packers, the journey ended one week later.

San Francisco, the defending NFC champs, knocked Green Bay out of the playoffs for a second straight year. Once again, the Packers struggled to contain Kaepernick and the visiting 49ers edged Green Bay 23–20.

"Yeah, I mean it's frustrating," Rodgers said afterward. "I think you have to start with yourself and…I could have definitely made a few more plays. So that's why it's disappointing.

"These opportunities are pretty special and you've got to make the most of them. It's nine years for me now, blessed to play that long, and would love to play another nine if possible, but this is an opportunity we let slip through our fingers."

Rodgers certainly wasn't at his best against the 49ers. He finished 17-of-26 for 177 yards, with one touchdown and a passer rating of 97.8.

Rodgers and the entire offense struggled early, never could get in complete rhythm, and fell to the 49ers for a fourth consecutive time.

"Frustrating way to end the season," Rodgers said. "I think a lot of us felt that the way things had gone the last four or five weeks, there was something special about this year and this might be everything aligning right for us to make a run. So, very disappointing. Personally, it's frustrating not to play your best game."

The finish ended a wild year for Rodgers, who had missed 55 days with his broken collarbone and endured the most trying season of his career.

Rodgers believed Green Bay had enough talent to make a deep postseason run. Instead, Rodgers and the Packers fell to 1–3 in the playoffs since their Super Bowl season of 2010.

"We did some great things this year but we came up a little short," Rodgers said.

Unfortunately for Green Bay, the 2014 season ended in more devastating fashion. But the ride itself was largely a thriller.

Rodgers had arguably the best season of his career and won his second MVP in four seasons. Rodgers completed 341 of 520 passes (65.6 percent) for 4,381 yards and 38 touchdowns. He also threw just five interceptions and finished with a 112.2 passer rating.

Rodgers again ranked No. 1 in touchdown-to-interception ratio (7.60, 38–5) and finished second in the NFL in passer rating and yards per attempt (8.43). Rodgers was third in touchdown passes and was the only quarterback in the NFL to finish in the top three in all four of those categories.

"I need to figure out new ways to compliment Aaron, frankly," McCarthy said.

There was plenty to compliment in 2014.

The Packers started slowly, much as they had in both 2012 and 2013. Green Bay lost two of its first three games before Rodgers and the offense got rolling in a 38–17 dismantling of host Chicago in Week 4.

Rodgers completed 22-of-28 passes for 302 yards and four touchdowns that afternoon at Soldier Field. Rodgers' final passer rating of 151.2 was the fourth-highest in franchise history and he averaged a remarkable 10.79 passing yards per attempt.

Just one week earlier, Rodgers and Green Bay's offense managed only seven points in an embarrassing loss at Detroit. Two days after that setback, Rodgers told Packer Nation to "R-E-L-A-X", then he delivered one of the better games of his career in Chicago.

"I just know it's a long season," Rodgers said. "There's always going to be mini-freakouts along the way.

"Just have to stick together and stay the course. I just wanted to remind everyone that it's a long season and at some point we are going to get this thing figured out."

Rodgers seemed to have the psyche of these Packers—and really all of Packer Nation—figured out. Instead of making a mountain out of Green Bay's early-season struggles, he settled everyone down with his message to "R-E-L-A-X."

The Packers responded with their best performance of the season, one that started a four-game winning streak.

"As a quarterback, you can get too much credit and too much blame at times," Rodgers said. "When you are getting too much credit, you need to be able to deflect properly and when you are getting too much blame sometimes you need to tell everyone to relax or just take it all and lead by example when you get on the field."

The Packers went to the bye week with a 5–3 record, then Rodgers went wild against the Bears for the second time in 2014.

Rodgers had an unforgettable performance on *Sunday Night Football*, joining Oakland's Daryle Lamonica as the only players in NFL history to throw six first-half touchdown passes. In the first half alone, Rodgers went a remarkable 18-of-24 with six touchdown strikes, 315 passing yards, and a nearly perfect quarter-back rating of 156.3.

Rodgers needed just seven possessions—and 36 offensive plays—to notch his accomplishment and power the Packers to a remarkably easy 55–14 rout of Chicago.

In a matter of three hours, Rodgers shined before a national audience, became a leading candidate for MVP honors, and showed that the Packers might be a legitimate contender in the NFC.

"He's just having probably a career year for him," Lang said. "He's been putting up touchdowns, but he's also a guy that doesn't turn the ball over a whole lot.

"I've seen so many great performances by him, that I don't think anything really surprises you anymore. Obviously, that's a little bit unprecedented, though, to have six touchdown passes in the first half."

To say the least.

Lamonica threw six touchdowns in the first half against Buffalo on October 19, 1969. In the 45 years since, no player had notched a six-pack by halftime—until Rodgers destroyed the Bears' atrocious defense.

Packers coach Mike McCarthy was asked afterward if he's ever seen Rodgers better.

"I'm going to have to wait until I'm sitting on that porch thinking back," McCarthy said. "But I mean, he was right on tonight. His statistics at halftime, I don't know if I've ever seen anything like that. He played a great game."

Rodgers had plenty of those during a memorable 2014 campaign.

Rodgers and the Packers rolled up 53 points during a rout of Philadelphia the following week. That marked the first time in franchise history that Green Bay scored 50 points in consecutive games and just the fifth time in NFL history that a team accomplished the feat.

Rodgers threw a pair of touchdowns in a highly impressive 26–21 home win over eventual Super Bowl champion New England. And Rodgers threw for 327 yards and three touchdowns in a 43–37 win over Atlanta.

But perhaps his most impressive performance came in the regular season finale against Detroit.

With the NFC North title on the line, Rodgers reinjured his left calf late in the first half and took a cart to the Packers locker room. Within the blink of an eye, Detroit turned a 14–0 deficit into a 14-all tie.

But with the Packers on the ropes, Rodgers returned and rallied Green Bay to a 30–20 win. Rodgers engineered touchdown drives on two of his first three second-half possessions, and completed 11 of 13 passes for 129 yards.

"I wanted to be back out there, compete with my guys," Rodgers said. "When I broke my collarbone (in 2013), I remember hearing Jon Gruden say that I was out for the game and I said, 'The hell with that.' (I) tried to get my pads back on and get back out there, but that didn't work obviously with the severity of that injury.

"This was different. Doc (McKenzie) came in, we talked about the risks and I was able to get him to allow me to do some movements on the sideline to see how I felt. I wasn't going to put myself in major harm's way, but at the same time, I feel like if I can be out there I can give our team a little jolt….I felt good on the

Aaron Rodgers' 2014 MVP season saw him throw for 38 touchdowns and a career-low five interceptions, with an interception rate of just 1.0 percent. He had a passer rating of 112.2, his highest since 2011, and showed his mettle by playing injured to lead the Packers to the NFC Championship Game. (AP Images)

sidelines throwing the ball, talked to Mike (McCarthy), asked him to just keep me in the shotgun because of my limited mobility, obviously, and we were able to do that and make some plays."

Rodgers' heroics helped Green Bay win its fourth straight NFC North title, earn the No. 2 seed in the playoffs, and clinch a first-round bye.

The Packers finished the year with an NFL-best 486 points, the second-highest total in franchise history. Rodgers was also historically good in games played at Lambeau Field.

During home games alone, Rodgers threw 24 touchdowns with no interceptions on 240 attempts. Rodgers joined New England quarterback Tom Brady (241 attempts in 2003) as the only quarterbacks in NFL history to throw 200-plus passes at home in a season with no interceptions.

Rodgers recorded a passer rating of 133.2 at home during the 2014 regular season, the highest in NFL history. And the Packers outscored their foes by an NFL-best 155 points in eight home games, the highest mark in franchise history.

"Right now, I'd say it's going to be tough for someone to beat us here," former Packers cornerback Tramon Williams said of Green Bay's home field advantage. "We haven't played like this, ever. We've played well, but not like this.

"If we are playing like this at home, then obviously people probably won't want to come here. It's not going to be easy at all, but it's pretty great how we're playing right now."

Green Bay opened the postseason by hosting longtime rival Dallas in the NFC Divisional playoff. And with Rodgers limited by his calf injury, the Packers were in a 21–13 hole late in the third quarter.

But with the season on the line, Rodgers scrapped the conservative nature he'd played with for three quarters and turned it loose down the stretch.

First, Rodgers engineered a seven-play, 90-yard touchdown march that pulled the Packers within 21–20. Rodgers fired a 46-yard touchdown to rookie wideout Davante Adams on a third-and-15, as the rookie wideout beat Sterling Moore and J.J. Wilcox for the score.

One series later, Rodgers led an eight-play, 80-yard scoring drive in which 78 of the yards came via his right arm. Rodgers capped the march with a 13-yard bullet touchdown to rookie tight end Richard Rodgers that gave Green Bay a lead it wouldn't relinquish.

The Packers prevailed and headed to their second NFC Championship Game under Rodgers.

"Just an incredible effort by (Rodgers), especially in the second half to go out there and grind and continue to make plays when he's not 100% healthy," Lang said. "But he's our leader and everything starts with him."

The Packers then headed to Seattle for the NFC Championship Game. The defending Super Bowl–champion Seahawks had routed the Packers 36–16 in the season opener and were a 7.5-point favorite in the rematch.

For most of the game, though, the Packers dominated the mighty Seahawks.

Green Bay held a 16–0 halftime lead. And according to Pro-Football-Reference .com, the Packers' chances of winning at that point were 89.9 percent.

Green Bay also led 19–7 with just more than 3 minutes left in the game. And at that moment, the Packers' chances of winning were 99.9 percent.

But somehow, someway, the Seahawks rallied for an improbable 28–22 win in overtime.

Green Bay's offense became conservative and predictable. The defense melted down. And former Packers reserve tight end Brandon Bostick fumbled away Seattle's onside kick that could have iced the game.

In overtime, Seahawks wideout Jermaine Kearse beat Tramon Williams for a 35-yard, game-winning touchdown when the Packers blitzed and had no safety help.

"I tried to watch the film…but I didn't," Packers left guard Josh Sitton said. "I couldn't watch it. I knew what happened. We kicked their ass up front the whole game. We handled them all day. We should've won the game."

Rodgers wasn't his typical self due to both the calf injury and Seattle's elite defense. Rodgers finished with two interceptions, one touchdown, and a 55.8 passer rating.

It marked his second disappointing individual performance in an NFC Championship Game.

But Green Bay was in control virtually the entire game. And afterward, every-one agreed that a golden opportunity was wasted.

"It's a missed opportunity that I will probably think about the rest of my career," Rodgers said. "We were the better team…and we played well enough to win and we can't blame anybody but ourselves."

2014 NFL MVP

The 2014 MVP race was going to be a photo finish.

Houston's J.J. Watt was in the midst of one of the finest defensive seasons in NFL history and had plenty of support. Dallas quarterback Tony Romo was having a career year. New England's Tom Brady was being Tom Brady. And Dallas' DeMarco Murray was having one of the finest seasons a running back has ever enjoyed.

Then there was Aaron Rodgers having arguably the finest season of his brilliant career.

As Week 17 arrived, the Packers were in a dogfight with Detroit for the NFC North title. And Rodgers was considered a slight favorite for the prestigious award.

But late in the first half of the regular season finale against the visiting Lions, all bets were off.

The Packers led 7–0 late in the first half when Rodgers rolled to his right and flipped a four-yard touchdown pass to wideout Randall Cobb. Just as he was delivering the ball, though, Rodgers collapsed as if he'd been shot in the back of the leg.

Rodgers, who had injured his left calf the previous week, had to be helped off the field. Then he was carted back to the Packers' locker room.

"Just moved out of the pocket there, felt a very similar feeling in a different spot as I did last week," Rodgers said afterward. "I was worried about the severity of the injury and my ability to walk off the field at that point. But once I got back in the locker room I was actually watching the game on TV with some heat on my calf thinking if I could finagle myself to go back in."

He did. And in the process, Rodgers solidified his second MVP award.

Rodgers and Dr. Pat McKenzie, Green Bay's team physician, had a long discussion at halftime. And McKenzie agreed to let Rodgers test out the calf.

Rodgers got retaped and also kept heat on the injury. And eventually, McKenzie gave him a thumbs up.

"Just felt like if I could get back in there it might give us a little jolt, and wanted to be out there with the guys competing," Rodgers said.

There was just one problem. In the brief time Rodgers was out, the Lions had roared back to tie the game at 14. And Green Bay's season now hung in the balance.

"It was make or break for us," former Packers cornerback Tramon Williams said. "When someone like A-Rod leaves the game, it's a little scary. We were just all happy he made it back."

It's easy to see why.

With the Packers on the ropes, Rodgers returned and rallied Green Bay to a thrilling 30–20 win. Rodgers engineered touchdown drives on two of his first three second-half posses-sions, and completed 11-of-13 passes for 129 yards after his return.

Rodgers' heroics helped Green Bay win its fourth straight NFC North division title, earn the No. 2 seed in the playoffs, and clinch a first-round bye. In the process, Rodgers locked up the MVP award—which he was presented one month later.

(continued)

2014 NFL MVP *(continued)*

"He's obviously the MVP for a reason," Packers linebacker Clay Matthews said of Rodgers. "If this doesn't solidify it today, I don't know what will."

Cobb, who caught a pair of touchdowns from Rodgers, agreed.

"Everything about him," Cobb said when asked what makes Rodgers the MVP. "Obviously, his numbers speak for themselves, but his leadership, his competitive nature…I mean, this guy is hurt, he was hurtin' out there, and you could see it on his face, and for him to come back out and play the way he did is huge."

On Rodgers' first series back, he hit Cobb for 29 yards on a crossing route to the Lions' 19-yard line. Three plays later, Cobb whipped Detroit nickel cornerback Cassius Vaughn and Rodgers hit him for an 18-yard touchdown.

Two series later, Rodgers drove Green Bay to the Lions' 1-yard line. On second-and-one, Rodgers called his own number, then fell forward for an awkward 1-yard touchdown that gave Green Bay a 28–14 lead.

A short time later, the Packers were NFC North champions. And Rodgers had locked up MVP honors.

"Aaron Rodgers, I don't know what to say about him," Packers coach Mike McCarthy said. "To come back after the calf injury, and to perform on a limited game plan and to play at a level that he continues to play at, I thought was extraordinary. It was clearly an MVP performance, another MVP performance, by Aaron Rodgers.

"Aaron Rodgers is the leader of our football team. He's, in my opinion, the Most Valuable Player in the National Football League this year. I think what he demonstrated tonight in a must-win game against an excellent opponent, I think it's clear what he means to our football team."

Rodgers finished the year with 38 touchdown passes and five interceptions. And his touch-down-to-interception ratio of 7.6 was by far the finest in football.

Rodgers' quarterback rating of 112.2 was second in football behind Romo. Rodgers threw for 4,381 yards and completed 65.6 percent of his passes.

But in an extremely tight race, Rodgers' performance against Detroit tipped the scales in his direction.

"If I had a vote, I would have cast it about a month ago," Packers right tackle Bryan Bulaga said. "The fact he came back in and helped us win this game, that's about as gutsy as it gets."

Afterward, some players compared Rodgers' heroics to Michael Jordan playing with the flu and leading Chicago to the 1997 NBA title. Others brought up the name Willis Reed, referring to the New York Knicks center's gallant effort in Game 7 of the 1970 NBA Finals.

"When I step back and think about this season and this game years from now, I'll probably take a lot of pride in getting back out there and letting my teammates know I'll put my body on the line for them," Rodgers said. "We're in the moment. It's about winning the division and getting a home playoff game.

"You're just out there competing. This is what we love to do. I'm passionate about this game. I love the competition, and I love being out there with my guys and having them count on me to be myself. This is a good night and good things to come."

In 2014, that included MVP honors.

While the ending to the 2014 season was heartbreaking, the first half of Rodgers' career has been remarkable.

In addition to a Super Bowl title and two MVP awards, Rodgers has led the Packers to six straight playoff appearances.

Rodgers and the Packers have won four straight NFC North Division titles, something that hadn't been done since Chicago won five in a row in the mid-1980s. And Rodgers has compiled a 70–33 record in the regular season (.680) and is 6–5 in the postseason (.545).

To think, Rodgers nearly gave the game up as an 18-year-old back in Chico, California. And as recently as 2009, a large segment of the fan base wanted to move on from the trio of Rodgers, McCarthy, and Thompson.

"We've all gained a lot by working together," Rodgers said. "All relationships that last are built on trust. And trust for me is not initially given. It's earned. And Mike's the same way.

"I'm kind of a laid-back, California guy. He's a loud Pittsburgh guy. So it took a while to get on the same page, I think, as far as our styles meshing together. But the thing that always helped was the preparation we always put in and how much we desired to be successful and it was only a matter of time before things started clicking the right way."

In the process, Rodgers has made himself the next great Packers quarterback. And that's something most never believed could be possible.

Late in the 2014 season, Rodgers was asked if there was a central characteristic that he shared with Favre and Starr.

"I think it's guys that fit in here well. Personalities mesh and it's bigger than football," he said. "I'm from a small town in California. We moved around a lot, but Chico's a small town. Brett's from a real small town in Mississippi, obviously. Bart has the roots in Alabama. This was a place I think we all fell in love with. The atmosphere, the environment.

"I don't know if those two guys feel like I do about the weather. I'm not crazy about the cold weather, but you just love the atmosphere, the commitment to the team that the community has, the expectations. And I think we all bring something a little different to the table, but we all have similar makeups with the mental and physical toughness. That makeup and character makeup helps. This is a blue-collar town and I think it warrants that kind of guy leading your team.

"I think we all do pretty well, too, with pressure. That's probably another character trait the three of us share is being pretty good under pressure and being able to handle that pressure. Football's bigger than it was when Brett began starting (1992) and Bart. It still is the main attraction in Green Bay. Football season is a year-round thing. The expectations are always there to win.

"Seeing Brett for those three years, he did a good job of handling the pressures on and off the field here. And I'm sure Bart did the same thing with all the championships they won. But that's just part of the job description. You play in Green Bay, there's no other professional teams in town. There's not a lot of nightlife or big attractions that distract people from what's going on. It's about the Packers and how they're doing. So to play quarterback in this town means there's a lot of expectations, but I think we all like it that way."

And right now, all of Packer Nation loves the results Rodgers has provided.

Part II

The Other Quarterback Trios

★ ★ ★

No. 2:
San Francisco 49ers

The combination of Joe Montana and Steve Young might be the best duo in league history.

Montana went a remarkable 4–0 in Super Bowls and was the MVP of the big game three times. Young was 1–0 in Super Bowls and was the MVP of that game, too.

Together, the duo were selected for 15 Pro Bowls and won a combined four MVP awards. Both are in the NFL Hall of Fame and are two of the game's all-time greats.

But this is a book that ranks quarterback trios—and that's where the 49ers slip behind the Packers.

San Francisco's third-best quarterback is Y.A. Tittle, who had 10 outstanding years with the 49ers, but never came close to a championship. Tittle's best seasons also came late in his career with the New York Giants.

While the 49ers have five championships with this trio, the Packers have seven with their threesome. Green Bay leads in MVP Awards (6–4) and virtually every statistical passing category.

The 49ers have enjoyed terrific quarterbacking play, but not to the level of Green Bay.

Joe Montana

It was crunch time in one of the biggest games of his life.

Lesser men have panicked, become flustered, unraveled. But few have ever been better in crisis moments than Joe Montana.

In the 1989 Super Bowl, Montana and the San Francisco 49ers trailed the Cincinnati Bengals 16–13 with 3:20 remaining. As Montana entered the huddle, he saw something that made everyone relax.

"There, in the stands, standing near the exit ramp," Montana said to tackle Harris Barton. "Isn't that John Candy?"

Suddenly, everybody exhaled. The magnitude of the moment didn't seem as large.

And Montana proceeded to lead a memorable 92-yard drive that he capped with a 10-yard touchdown pass to John Taylor for a 20–16 San Francisco win.

That was one of four Super Bowl titles Montana and the 49ers won. To this day, many consider Montana and New England's Tom Brady the finest to ever play the position.

"Joe was like a little kid on the football field and no doubt the best quarterback to ever play the game," said Jerry Rice, widely regarded as the best receiver in NFL history. "I remember Super Bowl XXIII when he ran into the huddle when we began that final drive, and the complete quietness in there as he started making his calls. There was no doubt in that huddle that we were going to take the ball down the field and win, and that was because of Joe, always cool and collected."

During his remarkable 13-year career in San Francisco, Montana and the 49ers went 4–0 in Super Bowls. The man nicknamed "Joe Cool" was the MVP in three of those.

Montana was an eight-time Pro Bowl selection and was the NFL's MVP twice. Montana also engineered 31 fourth-quarter come-from-behind wins during his illustrious career, including that memorable drive against the Bengals.

"With all the excitement, all the pressure, Joe has always appeared to be passive," said Bill Walsh, who was Montana's coach from 1979 to 1988. "But under the surface there was this tremendous energy, this magnetic ability to rise to the occasion."

Montana was lightly regarded early in his career.

Montana's arm strength, size (6'2", 205 pounds), and speed were all questioned when he came out of Notre Dame in 1979. And Montana wasn't drafted until the third round that year.

By Montana's third season, though, Walsh believed he had something special— and Montana delivered. The 49ers went 13–3 that year, then Montana led San Francisco to its most memorable win ever—a game that would simply become known as "The Catch."

In the NFC Championship Game that year, the host 49ers trailed mighty Dallas 27–21 late in regulation. But Montana—as only Montana could do— drove the 49ers from their own 11-yard line to the Dallas 6.

On third-and-3 with 58 seconds left, Montana sprinted to his right and looked for wideout Freddie Solomon. With Solomon covered up, though, Montana threw a high floater to the back right corner of the end zone.

It appeared the ball was destined to sail out of bounds. But at the last moment, 49ers wideout Dwight Clark made a fingertip grab in the back of the end zone to give San Francisco a 28–27 win.

"This is something we work on from day one in camp," Montana said that day. "If (Clark) doesn't catch it, nobody does…but I have great confidence in Dwight's leaping ability."

Two weeks later, San Francisco defeated Cincinnati 26–21 in Super Bowl XVI and Montana was the MVP. That was just the start of "Joe Cool's" dominance.

Montana and the 49ers went 15–1 in the 1984 season and steamrolled a pair of foes in the NFC playoffs. Montana then was the MVP of Super Bowl XIX as the 49ers rolled past Dan Marino's Miami Dolphins 38–16.

Montana threw three touchdowns and no interceptions that afternoon at Stanford Stadium. Montana also completed 24-of-35 passes for 331 yards.

Afterward, Walsh said: "Joe Montana is the greatest quarterback today, maybe the greatest quarterback of all time."

The 49ers reached the Super Bowl again during the 1988 season. But it was one of their tougher journeys.

San Francisco was 6–5 late in the regular season and Montana was trying to hold off Steve Young from taking his job. But the 49ers rallied to make the postseason, got hot in the playoffs, and eventually toppled the Bengals again in Super Bowl XXIII.

"This trip to the Super Bowl is more gratifying than the others because the road has been harder," Montana said.

Montana and the 49ers were at the peak of their powers in the 1989 season, finishing an NFL-best 14–2. Montana also threw 26 touchdowns to just eight interceptions, and finished with what was then the top single-season passer rating in NFL history (112.4).

Montana was named the NFL's MVP that season. Then he threw five touchdowns during a 55–10 destruction of Denver in Super Bowl XXIV.

"There have been, and will be, much better arms and legs and much better bodies on quarterbacks in the NFL," former 49ers teammate Randy Cross said. "But if you have to win a game or score a touchdown or win a championship, the only guy to get is Joe Montana."

Things began to unravel, though.

The 49ers were upset by the New York Giants in the 1990 NFC Championship Game, foiling their attempt to become the first team ever to win three straight Super Bowls. Montana then missed the entire 1990 season and most of the 1991 campaign with an elbow injury suffered against the Giants in that championship game.

In those two seasons, Young proved he was one of the best quarterbacks in football himself. He was also five years younger than Montana.

So in April 1993, the 49ers did the unthinkable and traded Montana to the Kansas City Chiefs.

"I didn't want to leave San Francisco," Montana said. "But I just wanted to play, and at that point the opportunity was not afforded to me."

Montana led the Chiefs to the AFC Championship Game in 1993 and the playoffs in 1994. But a fifth Super Bowl eluded him.

Montana retired in April 1995, with 40,551 passing yards, 273 touchdown passes, and just 139 interceptions. At the time of his retirement, Montana's career passer rating of 92.3 ranked second in NFL history.

Montana went a sensational 117–47 as a starter (.713). And he reached 100 wins faster than anyone in NFL history, a mark that stood until Brady surpassed it in 2008.

Montana completed a scintillating 83-of-122 passes in his four Super Bowls for 1,142 yards. He threw 11 touchdowns in those games and no interceptions, and had a passer rating of 127.8. And his postseason record was a terrific 16–7 (.696), including a 14–5 mark with San Francisco.

"When you're down, your leadership skills may be more important than your playing ability. If you stay positive, things start turning around, and in most cases you've still got plenty of time," Montana wrote in his 1997 book *Joe Montana's Art and Magic of Quarterbacking*.

"It's impossible to have any success as a quarterback without being a leader, since all eyes in the huddle will be on you. If you're uncertain about things, your teammates will know."

Joe Montana by the Numbers

4× Super Bowl champion (XVI, XIX, XXIII, XXIV)
3× Super Bowl MVP (XVI, XIX, XXIV)
8× Pro Bowl (1981, 1983, 1984, 1985, 1987,1989, 1990, 1993)
3× Associated Press First Team All-Pro (1987, 1989, 1990)
2× NFL MVP (1989, 1990) (AP, Pro Football Writers Association, Newspaper Enterprise Association, *Sporting News*, Maxwell Club)
2× AP Second Team All-Pro (1981, 1984)
1989 NFL Offensive Player of the Year (AP, PW)
4× NFC champion (1981, 1984, 1988, 1989)
PFW NFL Comeback Player of the Year (1986)
United Press International NFC Player of the Year (1989)
1989 Sportsman/Athlete of the Year (AP, *SN*)
1990 Sportsman/Athlete of the Year (AP, *Sports Illustrated*)
1977 NCAA Division I National Champion
Cotton Bowl Classic MVP (1979)
NFL 1980s All-Decade Team
NFL 75th Anniversary All-Time Team
San Francisco 49ers #16 retired
Pro Football Hall of Fame inductee (2000)

Career Stats
Pass attempts: 5,391
Completions: 3,409
Percentage: 63.2
TD–INT: 273–139
Passing yards: 40,551
QB rating: 92.3

That was never a problem with Montana. He was unflappable when things seemed the most chaotic. He was levelheaded when others were losing theirs.

In essence, he was "Joe Cool." And it's a huge reason he ranks among the greatest players in NFL history.

Steve Young

Steve Young hollered, "Somebody take the monkey off my back!"

Teammate Gary Plummer then did the honors.

Super Bowl XXIX was nearly complete and Young had just finished a performance for the ages.

Young had thrown a Super Bowl–record six touchdown passes. He was a sensational 24-of-36 for 325 yards.

And his 49ers routed an overmatched San Diego team 49–26.

Now, it was time for Young to celebrate—not only the win, but the moment where he officially escaped Joe Montana's enormous shadow.

"There were times when this was hard! But this is the greatest feeling in the world," Young said that night at Joe Robbie Stadium in Miami. "No one—no one—can ever take this away from us! No one, ever. It's ours!"

Today, it's easy to look at the numbers, the two MVP awards, and the eventual Hall of Fame honors and think things were easy for Young. But Young traveled one of the wilder roads before experiencing greatness in San Francisco.

Young played one year in the now-defunct United States Football League. Then he went just 3–16 as a starter during two miserable seasons with the Tampa Bay Buccaneers.

Tampa Bay viewed Young as a bust and traded him to Bill Walsh's San Francisco 49ers. And that proved to be the greatest break of Young's life.

"When I first came to San Francisco, I soon realized that I was watching the Michelangelo that Sid Gillman had years ago prior spoken about," Young said during his Hall of Fame induction in 2005. "It was art in action and I was privileged to be holding the palette.

"Joe Montana was the greatest quarterback that I had ever seen. I was in awe. I was tempted many times by the opportunity to play for other teams, but I was drawn to the inevitable challenge to live up to the standard that I was witnessing.

"I knew that I was a decent player, and for some reason God blessed me with the big-picture knowledge that if I was ever going to find out just how good I could get, I needed to stay in San Francisco and learn, even if it was brutally hard to do."

It was difficult for Young, because while he showed flashes of being a star, he was also stuck on the bench.

Montana was in the prime of his career, so from 1987 to 1990, Young was his backup. In that time, Young had moments of brilliance, throwing 23 touchdowns and just six interceptions.

Montana missed all of the 1991 season with an elbow injury. And while Young performed quite well, the 49ers failed to make the playoffs.

Montana missed almost the entire 1992 season, as well, and Young won league MVP honors. Young threw an NFL-best 25 touchdowns, led the league with a 107.0 passer rating, threw for 3,465 yards, and ran for another 537 yards.

When the 1993 season rolled around, the 49ers were a house divided. Montana had won four Super Bowls and had his share of loyal supporters. But Young was the future, and he had a segment of backers, as well.

Finally, in the spring of 1993, Montana requested a trade and the 49ers obliged, sending him to Kansas City. The 49ers were now officially Young's team.

"I had faith that the opportunity would create itself at the appropriate time," Young said. "I was tough to live with during some of those years, but as I look back, I am thankful for the struggles and trials that I had and for the opportunities that were given to me.

"When the opportunity for me opened up, being a regular quarterback was no longer an option. I would have gotten booed out of Candlestick Park so fast that I had to rise to the new standard of performance that Joe set."

Young did that—and then some.

San Francisco reached the 1993 NFC Championship Game before losing to Dallas. But the 49ers reached the pinnacle the following season.

San Francisco finished an NFL-best 13–3 during the regular season. The 49ers exacted revenge and defeated Dallas in the NFC title game, then Young & Co. had a Super Bowl for the ages.

Young's six touchdowns that night against San Diego broke the mark of five held by Montana. And that capped off a year in which Young won his second MVP award.

Steve Young by the Numbers

7× Pro Bowl selection (1992, 1993, 1994, 1995, 1996, 1997, 1998)

3× Associated Press First-Team All-Pro (1992, 1993, 1994)

3× AP Second-Team All-Pro (1995, 1997, 1998)

United Press International Second-Team All-NFC (1996)

3× Super Bowl champion (XXIII, XXIV, XXIX)

Super Bowl XXIX MVP

3× NFC champion (1988, 1989, 1994)

1992 NFL MVP (AP, Pro Football Writers Association, *Sporting News*, Maxwell Club)

1994 NFL MVP (AP, PFWA, Newspaper Enterprise Association, *SN*, MX)

AP NFL Offensive Player of the Year (1992)

2× UPI NFC Player of the Year (1992, 1994)

2× Kansas City Committee of 101 NFC

Offensive Player of the Year (1992, 1994)

San Francisco 49ers #8 retired

Pro Football Hall of Fame inductee (2005)

Career Stats
TD–INT: 232–107

Passing yards: 33,124

QB rating: 96.8

Rushing attempts: 722

Rushing yards: 4,239

Rushing touchdowns: 43

"The way (Young) played, he's got to be one of the greatest quarterbacks of all time," 49ers coach George Seifert said after Super Bowl XXIX. "To play a game as he did tonight and play the way he did this season. (But) the other thing you have to say is that we're fortunate, I'm fortunate, that I've been a part of an organization that had two of the greatest quarterbacks of all time.

"Joe Montana was phenomenal and he set the standard. And Steve Young is talented enough and worked hard enough that he could maintain the standard."

Indeed he did. But the 49ers could never get over the hump in the playoffs again with Young in charge.

The Green Bay Packers knocked the 49ers out of the postseason in 1995, '96, and '97. San Francisco defeated Green Bay in 1998, but lost the next week in the divisional playoffs to Atlanta.

In 1999, Young was sacked by Arizona's Aeneas Williams after running back Lawrence Phillips missed a block. Young suffered a concussion—the seventh of his career—and retired at the end of that season.

Young finished his career with a 96.8 passer rating that's the highest among retired players and the fourth-greatest in NFL history. Young was the NFL's top-rated passer in six different seasons and led the league in touchdown passes four times.

Young threw for more than 33,000 career yards and 232 touchdowns, and had just 107 interceptions. He also had 4,239 rushing yards—the third-most in NFL history by a quarterback—and 43 rushing touchdowns.

"The 49ers of that time will always be remembered for our successes," Young said. "Anyone who followed our team will remember all of the great moments. I'd guess there will never be another period of time like that in sports."

Y.A. Tittle

Yelberton Abraham Tittle Jr.

LSU athletic director Jim Corbett promoted that as "college football's most exciting name" in the 1940s. And anyone who saw Tittle play for the Tigers—or during his two years in the AAFC and 15 years in the NFL—would certainly concur.

Tittle—better known as Y.A. or "Yat"—played 10 of his 17 seasons in San Francisco.

Tittle was named to seven Pro Bowls and was a two-time NFL MVP. Tittle was the first quarterback to throw 30 touchdown passes in consecutive seasons and was inducted into the Pro Football Hall of Fame in 1971.

Tittle was ahead of his time, producing record-setting passing seasons in a running league. About the only thing Tittle didn't do during his memorable career was win a championship.

"After every game people ask me questions about how I figured the other team," Tittle once said. "You have to be in the league a long time and remember things, and at last you get a feel about it. If you could learn it by studying movies, a good smart college quarterback could learn all you've got to learn in three weeks and then come in and be as good as the old heads. But they can't."

Y.A. Tittle by the Numbers

7× Pro Bowl (1953, 1954, 1957, 1959, 1961, 1962, 1963)
3× Associated Press First-Team All-Pro (1957, 1962, 1963)
4× United Press International First-Team All-Pro (1957, 1961, 1962, 1963)
1957 NFL MVP (UPI)
1961 NFL MVP (Newspaper Enterprise Association)
1962 NFL MVP (NEA, UPI, *Sporting News*)
1963 NFL MVP (AP, NEA, *SN*)
First QB to throw 30 touchdowns in consecutive seasons
New York Giants No. 14 retired
Pro Football Hall of Fame inductee (1971)

Career Stats
Pass attempts: 4,395
Completions: 2,427
Percentage: 55.2
TD–INT: 242–248
Passing yards: 33,070
QB rating: 74.3

Tittle spent his first three seasons in Baltimore. But when the Colts became defunct, he joined the San Francisco 49ers.

Tittle spent the next 10 years in San Francisco, where the 49ers had just two losing seasons. But Tittle and the 49ers could never get over the hump.

The closest San Francisco came was in 1957, when it went 8–4 and tied for first in the Western Division. But the 49ers lost to Detroit 31–27 in the playoffs that year.

During Tittle's years in San Francisco, he was part of the 49ers' infamous "Million Dollar Backfield." At the time, San Francisco had four Hall of Fame Players in its backfield together—Tittle, along with running backs John Henry Johnson, Hugh McElhenny, and Joe Perry.

It didn't lead to any championships. But it did produce several memorable moments.

In fact, many that saw Tittle play said his style and passion were similar to Brett Favre's a generation later.

"Tittle has the enthusiasm of a high school kid," Giants great Frank Gifford once said of Tittle. "He loves to play."

The 49ers traded the 34-year old Tittle to the Giants in the spring of 1961. And Tittle proceeded to have some of his finest seasons in New York.

Tittle set an NFL record with his 33 touchdown passes in 1962, then broke that with 36 the following year. Remember, this came at a time when the NFL was a run-first league and there were just 14 regular season games.

On October 28, 1962, Tittle had one of the finest games in NFL history. He threw a remarkable seven touchdowns, and went 27-of-39 for 505 yards in a win over Washington.

Tittle remains one of just seven quarterbacks in NFL history to throw for seven touchdowns in a game.

Tittle chased an NFL Championship until he was 38. And in his 17th and final NFL season, Tittle was captured in one of the most iconic sports photos ever taken.

Tittle had just thrown an interception against Pittsburgh that was returned for a touchdown. Tittle was knocked to the ground by Pittsburgh's John Baker and suffered a concussion and a cracked sternum on the play.

Morris Berman of the *Pittsburgh Post-Gazette* captured a picture of Tittle kneeling, bloodied, and without a helmet. It captured the essence of one of the NFL's great quarterbacks, fighting for a championship until the very end.

"That was the end of the road," Tittle said in 2008. "It was the end of my dream. It was over."

Still, Tittle had a remarkable career.

He had 2,427 career completions, throwing for more than 33,000 yards and 242 touchdowns. Tittle also had 13 games in which he eclipsed 300 passing yards.

"My first Colts coach (Cecil Isbell) inspired me to become what I am—a great forward passer," Tittle said. "When I left college, I didn't know what kind of player I was, but Isbell believed in me. He was my confidence builder. He convinced me that I was the greatest player to ever throw the football."

★ ★ ★
No. 3: Baltimore/ Indianapolis Colts

Many consider Johnny Unitas the greatest quarterback of all time. He was a three-time NFL champion, won three MVP awards, and played in 10 Pro Bowls.

Peyton Manning has also been one of the best in league history. During his 14 years with the Colts franchise, Manning won a Super Bowl, went to 11 Pro Bowls, and was a four-time MVP.

But again, it's Green Bay's depth at this position that rules the day.

The Colts' third-best quarterback was Bert Jones, an extremely solid player throughout the 1970s who lacked talent around him.

Perhaps the Unitas-Manning duo would trump whichever two Green Bay quarterbacks you'd choose to nominate. But when each team plays its third card, the Packers are the runaway winner.

Johnny Unitas

Joe Montana. Tom Brady. John Elway.

These names are front and center when discussing the greatest quarterbacks in NFL history.

But those who saw Johnny Unitas play insist no one was better.

"John Unitas was the best quarterback ever," said Ernie Accorsi, who worked with the Colts during Unitas' final years and later became a general manager in Baltimore and with the New York Giants. "He was direct, and he expected you to be direct. If you crossed him, then there was trouble.

"He was in a class by himself as a quarterback. The rest can go in any order—Otto Graham, John Elway, Dan Marino, Joe Montana. They may have all had a little more than John in some ways as far as arm strength or physical attributes, but John Unitas won with what was in his stomach."

Nicknamed "The Golden Arm," Unitas amassed one record after another during a memorable 17-year run in Baltimore.

Unitas won league MVP honors in 1959, 1964, and 1967. He was named to 10 Pro Bowls and was a first-team All-Pro selection five times.

He led the Colts to NFL championships in 1958 and 1959, and through five games in 1968, before Earl Morrall stepped in. Then he and Morrall led Baltimore to a title in Super Bowl V.

Unitas held the record for most Pro Bowl appearances (10) by a quarterback until Brett Favre broke that mark in 2009. Unitas also posted 118 regular season victories, still a record when he retired.

In addition, Unitas threw a touchdown pass in a record 47 straight regular season games. That mark stood for nearly 52 years before New Orleans' Drew Brees broke it in 2012.

"Johnny Unitas is the greatest quarterback ever to play the game, better than I was, better than Sammy Baugh, better than anyone," Sid Luckman, the great Chicago Bears quarterback of the 1940s, once said.

Unitas' greatest legacy, though, came courtesy of the 1958 NFL Championship Game, widely called "The Greatest Game Ever Played."

At the time, the NFL was third in the pecking order with American sports fans. Baseball ruled the day, while boxing—especially heavyweight title fights—had the popularity of a Super Bowl today.

But Unitas and the Colts helped make the NFL what it is today.

On December 28, 1958, Unitas and the Colts defeated the New York Giants 23–17 in sudden-death overtime to win the NFL Championship. That was the first overtime game in NFL history and was seen by a national television audience on NBC.

Today, every NFL game can be accessed by fans. Nearly 60 years ago, though,

NFL games on television were a rarity, and this thriller has often been credited for sparking the rise in popularity of professional football during the 1960s.

"John really never knew how big he was when he played," Accorsi said. "He had that typical Western Pennsylvania working man's mentality. Hospitals would request him, and he would say, 'Why do they want me?' I would say, 'John, don't you understand how big you are?'"

Perhaps that's because Unitas was one of the ultimate rags-to-riches stories in league history.

Unitas, who played collegiately at Louisville, was drafted in the ninth round by Pittsburgh in 1955. But Steelers coach Walt Kiesling didn't think Unitas had the mental acumen to run an NFL team and cut him.

Unitas began working a construction job and was playing semipro football on weekends for $6 a game. In 1956, though, Unitas was invited to a tryout with the Colts. He needed to borrow gas money for the trip, but it was well worth it as Unitas eventually made the team.

By 1957, Unitas was the Colts' starter. And it didn't take long for him to set the game ablaze.

Unitas finished first in the NFL in passing yards (2,550) and touchdown passes (24) that season. He also led the Colts to a 7–5 record, the first winning record in franchise history.

One year later, the Colts won the first of their three championships under Unitas.

"He was one of the toughest competitors I ever knew, and overcame tremendous odds to become one of the greatest players in NFL history," said the legendary Don Shula, who coached Unitas from 1963 to 1969.

Hall of Fame wide receiver Raymond Berry agreed.

"To be in Baltimore as a receiver and get to play 12 years with him, I have to classify as the best break I ever got in my career," Berry said. "The type of quarterback he was, the leader he was, he was totally focused on moving the football, scoring points, and winning."

Unitas was named to the 1960s All-Decade Team and the NFL's 75th Anniversary All-Time Team. And in 1979, he was inducted into the Pro Football Hall of Fame.

When Unitas retired, he held records for most passing attempts (5,186); most completions (2,830); most total yards (40,239); most touchdowns (290); and most 300-yard passing games (26).

"A man never gets to this station in life without being helped, aided, shoved, pushed, and prodded to do better," Unitas said at his induction into the Hall of Fame in Canton, Ohio, in 1979. "I want to be honest with you: The players I played with and the coaches I had…they are directly responsible for my being here. I want you all to remember that. I always will."

Those who knew Unitas best, though, fully understand just how modest he was being.

Johnny Unitas by the Numbers

10× Pro Bowl selection (1957, 1958, 1959, 1960, 1961, 1962, 1963, 1964, 1966, 1967)
5× Associated Press First-Team All-Pro (1958, 1959, 1964, 1965, 1967)
2× AP Second-Team All-Pro (1957, 1963)
United Press International Second-Team All-Conference (1970)
1957 NFL MVP (Newspaper Enterprise Association)
1959 NFL MVP (AP, UPI, *Sporting News*, Maxwell Club)
1964 NFL MVP (AP, UPI, *SN*, MX)
1967 NFL MVP (AP, UPI, NEA, *SN*, MX)
3× Pro Bowl MVP (1959, 1960, 1963)
NFL Man of the Year Award (1970)
Super Bowl V Champion (1970)
3× NFL Champion (1958, 1959, 1968)
NFL 50th Anniversary All-Time Team
NFL 75th Anniversary All-Time Team
NFL 1960s All-Decade Team
Indianapolis Colts #19 retired
Louisville Cardinals #16 retired
Pro Football Hall of Fame inductee (1979)

Career Stats
Pass attempts: 5,186
Pass completions: 2,830
Percentage: 54.6
TD–INT: 290–253
Passing yards: 40,239
Passer rating: 78.2

"Johnny Unitas will always be a legendary name in NFL history," former NFL commissioner Paul Tagliabue said. "One of the greatest quarterbacks to ever play the game, he epitomized the position with his leadership skills and his ability to perform under pressure."

Added Accorsi: "What made him the greatest quarterback of all time wasn't his arm or his size, it was what was inside his stomach. I've always said the purest definition of leadership was watching Johnny Unitas get off the team bus."

Peyton Manning

One move can determine your legacy.

It can cement your place as one of the best ever in your field, or leave you on the unemployment line.

No one knows this better than former Indianapolis Colts general manager Bill Polian.

Back in April 1998 Polian held the No. 1 pick in the NFL Draft. And as draft day approached, Polian was struggling to decide between quarterbacks Peyton Manning and Ryan Leaf.

"The closer we got to the draft, the louder the 'noise'—opinions from draft media analysts far and wide—became, until it reached a crescendo," Polian said in his book, *The Game Plan*. "You were hearing all of the negatives about Peyton Manning: 'He's a product of the system. He's not a good athlete. He has a weak arm. He can't win the big one.'

"On the contrary, you were hearing nothing but accolades for Ryan Leaf: 'He's a natural thrower. He has a cannon arm. He can make people miss when he runs. He's the second coming of Roger Staubach.'

"Most of that was in the media, and largely, I'm sure, fueled by (agent) Leigh Steinberg, who was a master at getting favorable publicity for his clients. I reminded myself and others in the building, 'Tune out the noise! Tune out the noise!' I even delivered the same message in my public comments, saying, 'We are going to ignore the noise; it's not part of the equation. We are going to make the decision based on what we believe to be sound football reasons.'"

Polian did exactly that.

Then he picked one of the greatest quarterbacks in NFL history and passed on one of the league's all-time busts.

Manning spent 14 memorable years in Indianapolis, leading the Colts to the championship of Super Bowl XLI. Manning was selected to 11 Pro Bowls while in Indianapolis, was a four-time NFL MVP, won two AFC Championships, and was later named to the NFL's All-Decade Team of the 2000s.

Leaf, meanwhile, was drafted second overall by San Diego but lasted just three years with the Chargers and was out of the NFL after only four seasons.

Polian recalled a conversation he had with owner Jim Irsay shortly before he selected Manning.

"I can't tell you if either of these guys is going to win a Super Bowl or become a Hall of Famer," Polian remembers telling Irsay. "We are just trying to find a quarterback that we can win with. But I'll tell you this: If we bust out with Leaf, we have busted out everything. If he busts out, we've lost. If we are wrong on Peyton Manning, the worst we have is Bernie Kosar—a really good, winning quarterback.

"So much for my scouting acumen. I can't say that I envisioned everything that Peyton Manning would become, but after you have been through this process, which you trust, everything pointed to him. You hoped that he would become half of what he became, but there was no question that he would be a winning quarterback in the National Football League."

Manning was that—and so much more—for a Colts team in desperate need of a spark.

Between 1978 and 1998, the Colts had just five winning seasons. Indianapolis reached the postseason just three times in that 21-year span, and its best record in that time was 9–6.

But Manning changed all of that.

After a somewhat rocky rookie season, Manning and the Colts went to the playoffs 11 of the next 12 years. Indianapolis reached double-digit victories in each of those seasons, as well.

Manning was the NFL's leader for touchdown passes three times while in Indianapolis. And he's the Colts' all-time leader in career wins, passing touchdowns, pass attempts, pass completions, and passing yards.

Indianapolis broke the NFL record for most regular season wins in a decade (115) with Manning running the show and tied Dallas' mark for most consecutive playoff appearances (nine). Manning also broke all of the franchise's major career passing records, previously held by Hall of Fame Player Johnny Unitas.

"He's been such a highly accomplished performer year in and year out. Just when you think you've seen his best, he improves upon it," said Jim Caldwell, who coached the Colts from 2009 to 2011. "You look at his numbers and how he's been able to play consistently well over a long period of time. It's been remarkable. I think a lot of it has to do with his drive. He just has an innate sort of will to excel. He never gets bored with it. That, I think, is highly unusual."

Manning's arm was better than scouts gave him credit for before the draft in 1998. His accuracy has always been first rate.

But what always set Manning apart were his preparation, work ethic, and drive.

Tony Dungy, who coached Manning from 2002 to '08, said Manning was the "smartest player I've ever been around."

But Dungy said that was both a blessing and a curse. And Dungy once joked how Manning's legendary study habits would make the task of being a head coach too frustrating for the all-everything quarterback.

"He doesn't realize, everybody's not Peyton Manning," Dungy said. "Everybody doesn't work that hard, everybody can't be at that level all the time. It would frustrate him to death.

"He's got 25 things we can run and he knows they'll be touchdown plays. You have to say, 'Peyton, they are great plays—they probably would be touchdowns. You could put them in just like that. Everybody can't. The other 10 guys can't handle those 25 new plays.'"

Manning handled everything that came his way in Indianapolis and turned a franchise of loveable losers into a juggernaut.

But Manning missed the entire 2011 season after undergoing two neck surgeries. Up until that point, Manning had never missed an NFL game.

With his future in doubt, the Colts released him the following offseason.

"Nobody loves their job more than I do," Manning said on the day he was released. "Nobody loves playing quarterback more than I do. I still want to play. But there is no other team I wanted to play for. I'll always be a Colt. I always will be. That'll never change."

Manning found new life in Denver, where he resuscitated his career. But his 14 seasons in Indianapolis provided one of the greatest runs in NFL history.

About the only knock on Manning was a 9–10 playoff record during his time in Indianapolis.

"I mean, he's great, he's obviously a great quarterback," New England head coach Bill Belichick said of Manning. "The best quarterback I've coached against....Not to take anything away from the Montanas, Marinos, and Elways or whoever is up there with those guys, but (Manning) is tough.

"He's very smart. He has a great understanding of concepts and timing, game management, clock management, situational football—third down, red area—great utilization of the field from sideline to sideline and attacking the deep part

Peyton Manning by the Numbers

Super Bowl champion (XLI)
Super Bowl MVP (XLI)
14× Pro Bowl (1999, 2000, 2002, 2003, 2004, 2005, 2006, 2007, 2008, 2009, 2010, 2012, 2013, 2014)
7× First-team All-Pro (2003, 2004, 2005, 2008, 2009, 2012, 2013)
3× Second-team All-Pro (1999, 2000, 2006)
3× AFC Champion (2006, 2009, 2013)
5× Associated Press NFL MVP (2003, 2004, 2008, 2009, 2013)
2× AP NFL Offensive Player of the Year (2004, 2013)
AP NFL Comeback Player of the Year (2012)
4× NFL passing touchdown leader (2000, 2004, 2006, 2013)
Indianapolis Colts all-time leader (Career Wins, Passing Touchdowns, Pass Attempts, Pass Completions. and Passing Yards)
NFL's all-time leader in career touchdown passes
Tied most Pro Bowl appearances by any player
Pro Bowl MVP (2005)
NFL 2000s All-Decade Team

Career Stats
Pass attempts: 9,049
Completions: 5,927
Percentage: 65.5
TD–INT: 530–234
Passing yards: 69,691
QB rating: 97.5

of the field, very accurate, great decision maker, quick release....I don't think there are any weaknesses in his game."

Today, Polian agrees with everything Belichick says. And Polian remembers his final encounter with Manning prior to the 1998 draft.

"He turned to me and he said, 'Listen, I just want to leave you with this one thought: if you draft me, I promise we will win a championship. And if you don't, I promise I will come back and kick your ass.'"

Polian made the right pick, Manning delivered on that championship, and the Colts were the big winners.

Bert Jones

Pressure?

How's this for pressure?

Bert Jones was selected with the No. 2 overall pick in the 1973 NFL Draft. His mission? Oh, just to replace Johnny Unitas, widely regarded as the finest quarterback in NFL history.

"I don't think initially I felt any pressure," Jones said. "Of course, I held (Unitas) in high esteem. I was a fan of the NFL since my father (Dub) played and then coached for the Cleveland Browns until I was a senior in high school. So I was pretty dialed in on what was going on. I thought it was a great place to go and an opportunity to play quarterback where a great one had recently just played."

Jones didn't reach the status of Unitas, but he was one of the NFL's top quarterbacks throughout the 1970s. Jones had a cannon for an arm and could throw the ball farther than anyone in football.

Jones' best season came in 1976, when he won the NFL's MVP and Offensive Player of the Year. Jones threw for a career-high 24 touchdowns that season and posted a passer rating of 102.5. Interestingly, that was the third-highest passer rating of the entire decade.

In 1977, Jones ranked first in the NFL in completions, second in passing yards and fifth in touchdowns. The Colts also finished sixth that season in total offense.

With Jones in his prime, the Colts won three straight AFC East division titles from 1975–77. Each of those seasons, though, Baltimore lost in the first round of the playoffs.

Bert Jones by the Numbers

Pro Bowl selection (1976)
First-team All-Pro selection (1976)
Second-team All-Pro selection (1977)
1976 Associated Press NFL MVP
1976 Pro Football Writers Association NFL MVP
1976 Newspaper Enterprise Association NFL MVP
All-American (1972)
1972 *Sporting News* College Football Player of the Year

Career Stats

Passing attempts: 2,551
Completions: 1,430
Percentage: 56.1
TD–INT: 124–101
Passing yards: 18,190
QB rating: 78.2

In the final preseason game of 1978, Jones separated his throwing shoulder. Jones tried returning in mid-October that year, but separated the same shoulder again.

Over the 1978 and '79 seasons, Jones' shoulder caused him to miss 25 total games. With Jones, the Colts were 5–2 (.714). Without him, they were just 5–20 (.200).

Ernie Accorsi, the Colts' assistant general manager at the time, said of Jones: "If he had played under different circumstances, he probably would have been the greatest player ever."

Patriots coach Bill Belichick once called Jones the "best pure passer" he ever saw.

Jones understands he was snakebit. But playing football in the 1970s was much tougher that today, when most of the rules favor the offense—and in particular, quarterbacks.

Jones returned in 1980, but the Colts were a team on the decline.

Jones was sacked an NFL-record 12 times in a 1980 game. And after going 7–9 that year, Baltimore went 2–14 in 1981.

Jones finished up with the Los Angeles Rams, where he played just four games in the 1982 campaign. Eventually a neck injury forced Jones to retire at just 31 years old.

"I had a pretty good run until I hurt my shoulder, and then it took me two years to get well," Jones said. "After I got that well, I had good performances thereafter. I'm not so sure that my best performing days were not later in my career. We just didn't have near the team or near the success."

The Colts never had the team success they hoped for under Jones. And injuries robbed Jones of some of his prime years.

But for a stretch, Jones was one of the most dynamic players of the 1970s.

"I played 10 years in the NFL and enjoyed a lot of good things," Jones said on the day he retired. "That's what I'll remember. The players, the coaches, fulfilling our goals."

★ ★ ★

No. 4:
Dallas Cowboys

The trio of Troy Aikman, Roger Staubach, and Tony Romo have five Super Bowl titles between them. Aikman was a perfect 3–0 in Super Bowls, while Staubach was 2–2.

Aikman and Staubach certainly enjoyed the type of team success everyone strives for. Aikman helped make Dallas the 'Team of the 90s,' while Staubach and the Cowboys were the NFL's second-most-successful operation in the 1970s, behind only Pittsburgh.

Romo hasn't achieved as much team success. But he also hasn't been surrounded by the same kind of talent, yet he's still set virtually every meaningful team passing record.

This trio really can't make a case against the Starr-Favre-Rodgers triumvirate. But the three certainly trump most other organizations.

Troy Aikman

Steady. Consistent. Stable. Firm.

Week after week, season after season, the Dallas Cowboys sent "Mr. Reliability" out under center. While other franchises often experienced seismic shifts in performance from their signal callers, Troy Aikman was always the Cowboys' rock.

"Troy was consistently the most accurate passer I've ever seen," former Cowboys offensive coordinator Norv Turner said during Aikman's Hall of Fame induction in 2004. "What fans saw on Sundays, his teammates saw every day of the week. Troy was driven to be the best, and he expected the same from everyone around him."

Aikman was arguably the finest quarterback in Cowboys history. He led Dallas to three Super Bowl titles between the 1992–95 seasons. He was selected to six Pro Bowls and was inducted into the Pro Football Hall of Fame in 2006.

Aikman was remarkably accurate, a terrific leader, and tough as nails.

While those great Dallas teams of the early and mid-1990s experienced their share of off-the-field trouble, Aikman was always the glue. Aikman didn't put up video game numbers like the Brett Favres or Steve Youngs of his era, but he won.

Boy, did he win.

"In Dallas, my role as the quarterback was to move our team down the field and score points," Aikman said. "Sometimes that meant passing. Sometimes it meant handing off.

"We had a good system in Dallas, although it wasn't one that allowed me to put up big numbers, that was fine. I did what was asked to help the team win."

Dallas was a laughingstock when Aikman arrived as the first pick in the 1989 NFL Draft. The Cowboys had just finished a 3–13 campaign, then went 1–15 in Aikman's rookie season.

But Dallas had one of the game's best young trios in Aikman, running back Emmitt Smith, and wideout Michael Irvin. That group became known as "The Triplets," and today, all three are in the Hall of Fame.

Dallas also benefitted immensely from the 1989 trade that sent All-Pro running back Herschel Walker to Minnesota. The Cowboys traded Walker and four draft picks for five players and eight draft picks—including three first rounders and three second rounders.

That fast, the Cowboys had a young franchise quarterback and plenty of draft picks to begin a massive turnaround. And that's exactly what happened.

By 1992, Dallas went 13–3 and defeated San Francisco in the NFC Championship Game. The Cowboys then routed Buffalo 52–17 in Super Bowl XXVII.

Aikman was the game's MVP after throwing for four touchdowns and 273 yards.

"It's as great a feeling as I've ever had in my life," Aikman said that night in Pasadena, California. "I wish every player could experience it."

He would—two more times.

Dallas returned for Super Bowl XXVIII and again cruised past Buffalo 30–13.

Aikman's numbers in those two Super Bowl seasons weren't eye-popping. Instead, he ran football's best team with precision and meticulousness.

"You know, after a game, a lot of times you have those 'ifs,'" Turner said. "You know what I'm talking about. 'If we completed that ball on third-and-4, we would have won the game.' You also have those 'whys.' Why did they throw the ball in that situation? We could have given it to Emmitt. With Troy, you didn't have those 'ifs' and 'whys.'"

Aikman—and many of his teammates—were wondering 'why' though, after head coach Jimmy Johnson left after the second Super Bowl win.

Johnson and owner Jerry Jones were in a power struggle over player personnel decisions. Johnson had sole control over football decisions, but Jones wanted a greater involvement and Johnson scoffed.

When the two couldn't see eye to eye, Johnson left that offseason.

"What struck me most about Jimmy was his fearlessness," Aikman said. "Some coaches play not to lose. Jimmy always played to win. Some guard against over-confidence. Jimmy insisted on it.

"Jimmy's boldness set the tone for a young group of players who didn't know much about winning, but were eager to learn. Jimmy was the right coach at the right time for the Dallas Cowboys, and I'm grateful to have been given the opportunity to play for him."

The Cowboys hired Barry Switzer, a former teammate of Jones at the University of Arkansas. Dallas then reached the 1994 NFC Championship Game, but lost to San Francisco.

The following season, the Cowboys defeated Green Bay 38–27 in the NFC Championship Game. Aikman then threw for 209 yards and a touchdown as Dallas toppled Pittsburgh 27–17 in Super Bowl XXX.

"If you look at Troy's greatest plays, they came in the most critical situations," Turner said. "If you look at his greatest games, they came against the best teams and they came in the playoffs. Troy is one of the most unselfish players to have played. He knew the things he had to do to give his team the best chance to win. In an era of super egos, he never let his get in the way of winning. Super Bowls were more important than statistics."

Troy Aikman by the Numbers

6× Pro Bowl (1991, 1992, 1993, 1994, 1995, 1996)
Sporting News First-Team All-Pro (1993)
3× United Press International Second-Team All-NFC (1994, 1995)
3× Super Bowl champion (XXVII, XXVIII, XXX)
Super Bowl MVP (XXVII)
3× NFC Champion (1992, 1993, 1995)
Walter Payton Man of the Year (1997)
Dallas Cowboys Ring of Honor inductee (2005)
Pro Football Hall of Fame inductee (2006)

Career Stats

Pass attempts: 4,715
Completions: 2,898
Percentage: 61.5
TD–INT: 165–141
Passing yards: 32,942
QB rating: 81.6

The Cowboys' run of greatness was about to end, though.

Dallas' young stars began getting long in the tooth. Johnson, who had masterfully built the Cowboys into a power, proved irreplaceable.

And from 1996 to 2000, the Cowboys went 39–41 in the regular season and won just one playoff game. Many former Cowboys believe that if Johnson had stayed longer, they would have had more than three rings.

"As blessed and as fortunate as we've been, when I'm with Troy (Aikman)—to this day—we still talk about, 'We should have at least five rings,'" Irvin said.

Added Aikman: "I'm disappointed that we didn't get a chance to really exhaust that relationship and find out how great could it have been."

But Aikman isn't disappointed by much else.

Aikman threw for nearly 33,000 career yards and 165 touchdowns. He also went 11–4 in the postseason, highlighted by a seven-game winning streak at one point.

Aikman suffered as many as 10 concussions though. He also had back issues, and retired after the 2000 season.

To this day, the debate rages on whether Aikman or Staubach was the greatest Dallas quarterback ever.

"If you're in my shoes and you've been able to wake up with a franchise quarterback for the last 12 years, that's a luxury," Jones said. "Troy will always be a Dallas Cowboy. When people look at him, they will always see him with a star on the side of his helmet."

Roger Staubach

By the age of 27, many NFL players are already finishing their careers—whether they like it or not.

At age 27, Roger Staubach was just getting started.

Staubach, considered by many the greatest quarterback in Dallas Cowboys history, fulfilled a four-year commitment in the Navy before his NFL career could ever begin. Then he took the football world by storm.

By the time Staubach finished his brilliant career, he led Dallas to a pair of Super Bowl wins and was the MVP in one of those games. Staubach was also a four-time NFL passing leader, retired with what was then the highest passer rating in NFL history (83.4), and earned the nickname "Captain Comeback" for his fourth-quarter heroics.

Oh yeah, and that term "Hail Mary" that gets thrown around today, you can credit Staubach for that, too. Staubach used that phrase after a 1975 playoff win over Minnesota, in which he threw a 50-yard touchdown pass to Drew Pearson in the final seconds.

Afterward, Staubach told reporters that he closed his eyes and "said a Hail Mary." The term has remained in the sports lexicon since.

"Quarterbacking is a mental deal," Staubach once said. "You've got to be able to transfer your confidence to your teammates. There are players with less talent as quarterbacks that are better than players with more talent. If those players with less talent have total team confidence, they're leaders and make things happen."

Make no mistake: Staubach had all the mental and physical skills a player could dream of.

Staubach had his pick of colleges. But he was drawn to the U.S. Naval Academy, where he became a household name.

As a junior in 1963, Staubach led the Midshipmen to a 9–1 record and the

No. 2 ranking in the country, and won the Heisman Trophy. To this day, that trophy means as much—if not more—to Staubach than any award he ever received.

"(The trophy) sits in my home office in a case," Staubach said. "My wife (Marianne) and I do a lot of entertaining, and the Heisman is the one thing people still ask to see when they come over. It's the only trophy in my house that people always ask to be photographed with."

When Staubach's eligibility ended, he had a four-year Navy commitment to fulfill. So Dallas—which had used a 10th-round draft choice on Staubach in 1964—patiently awaited his arrival.

Staubach sat behind incumbent Craig Morton in 1969 and '70. Dallas coach Tom Landry couldn't decide between the two in 1971, and during a midseason game against Chicago, had the two quarterbacks alternate every play.

By the following week, Landry decided on Staubach—and for the next nine seasons, he refused to give the job back.

Staubach led the Cowboys on a 10-game winning streak, highlighted by a 24–3 victory over Miami in Super Bowl VI. Staubach threw a pair of touchdowns in that game and finished with a passer rating of 115.9.

Dallas had been on the doorstep of winning a championship for five seasons. But the wait was finally over—for both the Cowboys and Staubach.

"It meant so much to a team that couldn't win the big one for years," Landry said. "Those players, for that game, they really knew they could win. And they went out and won."

Staubach missed most of the 1972 campaign with a separated shoulder and Morton and the Cowboys excelled throughout that season. But in the NFC divisional playoffs, Staubach relieved Morton, threw a pair of touchdowns in the final 90 seconds, and propelled Dallas to a 30–28 win.

Never was there another peep about a quarterback controversy while Staubach was around.

Staubach led the Cowboys to Super Bowl X following the 1975 season. But Pittsburgh's Terry Bradshaw outdueled Staubach and the Steelers prevailed 21–17.

Bradshaw threw two touchdowns that afternoon and had a 122.5 passer rating. Staubach, on the other hand, fired two touchdown passes, but also had three interceptions.

"We played a very good football game against a very great football team,"

Staubach said. "Their defensive team, I think was the best defense that's ever played in the NFL. And they intimidated us.

"I screamed at (Steelers linebacker) Jack Lambert, calling him every name in the book when I saw Lambert kick Preston Pearson. But we didn't retaliate against him. We let him get away with that, so they won the war of intimidation."

After losing in the divisional playoffs the following season, Dallas was back in Super Bowl XXII. And the Cowboys won their second championship with Staubach at the helm, rolling past Denver 27–10.

Cowboys defensive standouts Harvey Martin and Randy White shared MVP honors. Staubach was also as steady as it gets, completing 17-of-25 passes for 183 yards, while posting a quarterback rating of 102.6.

"That was the best football team I played on," Cowboys safety Charlie Waters said. "I'd put that team against any team of any era. There was no weakness on that team."

Staubach led the Cowboys back to Super Bowl XIII the following season. Staubach threw 25 touchdowns and for 3,190 yards during the 1978 campaign, which were both career-highs at the time.

But Pittsburgh—the Cowboys' No. 1 nemesis during the Staubach years—again prevailed 35–31 in a thrilling Super Bowl.

Staubach certainly did his part, throwing for three touchdowns and 228 yards. But Pittsburgh's Bradshaw was a notch better, throwing for 318 yards and four touchdowns.

Most agreed it was the best Super Bowl played up until that point, a game matching the NFL's top two franchises of the 1970s. And years later, it was still a loss that sat with Staubach and the Cowboys.

"This was the most disappointing game I ever played in, because we had this great team," Staubach said. "Breaks were going to determine that game. No one dominated the other. To me, the 1978 team was the best team we ever had in Dallas."

Statistically, Staubach had the best year of his career in 1979, throwing for 27 touchdowns and nearly 3,600 yards. Those Cowboys won the NFC East for a fourth straight year, but lost in the divisional playoffs.

And when the season was finished, Staubach elected to retire shortly before his 38th birthday. Staubach had suffered 20 concussions during his career, and stepped away to protect his long-term health.

Roger Staubach by the Numbers

6× Pro Bowl selection (1971, 1975, 1976, 1977, 1978, 1979)
2× Associated Press All-NFC (1971, 1976)
2× Super Bowl champion (VI, XII)
5× NFC champion (1970, 1971, 1975, 1977, 1978)
1971 NFL MVP (Maxwell Club)
1971 NFC Player of the Year (*Sporting News*)
Super Bowl MVP (VI)
NFL 1970s All-Decade Team
Dallas Cowboys Ring of Honor
Pro Football Hall of Fame inductee (1985)

Career Stats
Pass attempts: 2,958
Completions: 1,685
Percentage: 57.0
TD–INT: 153–109
Passing yards: 22,700
QB rating: 83.4

Staubach finished his 11 NFL seasons with 153 touchdowns, 109 interceptions, and 22,700 passing yards at a time when most teams were run-first outfits. Staubach, a sensational scrambler known as "Rodger Dodger," also gained 2,264 rushing yards and scored 20 touchdowns.

Staubach went a remarkable 85–29 in the regular season (.746) and 12–6 in the postseason. In addition, he earned the nickname "Captain Comeback" after leading Dallas to 23 game-winning drives (15 comebacks) in the fourth quarter, with 17 of those coming in the final two minutes or in overtime.

"Confidence doesn't come out of nowhere," Staubach said. "It's a result of something... hours and days and weeks and years of constant work and dedication."

Staubach had it all. And even though he started his NFL career later than most, few have ever accomplished more.

Tony Romo

America loves a great underdog story.

Good luck finding many that are better than the rise of Tony Romo.

Romo attended NCAA Division I-AA Eastern Illinois. He went undrafted in 2003 and rode the bench for three seasons in Dallas.

Today, Romo holds franchise records for career passing yards (33,270), career touchdown passes (242), and most game-winning drives (28).

Romo has just two playoff wins in his nine years as a starter. But for the majority of his time in Dallas, Romo has been surrounded by mid-level talent, at best.

And many would argue that Romo is the No. 1 reason the Cowboys haven't fallen off the football map in the past decade.

"I've always felt Tony is an excellent player," Green Bay Packers head coach Mike McCarthy said of Romo. "I think Tony, his ability to get in and out of plays, command the whole offense at the line of scrimmage, and their run-pass balance helps any quarterback. He still has that unique ability to extend plays. He sees the field very well, he's very instinctive, has an excellent awareness. He's a dangerous player."

Packers quarterback Aaron Rodgers agreed.

"He's a really talented guy and I enjoy watching the film of him playing," Rodgers said of Romo. "He does a great job in the pocket, does some great things out of the pocket as well."

Not many people could have predicted this for Romo.

The Cowboys gave Romo a paltry $10,000 signing bonus after he was ignored in the 2003 NFL Draft. Romo was Dallas' No. 3 quarterback in 2003, then was in danger of being cut in 2004. Instead, Quincy Carter was released following allegations of substance abuse and Romo had new life.

"If I had put in Romo in his first year and just let him play, he would have been out of football in a year and a half," former Cowboys coach Bill Parcells said in his biography, *Parcells: A Football Life*. "He was just a gunslinger. He was indiscriminate. And he would do [expletive] that you just can't succeed doing. But after a year or two of practicing in the preseason, getting his [reps], you could see he had a real good chance to come along."

Romo began to impress in his limited opportunities, then was elevated to the Cowboys' No. 2 quarterback in 2005. By the middle of the 2006 season, Parcells named Romo his starter over incumbent Drew Bledsoe.

"Any time you do something like this, it's not without a lot of consideration," Parcells said at the time. "I've been thinking about it for some time....Hopefully, maybe as the team is comprised right now, he might be able to do a couple of things that assist us."

He did—and then some.

Romo had a sensational second half to the 2006 season and powered the Cowboys to just their second playoff appearance of the decade. Unfortunately for Romo, his first playoff appearance included a nightmarish ending.

Trailing 21–20 against Seattle with just 1:19 remaining, Dallas lined up for a potential game-winning 19-yard field goal. But Romo—the holder on the kick—bobbled the snap, then was tackled short of the end zone and the Cowboys lost.

Over the next several seasons, Romo and the Cowboys suffered several late-season losses that raised questions about his resolve in "big games."

Dallas, the No. 1 seed in the 2007 playoffs, lost its first postseason game that year to the New York Giants. With a playoff berth on the line in 2008, Philadelphia routed Dallas 44–6.

The Cowboys won their first postseason game in 13 years in 2009. But Minnesota then drilled Dallas in the Divisional playoff.

Dallas missed the postseason the following three years—and twice was eliminated after losses in the final game of the season.

Romo was playing the game at an extremely high level. He was named to four Pro Bowls. He led the NFC in passing yards in 2009. And he led the conference in passing touchdowns in 2007.

But for the most part, Dallas was a .500 team stuck in the middle of the football universe. And Romo was taking his share of heat for the Cowboys' inability to escape mediocrity.

"I think teams win 'win or go home' games," Cowboys coach Jason Garrett said. "I think teams win playoff games. I think teams win championships.

"The quarterback has a big role in having a really good football team, a championship football team. Tony's done a great job helping us get into some of those games, helping us get an opportunity to win the division, to go to the playoffs, and sometimes it hasn't worked out for our football team."

It finally started to in 2014.

Dallas went 12–4 in the regular season, its best record since 2007. The Cowboys also won the NFC East for the first time since 2009.

Tony Romo by the Numbers

4× Pro Bowl (2006, 2007, 2009, 2014)
Second-team All-Pro (2014)
NFC passing yards leader (2009)
NFC passing touchdowns leader (2007)
NFL passer rating leader (2014)
2× NFC passer rating leader (2007, 2014)

Career Stats
Pass attempts: 4,210
Completions: 2,743
Percentage: 65.2
TD–INT: 242–110
Passing yards: 33,270
QB rating: 97.6

Romo's quarterback rating of 113.2 was the best of his career and ranked No. 1 in the NFL. And his 34 touchdown passes were the second-most of his career.

Dallas defeated Detroit in the Wild Card round, before losing to Green Bay in the Divisional playoff. Making it all even more impressive is Romo had the best season of his career despite playing with two fractures in his spinal vertebrae.

"I'm a better version of myself then I was in years past," Romo said during the 2014 campaign. "And I'm excited about the trend that's continuing to go on that route."

The Cowboys were awfully excited, too.

Romo signed a six-year, $108 million contract in 2013—a far cry from that $10,000 signing bonus a decade earlier.

"He's a stud. We've said it all along, and we paid him accordingly. He's one of the best in the business, if not the best," Cowboys executive vice president Stephen Jones said. "The only thing he's missing is a championship. I don't know when that's coming. Hopefully it's sooner rather than later, but when that comes, he'll go down as one of the all-time greats."

Right now, that still hasn't happened. But Romo definitely goes down as one of the great Cinderella stories.

★ ★ ★

No. 5: Pittsburgh Steelers

Terry Bradshaw was a remarkable 4–0 in Super Bowls. Ben Roethlisberger is 2–1.

Together, this duo can match up with Young-Montana, Unitas-Manning, and any pair the Packers have had. Once again, though, the fall after the top two is steep.

Bobby Layne was a terrific NFL quarterback, but most of his elite years came in Detroit. Layne had five highly productive years in Pittsburgh, but was not in the class of the NFL greats when he was a Steeler.

When Layne enters the equation, Pittsburgh tumbles down the list.

Terry Bradshaw

Greatness was always predicted for Terry Bradshaw.

Bradshaw was an All-American at Louisiana Tech. He was big, strong, and had a rocket for an arm. And the Pittsburgh Steelers made him the No. 1 pick in the 1970 NFL Draft.

But even the Steelers couldn't have forecasted this level of success.

Four Super Bowl titles in just six years. Six trips to the AFC Championship Game. Eight AFC Central titles. And a Hall of Fame career.

Yes, Bradshaw did it all.

"Next to Johnny Unitas, I think Terry Bradshaw is the greatest quarterback in history," said former Steelers chairman Dan Rooney. "They called him the 'Blond Bomber,' and his teammates loved his sense of humor and bravado. The press tormented him with stories about his intelligence. Pittsburgh fans were tough on him—I thought maybe too tough. But he got through all this and became a real team leader."

Indeed.

The Steelers had never won much of anything when Bradshaw arrived. By the time his 14-year career ended, Pittsburgh was the NFL's most dominant franchise.

Bradshaw benefitted from Pittsburgh's "Steel Curtain" defense. And elite running backs Franco Harris and Rocky Bleier certainly made Bradshaw's life easier.

But Bradshaw was also one of the game's elite long-ball throwers. And his connection with standout wide receivers Lynn Swann and John Stallworth was legendary.

Today, video-game passing numbers are the norm. But 40 years ago, Bradshaw's prowess finding his Pro Bowl receivers helped lead to the rise of the passing game.

"Imagine yourself sitting on top of a great thoroughbred horse," Bradshaw said. "You sit up there and you just feel that power. That's what it was like playing quarterback on that team [the Steelers]. It was a great ride."

To this day, many argue that Bradshaw was the greatest Super Bowl quarterback ever. Not only were Bradshaw and the Steelers 4–0 in Super Bowls, he was dominant in the fourth quarter and led two come-from-behind wins.

Getting there wasn't easy, though. Bradshaw briefly lost his starting job in 1974, his fifth season in the league, and many were quick to label him a bust.

"I always wanted everyone to like me. I wanted the city of Pittsburgh to be proud of me, Bradshaw said. "But my first few seasons, I could count the number of people on my bandwagon on one finger."

Bradshaw rebounded, though, and led the Steelers to a championship in Super Bowl IX.

Bradshaw wasn't great that day, as Pittsburgh defeated Minnesota 16–6. But the defense and running game were terrific, and Bradshaw's fourth-quarter touchdown pass to tight end Larry Brown iced the game.

Bradshaw and the Steelers repeated as champions the following year with a 21–17 win over Dallas in Super Bowl X. Bradshaw and Swann hooked up for a 64-yard touchdown pass in the fourth quarter that iced the game.

Bradshaw was leveled on the play and suffered a concussion. But he finished the day with 209 passing yards and two touchdowns.

Bradshaw's finest season came in 1978, when he threw a league-best 28 touchdowns, passed for 2,915 yards, and won league MVP honors. Bradshaw then led the Steelers to Super Bowl XIII for a rematch with the mighty Cowboys.

Bradshaw's intellect was always questioned. And before the game, Cowboys linebacker Thomas "Hollywood" Henderson said of Bradshaw: "He couldn't spell 'cat' if you spotted him the 'c' and the 'a'."

But Bradshaw could spell touchdown, and he threw four of them to power the Steelers to a 35–31 win. Bradshaw also threw for a then-record 318 yards and was named the game's MVP.

Bradshaw captured Super Bowl MVP honors the following year, as well, after powering the Steelers to a memorable 31–19 win over the Los Angeles Rams.

The Rams entered the game as a 10-point underdog. But Los Angeles held a 19–17 lead heading to the fourth quarter.

Early in the final period, though, Bradshaw hit Stallworth with a 73-yard touchdown pass. And the Steelers went on to their fourth Super Bowl title in six years.

"No one will ever win four [Super Bowls] in six years again," Bradshaw said in 2012. "It won't happen. You can chisel that sucker in stone."

Injuries began to take their toll on Bradshaw. And by the early 1980s, he was taking cortisone shots in his throwing elbow before every game.

Bradshaw had elbow surgery after the 1982 season, and missed the first 14 games the following season. When he returned, he felt a pop in his elbow on what wound up being the final pass of his NFL career.

Fittingly, that pass was a 10-yard touchdown to Calvin Sweeney.

Bradshaw finished with a 107–51 record as a starter and a remarkable 14–5 mark in the playoffs (.737). He threw for nearly 28,000 career yards and 212 touchdowns at a time when running games ruled the day.

"There was no quit in him. When he threw an interception, he came right back gunning," Rooney said. "Some sportswriters said he had a problem with (head coach) Chuck Noll, but he didn't, not really. They were about as different as two people could be, but working together they won four Super Bowls. If you call that having a problem, I'll take it any day."

Terry Bradshaw by the Numbers

4× Super Bowl champion (IX, X, XIII, XIV)
2× Super Bowl MVP (XIII, XIV)
3× Pro Bowl selection (1975, 1978, 1979)
Associated Press First-Team All-Pro (1978)
1978 NFL MVP (AP, Maxwell Club)
NFL 1970s All-Decade Team
2011 Pittsburgh Pro Football Hall of Fame
Pittsburgh Steelers All-Time Team (50th Season)
Pittsburgh Steelers #12 no longer issued
Louisiana Tech Athletic Hall of Fame (1984)
Pro Football Hall of Fame inductee (1989)
Led the NFL in touchdown passes in 1978 and 1982

Career Stats

Pass attempts: 3,901
Completions: 2,025
Percentage: 51.9
TD–INT: 212–210
Passing yards: 27,989
QB rating: 70.9

Ben Roethlisberger

Discussions of the great quarterbacks of today almost always include the names Brady, Manning, Rodgers, and Brees.

At times, the remarkable Ben Roethlisberger gets overlooked. And that's a preposterous mistake.

Roethlisberger is one of the game's great pocket passers. At 6'5" and 241 pounds he's built like a truck and is arguably the hardest quarterback in football to bring down.

After just 11 seasons, Roethlisberger holds almost every Steelers team passing record there is. And most importantly, he's led Pittsburgh to a pair of Super Bowl wins.

Most agree Terry Bradshaw is the top quarterback in Steelers history. But by the time he's finished, Roethlisberger could trump him.

"He is a big man. I think he is a special player, the way he extends plays," Packers coach Mike McCarthy said of Roethlisberger. "The length of the play with Ben is always longer.

"The way their passing game is designed, his ability to step up in the rush and do the things he does. He can make any throw on the field. He has the arm to step up, roll to his right, and still make the 60-plus throw."

Oakland Raiders safety Charles Woodson is a big Roethlisberger fan himself.

"Ben is just one of those guys that knows how to get it done," Woodson said. "He's not going to always kill you with numbers and those sorts of things. But when their team needs a play, he being their guy, he can get it done.

"And he makes a lot of guys look bad out there on the field during the course of the games with making guys miss who have free rushes, free shots at him. Or if they get to him, breaking tackles, and still being able to keep a play alive. And he's done that his whole career, and he has hardware to show for that, two championships."

Roethlisberger, the 11th overall pick in the 2004 draft, had success from the start.

Roethlisberger went 13–0 during the regular season as a rookie. But his Steelers lost to New England in the AFC Championship Game.

The following year, Roethlisberger led the Steelers to Super Bowl XL as a No. 6 seed. Pittsburgh then defeated Seattle 21–10 in the Super Bowl, despite a rough outing from Roethlisberger. That night, Roethlisberger completed just 9-of-21 passes for 123 yards and two interceptions, and his passer rating of 22.6 was the lowest in Super Bowl history by a winning quarterback.

"We got the win, and that's all that matters," Roethlisberger said that night.

Roethlisberger led the Steelers back to the big game three years later and was light years better.

Roethlisberger completed 21-of-30 passes for 256 yards. And his six-yard touchdown pass to Santonio Holmes with just 35 seconds left lifted the Steelers to a 27–23 win over Arizona.

"He's a winner, first and foremost," Arizona defensive end Bertrand Berry said of Roethlisberger. "He's about [buying] time in the pocket and making big plays. He did what he's always done. Most quarterbacks wouldn't have been able to do what he did. You have to give him credit. They're the champions because of the way he played."

Roethlisberger became just the 10th quarterback in NFL history to win multiple Super Bowl titles. And he was still just 26 years old.

Roethlisberger had a chance to join Joe Montana, Bradshaw, Tom Brady, and Troy Aikman as the only quarterbacks to win three or more Super Bowl titles. But Green Bay's Rodgers outdueled Roethlisberger in Super Bowl XLV and the Packers prevailed 31–25.

Roethlisberger was terrific, though, in defeat. He completed 25-of-40 passes for 263 yards, two touchdowns and two interceptions.

"I feel like I let the city of Pittsburgh down, the fans, my coaches, and my teammates and it's not a good feeling," Roethlisberger said.

Truth is, Roethlisberger hasn't let anybody down. Instead, he's already cemented his place as one of the top players in franchise history and might have already accomplished enough to lock down a trip to Canton, Ohio, one day.

Roethlisberger was just the third quarterback taken in the 2004 draft. But he's arguably had a better career than top pick Eli Manning and Philip Rivers, who was the fourth overall selection.

Roethlisberger has thrown for at least 4,000 yards four times, including a franchise record 4,952 in 2014. He's thrown a team-record 32 touchdowns on two different occasions (2007, 2014). And he completed a career-best 67.1 percent of his passes in 2014.

Roethlisberger also had a career game in 2014, when he completed 40-of-49 passes for 522 yards and six touchdowns in a 51–34 rout of Indianapolis.

"It was probably the single best regular season performance I have ever seen a quarterback put together," former NFL standout and current broadcaster Boomer Esiason said. "I would put that performance up against any other regular season performance in the history of the NFL."

Year by year, Roethlisberger has become a more dynamic passer. And from day one, Roethlisberger has been among the hardest quarterbacks in football to sack.

"You see quarterbacks who sometimes go down easily, and you can bring them down," Packers linebacker Clay Matthews said. "But he's one of those guys who will fight and gets out of a lot of sacks, and the sacks that he does give up, he's still standing. He continues to make plays by breaking those sacks and those tackles and letting his receivers get open down field."

Ben Roethlisberger by the Numbers

3× Pro Bowl (2007, 2011, 2014)
2× Super Bowl champion (XL, XLIII)
3× AFC champion (2005, 2008, 2010)
NFL Offensive Rookie of the Year (Associated Press, Diet Pepsi, Pro Football Writers Association, *Sporting News*) (2004)
NFL passing yards co-leader (2014)
Joe Greene Great Performance Award (2004)
Pittsburgh Steelers Rookie of the Year (2004)
Pittsburgh Steelers Team MVP (2009)
Pittsburgh Steelers all-time leader (career wins, passing touchdowns, pass attempts, pass completions, and passing yards)

Career Stats
Pass attempts: 4,954
Completions: 3,157
Percentage: 63.7
TD–INT: 251–131
Passing yards: 39,057
QB rating: 93.9

Roethlisberger has already led the Steelers to seven playoff appearances in 11 seasons. Pittsburgh hasn't had a losing season in Roethlisberger's 11 years with the franchise. And Roethlisberger is a sensational 10–5 in the postseason.

"He's got a real unique ability to pump fake, get (people) off balance, has very good pocket instincts, and he has very good vision in terms of where the pressure's coming from," Green Bay Packers defensive coordinator Dom Capers said of Roethlisberger. "He's so big and strong that he's hard to get off his feet. And then he'll step up in and flush, and the receivers will uncover down the field because he buys a lot of time for those receivers to uncover off the coverage."

Those skills have made Roethlisberger one of the game's best. And what has to scare foes is he's a long ways from being done.

Bobby Layne

Today, the Pittsburgh Steelers are seen as one of the NFL's model franchises. Successful. Popular. Thriving.

The Steelers are a model organization.

But Pittsburgh's first 25 years in the league were largely a joke. In that time, the Steelers had just three winning seasons and never finished higher than second in their own division.

But at a time the franchise was a laughingstock, Bobby Layne came along and gave it plenty of credibility.

Layne spent eight memorable seasons in Detroit and led the Lions to three NFL Championships. But after the second game of the 1958 season, Layne was traded to Pittsburgh.

Over the next five seasons, Layne helped the Steelers go 27–22–2. And to this day, he still ranks sixth on the Steelers' all-time passing list.

"My reaction, like everyone else, was 'why?'" Alex Karras, who was Layne's teammate in Detroit, once said of the trade. "No one could give us a real explanation and that disturbed a lot of us. Once he was gone the team just wasn't what it used to be."

The Steelers made immense strides, though.

Over the next five years, Pittsburgh had three winning seasons—as many as they had in the previous quarter century.

Layne threw for 2,339 yards with the Steelers in 1958—the second-highest total of his career. He threw 20 touchdown passes in 1959, also the second-most of his career.

And he helped lay the groundwork for a Pittsburgh team that was beginning to trend upward. Layne later said the greatest regret of his career was not winning a championship for Pittsburgh and owner Art Rooney.

"Winning's the big thing, not records," Layne said. "Look at Fran Tarkenton. He set all those records, but he was throwing three-yard passes to his backs and getting them killed. How many championship rings does he have?"

"He was a unique leader," said Yale Lary, who played on the great Detroit teams with Layne and later joined him in the Hall of Fame. "When he said block, you blocked. And when he said drink, you drank."

Layne's drinking was downright legendary. Layne died at just 59 years old from cardiac arrest, but he got the most out of his time.

Bobby Layne by the Numbers

6× Pro Bowl selection (1951, 1952, 1953, 1956, 1958, 1959)
2× Associated Press First-Team All-Pro (1952, 1956)
3× AP Second-Team All-Pro (1954, 1958, 1959)
3× NFL champion (1952, 1953, 1957)
Led NFL in passing touchdowns (1951)
Led NFL in passing yards (1950, 1951)
NFL 1950s All-Decade Team
Texas Longhorns No. 22 retired
Detroit Lions No. 22 retired
Pro Football Hall of Fame inductee (1967)

Career Stats
Pass attempts: 3,700
Completions: 1,814
Percentage: 49.0
TD–INT: 196–243
Passing yards: 26,768
QB rating: 63.4

Layne had a reputation of closing down bars on a Saturday night, then excelling the next afternoon.

He once crashed into a streetcar after leaving a party. Then he beat the rap when his lawyer argued Layne's Southern drawl was mistaken for drunken slurring.

"Knocked it off the track, just like they wrote," Layne said of the streetcar. "But it wasn't at dawn, like they keep writing. I'd left the party about 10:30 PM because I wanted to do real good in the game the next day. Next thing I knew I was bleeding in the hospital and there were reporters all over the place. I got out of the hospital and played the whole game. The worst part of the whole thing was I finished second that day and it was my last game."

Layne was also legendary for the alleged "curse" he put on the Detroit Lions.

After Layne was traded to Pittsburgh, he supposedly said the Lions would "not win for 50 years." Over the next 50 years, Detroit had the worst winning percentage in the NFL. And Detroit and Cleveland are the only teams that have been in the NFL since the 1970 merger not to play in a Super Bowl.

"He wasn't too happy with the way it went about," Alan Layne, Bobby's son, once said. "I think he heard about (the trade) in the media. That created a little dissension."

But Layne created a buzz in Pittsburgh. He helped pull the Steelers out of the doldrums. And he helped Pittsburgh in its quest to become a championship outfit.

Layne was inducted into the Pro Football Hall of Fame in 1967. And when Layne retired, he owned NFL records for passing attempts (3,700), completions (1,814), touchdowns (196), yards (26,768), and interceptions (243).

Layne was also credited with beginning the two-minute offense. And the hard-nosed Layne was one of the last players to go without a face mask.

"Bobby never lost a game," said Doak Walker, a fellow Hall of Fame Player who played with Layne in Detroit. "Some days, time just ran out on him."

★ ★ ★

No. 6: New England Patriots

The belief here is Tom Brady is the greatest quarterback the NFL has ever known.

Four Super Bowl championships. Six Super Bowl appearances and nine trips to the AFC title game. And amazingly, Brady isn't done.

If this was a game of one-on-one, New England would win the title. But it's not.

Drew Bledsoe was the second-best quarterback in team history. Steve Grogan was No. 3.

Both played in one Super Bowl and lost. Both had solid careers, but far from spectacular.

The decline from Brady to Nos. 2 and 3 is immense, and it's why New England sits at No. 6.

Tom Brady

The National Football League has been filled with remarkable long-shot stories for generations now.

Green Bay's Bart Starr was a 17th-round draft choice in 1956, then won five championships. Warren Moon was trapped in the Canadian Football league, then finally got a chance in the NFL and threw for nearly 50,000 career yards. Kurt Warner went from grocery store shelf stocker to three Super Bowl appearances.

But the game has never seen a more improbable story than that of Thomas Edward Patrick Brady Jr.

Fifteen years ago, Brady was a skinny, underdeveloped NFL hopeful who somehow lasted until the 199th pick of the 2000 Draft. Today, Brady is widely regarded as not only the best quarterback in NFL history, but perhaps the best player ever.

"It's one of the most remarkable stories you'll find," said Gil Brandt, a 30-year executive for the Dallas Cowboys and a senior analyst today at NFL.com. "Not just in our sport, but any sport anywhere."

There's no doubt about that.

Today, Brady is the gold standard for quarterback play. And his list of accomplishments reads like *War and Peace*:

- Four Super Bowl championships (XXXVI, XXXVIII, XXXIX, XLIX)
- Three Super Bowl MVP awards (XXXVI, XXXVIII, XLIX)
- Six-time AFC Champion (2001, 2003, 2004, 2007, 2011, 2014)
- Two NFL MVP awards (2007, 2010)
- 10 Pro Bowls
- Three-time NFL passing touchdown leader (2002, 2007, 2010)

Brady has recorded a remarkable 21–8 record in the postseason (.724). And those 21 wins are five ahead of runner-up Joe Montana.

Brady is also a sensational 160–47 in the regular season and has led the Patriots to the playoffs in 12 of his 13 years. Brady missed the 2008 season with a torn ACL and New England missed the postseason.

"He's the greatest quarterback ever to live on this Earth," Patriots wide receiver Julian Edelman said after New England won Super Bowl XLIX. "He's won four Super Bowls in the modern-day era with a salary cap. He's been to six. I'm a huge Joe Montana fan, I love him to death, but Tommy's No. 1."

New York Jets cornerback Darrelle Revis, widely regarded as the NFL's top cornerback of the past decade, agreed with his former teammate.

"He is going to go down as the greatest quarterback to ever play this game," Revis said. "He is clutch. He is Michael Jordan. You put him in that category of Magic Johnson, all of them, man. Go down the list. He is one of the greatest to ever do it."

Back in April 2000, though, there wasn't an NFL team anywhere that saw this coming.

Brady was optimistically hoping to go in the second round. He felt the third round was probably more realistic.

Never did Brady anticipate sliding to the sixth round.

During a 2011 ESPN documentary, Brady was asked about that draft weekend and was brought to tears.

"It was hard," Brady said. "I remember taking a walk with my dad and mom around the block…."

After pausing and crying, Brady continued.

"It was just a tough day, you know?" he said. "I just remember being there with my mom and dad. You know, they were just so supportive of me. They take it as emotional as I do. Finally, when the Patriots called, I was so excited. I was like, 'I don't have to be an insurance salesman,' you know?"

Brady's slide didn't draw much attention back in 2000. But Lloyd Carr, Brady's coach at Michigan, insisted NFL teams would regret overlooking Brady.

"He's everything you want in a quarterback," Carr said. "First of all, he's tough-minded and tough physically. He's very, very smart and makes good decisions. He's a lot like Brian Griese. He'll play in the NFL.

"There's a lot of guys out there who doubted Griese, and they've lived to see how wrong they could be. And anybody who doubts that Brady can play in the NFL they'll find themselves in the same situation. The kid just can see things. And the guys around him, they love him. If you knew him, you'd love him, too."

Patriots fans—and really an entire generation of football fans—have certainly grown to love Brady.

Brady threw just three passes as a rookie. But Brady's big break came early in the 2001 season when starter and franchise quarterback Drew Bledsoe sheared a blood vessel in his chest.

Brady was lights out the rest of the year and never gave the job back. In that memorable 2001 season, Brady led the Patriots to the Super Bowl. Then as a 14-point underdog, New England stunned St. Louis 20–17 in one of the biggest Super Bowl upsets ever.

Brady wasn't ready for a starring role yet. But he was the ultimate game manager, throwing for one touchdown and 145 yards in the win.

Brady also engineered a nine-play, 53-yard drive in the final two minutes that set up Adam Vinatieri's game-winning 48-yard field goal as time expired. The win gave the Patriots their first-ever Super Bowl title.

Brady (24) became the youngest quarterback to win a Super Bowl and the second-youngest player to earn MVP honors.

"The emotional ride," Brady said that night. "It's been straight up, there hasn't been a downer yet."

There haven't been many since, either.

Bledsoe was traded inside the division to Buffalo that offseason. And Brady, the man who was almost forgotten about on draft weekend just two years earlier, was given the keys to the Patriots empire.

Two years later, Brady and the Patriots were back in the Super Bowl and posted a memorable 32–29 win over upstart Carolina.

Brady, who was now in total control of the offense, was again the MVP. This time, Brady threw for 354 yards and three touchdowns, and completed 32 of 48 passes (66.7 percent).

And once again, Brady engineered a late-game drive, setting up Vinatieri with a 41-yard field goal with four seconds remaining.

"To win this the way we did is incredible, unbelievable," Brady said. "A great all-around game."

Brady and the Patriots made it three Super Bowl titles in four years after edging Philadelphia 24–21 the following year. New England joined Dallas (1992, 1993, 1995) as the only teams in NFL history to win three Super Bowls in four years.

Brady also improved to a remarkable 9–0 in playoff games.

"We've never really self-proclaimed ourselves anything," Brady said. "If you guys say we're great, we'll accept the compliment."

Brady was extremely steady against the Eagles, completing 23 of 33 passes for 236 yards and two touchdowns. But Deion Branch, who caught 11 passes, was named the game's MVP.

"I felt I was very prepared tonight, more so than ever before," Brady said. "I wish we had gotten things going a little quicker, but I knew I was looking in the right places."

For the next nine seasons, Brady and the Patriots enjoyed as much success as any team in football. New England went 110–34 in the regular season in that time, reached the playoffs eight times, and won at least 10 games every season.

But the Patriots also suffered a bevy of brutal postseason losses in that time, and many wondered if Brady would ever hoist another Super Bowl trophy.

New England suffered heartbreaking Super Bowl losses to the New York Giants in both 2007 and '11.

The 2007 Patriots were a perfect 18–0 heading to the Super Bowl. Brady also threw for a then-NFL-record 50 touchdowns that regular season.

But the Giants—a 12-point underdog—stunned New England 17–14 in Super Bowl XLII. Giants wideout David Tyree made a leaping, one-handed catch and pinned the football against his helmet for a 32-yard gain on New York's game-winning drive. Wideout Plaxico Burress then scored the game-winning touchdown on a 13-yard reception with 35 seconds remaining.

Four years later, the Giants' Eli Manning outplayed Brady in Super Bowl XLVI and powered New York to a 21–17 win.

The Patriots also lost AFC title games in 2006, 2012, and 2013. And after Brady struggled—particularly with the deep ball—in a 2013 AFC title game loss to Denver, many wondered if the end of his dominance was near.

"When you play good teams, the margin of error is pretty slim all day," Brady said that day. "We just couldn't do enough. They have a good team and made a lot of plays."

New England began the 2014 season 2–2, Brady was struggling, and some even suggested it was time to turn the team over to backup Jimmy Garoppolo.

Brady, who's always enjoyed beating the odds, did so again.

Brady and the Patriots rallied back, finished the year 12–4, and clinched the No. 1 seed in the AFC. New England then edged Baltimore 35–31 and routed Indianapolis 45–7 on its way to Super Bowl XLIX.

New England trailed defending Super Bowl champion Seattle 24–14 in the fourth quarter. But Brady threw touchdown passes to Danny Amendola and Julian Edelman and the Patriots rallied for a stunning 28–24 win.

Brady captured MVP honors for a third time after throwing four touchdown passes against a Seattle defense that was being discussed among the greatest in a generation. Brady also threw for 328 yards and completed 37 of 50 passes.

Brady went a sensational 13-of-15 in the fourth quarter for 124 yards as the Patriots stormed back.

"Every team has a journey and a lot of people lost faith in us," Brady said. "But we held strong, we held together, and it's a great feeling."

While Brady was the MVP, Malcolm Butler was the hero. Seattle had second-and-goal from the Patriots' 1-yard line with 26 seconds to go.

But Butler—the Patriots' rookie defensive back—stepped in front of wideout Ricardo Lockette and intercepted a Russell Wilson pass. The most dramatic

Tom Brady by the Numbers

4× Super Bowl champion (XXXVI, XXXVIII, XXXIX, XLIX)
3× Super Bowl MVP (XXXVI, XXXVIII, XLIX)
6× AFC champion (2001, 2003, 2004, 2007, 2011, 2014)
2× NFL MVP (2007, 2010)
2× First Team All-Pro (2007, 2010)
Second Team All-Pro (2005)
10× Pro Bowl (2001, 2004, 2005, 2007, 2009, 2010, 2011, 2012, 2013, 2014)
3× NFL passing touchdowns leader (2002, 2007, 2010)
2× NFL passing yards leader (2005, 2007)
Sports Illustrated Sportsman of the Year (2005)
Sporting News Sportsman of the Year (2004, 2007)
Associated Press Male Athlete of the Year (2007)
2× NFL Offensive Player of the Year (2007, 2010)
3× AFC Offensive Player of the Year (2007, 2010, 2011)
AP NFL Comeback Player of the Year (2009)
Pro Football Writers Association NFL Comeback Player of the Year (2009)
New England Patriots all-time leader (passing touchdowns, passing yards, pass completions, pass attempts, career wins)
NFL 2000s All-Decade Team

Career Stats
Pass attempts: 7,168
Completions: 4,551
Percentage: 63.5
TD–INT: 392–143
Passing yards: 53,258
QB rating: 95.9

ending in Super Bowl history made Brady and the Patriots champions again.

"I just had a vision that I was going to make a big play and it came true," Butler said. "I'm just blessed. I can't explain it right now. It's crazy."

It's not crazy, though, to suggest Brady is now the best quarterback the NFL has ever seen.

Brady, Terry Bradshaw, and Joe Montana are tied for the most Super Bowl wins with four. Brady has appeared in a record six Super Bowls.

Brady's 13 touchdown passes in Super Bowls is a record. His 21 postseason wins dwarf the competition.

The best? Most would argue yes.

Not Brady, though.

"I never put myself in those discussions," Brady said. "That's not how I think. There are so many great players that have been on so many great teams, and we've had some great teams that haven't won it. I think you just enjoy the moment."

For New England fans, it's been 15 years of magical moments...and counting.

Drew Bledsoe

Drew Bledsoe was helpless. And for a player who had dominated his sport his entire life, it was the most terrifying stretch of his career.

Bledsoe was an accomplished, three-time Pro Bowl quarterback for the New England Patriots in 2001. He was the No. 1 pick in the 1993 NFL Draft and had led the Patriots to a Super Bowl appearance in the 1996 season.

But during the 2001 campaign, Bledsoe sheared a blood vessel in his chest after being drilled by the New York Jets' Mo Lewis. From there, the legend of Tom Brady was born.

Brady, of course, came off the bench that season and led the Patriots to a stunning win in Super Bowl XXXVI. Bledsoe was traded to Buffalo the following offseason.

And that quickly, Bledsoe's terrific nine-year career in New England was over.

"While the team was having great success (in 2001), and I was a part of that to an extent, it was personally a very difficult time for me," Bledsoe said. "It was tough to watch this team take off and run while I'm standing on the sidelines. I kind of bottled that all up and put the team first. It wasn't easy."

Of course it wasn't. Up until that point, Bledsoe was playing the quarterback position better than anyone in franchise history.

New England selected the 6'5", 238-pound, strong-armed Bledsoe over Rick Mirer with the top pick in the 1993 NFL Draft. And Bledsoe immediately began to pay dividends.

By Bledsoe's second year, he threw for a franchise-record 4,555 yards and led the Patriots to the playoffs. That team finished the year on a seven-game winning streak and reached the postseason for the first time in eight years.

"The Patriots, when I came in, they did make some efforts, at least in my first year, to try and make things simpler for me and allowed me to have success early," Bledsoe said. "That was beneficial. We did a decent job in those first few years, because we were starting to put together some good personnel with the team that allowed us to start climbing reasonably quickly."

Bledsoe became the youngest quarterback in NFL history to play in the Pro Bowl and to reach the 10,000-yard mark. Then he led the Patriots to an appearance in Super Bowl XXXI, where they lost to the Green Bay Packers 35–21.

Bledsoe threw four interceptions that night, a major reason the Packers prevailed. And many rank Bledsoe's effort that night among the poorest by a quarterback in Super Bowl history.

"We definitely had our way with Bledsoe in that game," former Packers safety LeRoy Butler said. "We definitely rattled him."

New England qualified for the playoffs each of the next two years. But Bledsoe struggled and New England was just 13–19 overall in the 1999–2000 seasons.

Still, the Patriots viewed Bledsoe as their franchise quarterback and signed him to a then-record 10-year, $103 million contract before the 2001 season. Little could anyone have known that Brady—the 199th overall selection in the 2000 NFL Draft—would became an all-time great.

The Patriots had a tough decision to make choosing between Bledsoe and Brady. But they clearly made the right one by trading Bledsoe to Buffalo, as Brady has led New England to six Super Bowl appearances and four titles.

"Drew Bledsoe is a special player," Patriots owner Bob Kraft said after making the trade. "I have great respect for all he has done for this franchise. He gave our fans some of the greatest memories in the franchise's history, and there will always be a special place reserved for him in the hearts of Patriots fans. For many reasons, and at many levels, this was a difficult trade to make."

It wasn't any easier on Bledsoe.

"It was a very difficult situation," Bledsoe said. "A lot of blood, sweat, and tears for 8½ years for the organization and to just be dismissed, it was a pretty difficult thing."

These days, Bledsoe isn't bitter. He seems at peace that an all-time great took his job.

"There were some unique things about Tom," Bledsoe said. "He was just a sponge. He was in my hip pocket all the time, asking questions, trying to understand what I was looking at, how I was approaching the game. He was a great student of everything going on around him. And he's that way today. When you watch him, you see someone who's continuously trying to improve and look for advantages.

"It led me to believe he was going to be around the game a long time, because of the way he approached the game. Certainly I was in the same boat with everyone else from the standpoint that nobody saw this coming, with what he's done in his career. But he was definitely going to be around a long time."

Unfortunately for Bledsoe, that meant his New England career was shorter than anyone could have imagined.

Drew Bledsoe by the Numbers

Super Bowl champion (XXXVI)
4× Pro Bowl (1994, 1996, 1997, 2002)
2× United Press International Second-Team All-AFC (1994, 1996)
2× AFC Champion (1996, 2001)
New England Patriots Hall of Fame (2011)

Career Stats
Pass attempts: 6,717
Completions: 3,839
Percentage: 57.2
TD–INT: 251–206
Passing yards: 44,611
QB rating: 77.1

Steve Grogan

Underappreciated. Overlooked. Disregarded.

All of the following would be applicable to Steve Grogan.

No, Grogan didn't guide the New England Patriots to the promised land during his 16 years with the franchise. But he did lead the Patriots to four playoff appearances after they had just one total before Grogan arrived.

Grogan's toughness was legendary, as he had a bevy of major injuries, including five knee surgeries. He also survived a string of quarterback competitions throughout his time.

And when Grogan's run ended in 1990, he was the franchise's all-time leader in passing yards (26,886) and passing touchdowns (182). Today, Grogan ranks third in both categories.

"When Grogan plays, he's an offensive coordinator on the field," defensive tackle Fred Smerlas once said. "That gives them a big edge."

Grogan wasn't supposed to be the player that gave the Patriots such an edge. Grogan was a fifth-round draft choice in 1975 and was a long shot to even make the team.

"They already had three veterans," Grogan said. "I was told they were only going to keep two on the active roster that year. My chances didn't look too good.

"One of the veterans retires and Jim Plunkett, who was the starter, got hurt in the final preseason game. They had to keep me as the backup."

Grogan wasn't the backup for long. In fact, by his second season in 1976, Grogan was the starter.

That year, Grogan helped the Patriots reach the playoffs for just the second time in franchise history. New England went 11–3, establishing a franchise record for wins.

Grogan also ran for an NFL-record 12 touchdowns by a quarterback that season. That mark would stand for 35 years until Carolina's Cam Newton ran for 14 in 2011.

"I really didn't have any idea of what I was doing out there," Grogan said. "I was just having fun. I'd drop back and if my first or second options weren't there, I'd take off and run with it because it was something I had done most of my football career.

"I did that the first four or five years, then I had knee problems. I think one of the things I'm most proud of is that I was able to adapt my skills from being

Steve Grogan by the Numbers

Career Stats
TD–INT: 182–208
Passing yards: 26,886
QB rating: 69.6
Rushing yards: 2,176
Rushing touchdowns: 35

a running quarterback to a pocket passer later in my career when my running ability had diminished."

Grogan was the centerpiece of the Patriots for the next several seasons. And in 1978, Grogan led New England to the AFC East title and the franchise's first-ever home playoff game.

But injuries began to take their toll.

In addition to Grogan's knee surgeries, he had screws placed in his leg after the tip of his fibula snapped; a cracked fibula; two ruptured disks in his neck, which he played with for 1½ seasons; a broken left hand (he simply handed off with his right hand); two separated shoulders on each side; the reattachment of a tendon to his throwing elbow; and three concussions.

For the most part, Grogan kept getting off the mat and battling back.

"It was interesting. Everybody talks about how tough I was when I was playing," Grogan said. "I do appreciate that, but I hope that I was a pretty good player too, for the 16 years I played in the league. I wish they would talk about that a little more. But it feels good to be respected for what I did."

With injuries almost always an issue, Grogan was often forced to battle for his job. Along the way, he survived quarterback competitions with Matt Cavanaugh, Tony Eason, Doug Flutie, and Marc Wilson.

Grogan had a huge role in helping the Patriots reach Super Bowl XX in the 1985 season. But Grogan broke his leg late that year and missed most of the season.

Grogan did return for the Super Bowl against the mighty Chicago Bears. And after Eason was ineffective early, Grogan went 17-of-30 for 177 yards and a touchdown in New England's eventual 46–10 loss.

"The Super Bowl was a tremendous experience," Grogan said. "I think all of us remember the time leading up to the game and how much excitement there was around here. The game was a disappointing loss. But with the year we had, with the new coaching staff and no one expecting us to do much, the outcome of the Super Bowl didn't diminish the fun that we had that year.

"I remember riding in on buses to the airport, and people pulling over their cars and honking and waving. I had never seen anything like that in New England, at least for a football team."

Grogan set a franchise record for longevity with his 16 seasons in New England. And in addition to Grogan's terrific passing numbers, he still ranks fourth in franchise history with his 35 career rushing touchdowns.

"I know talent doesn't last forever," Grogan once said. "I just want to make sure I don't leave anything on the field."

He didn't, which is why he's a Patriots great.

★ ★ ★

No. 7: Washington Redskins

Sammy Baugh and Sonny Jurgensen are both in the Pro Football Hall of Fame. Joe Theismann won a Super Bowl and NFL MVP, while Baugh won a pair of titles and two MVP awards.

There's no doubt, Washington produced a sensational trio of quarterbacks. But compared with the teams above them, these three are a step behind.

Sammy Baugh

The National Football League experienced an offensive explosion in the late 1930s and early 1940s. And at the heart of it was Sammy Baugh—better known as "Slingin' Sammy."

When Baugh began his NFL career in 1937, teams never threw the ball from inside their 30-yard line. They believed it was simply too dangerous.

Football was a run-first, grind-it-out sport. The forward pass was more terrifying than exciting to most coaches.

"There wasn't one rule in the rulebook that made you want to throw a pass back when I started playing," Baugh said. "Everything was against the pass."

By the time Baugh was finished in 1953, he was the biggest reason the NFL was quickly becoming a passing league.

Baugh's accuracy was off the charts. And Baugh helped make the forward pass a routine play from scrimmage rather than an anomaly.

Baugh led the Redskins to two NFL Championships and was named an All-Pro six times. Baugh also led the NFL in passing a record six times.

Baugh, who was also a standout defensive back and punter, was among the 17 charter members of the Pro Football Hall of Fame in 1963. He is also on the NFL's 50th and 75th Anniversary Teams and on the 1940s All-Decade team.

"Sammy Baugh embodied all we aspire to at the Washington Redskins," said Daniel Snyder, the Redskins owner since 1999. "He was a competitor in everything he did and a winner. He was one of the greatest to ever play the game of football, and one of the greatest the Redskins ever had."

No one would argue that.

Baugh had options to play both baseball and football when he left Texas Christian University in 1937. Baugh was signed by the St. Louis Cardinals and thought he might have a longer, more prosperous baseball career.

Eventually, though, he settled on football.

"I couldn't hit that curve very well," Baugh said. "So I left in August to play football, and after that I stuck with football."

The 6'2" Baugh was skinny, no more than 180 pounds. But his toughness and accuracy were both legendary.

Former Washington coach Ray Flaherty often told the story of the first time he met Baugh.

Flaherty remembered telling Baugh, "These receivers in the pro league expect their passers to be good. None of those wild heaves you see the college boys throw. When they go down field, our eligible pass receivers want that ball where they can catch it. They like to be hit right in the eye, understand?"

Baugh allegedly took in Flaherty's message, and responded, "Which eye, coach?"

And for 16 seasons—a remarkably long career in the 1940s blood-and-guts world of football—Baugh did exactly that.

When Baugh entered the NFL, the forward pass was used largely at the end of games and at times of desperation. But Baugh helped introduce the short- and medium passing game, and he became the first man to play the quarterback position like it's played today.

Sammy Baugh by the Numbers

5× All-Star (1938, 1939, 1940, 1941, 1942)
Pro Bowl selection (1951)
6× United Press International First-Team All-Pro (1937, 1940, 1943, 1945, 1947, 1948)
3× Associated Press First-Team All-Pro (1940, 1942, 1943)
2× AP Second-Team All-Pro (1947, 1948)
2× NFL Player of the Year (1947, 1948)
2× NFL champion (1937, 1942)
NFL record 6× league passing champion (tied with Steve Young)
NFL 50th Anniversary All-Time Team
NFL 75th Anniversary All-Time Team
NFL 1940s All-Decade Team
70 Greatest Redskins
Redskins Ring of Fame
Washington Redskins #33 retired
Pro Football Hall of Fame inductee (1963)

Career Stats

Pass attempts: 2,995
Completions: 1,693
Percentage: 56.5
TD–INT: 187–203
Passing yards: 21,886
QB rating: 72.2

Baugh's accuracy was developed through countless hours of throwing footballs through a tire swing. And that dedication certainly paid off.

Baugh threw for nearly 22,000 yards and held 13 NFL records at the time of his retirement. He also completed 56.5 percent of his passes at a time the league average was 42.0 percent.

Perhaps even more amazing was how dominant Baugh was at other positions, as well.

Baugh was a sensational defensive back and punter. And in 1943, Baugh led the NFL in passing, punting, and interceptions (11). That's widely regarded as the greatest individual season in NFL history.

During a game in 1943, Baugh threw four touchdowns and intercepted four passes from his defensive back position. It's a safe prediction that will never happen again.

Baugh led the NFL in punting each season between 1940 and 1943. And he finished his career with 31 interceptions.

One of Baugh's most memorable performances came on "Sammy Baugh Day" in 1947. Baugh passed for 355 yards and six touchdowns that day.

"He could not only throw the ball, he could play defense, he could punt the football and he ran it when he had to," said Baugh's former teammate Bill Dudley. "He and I roomed together and he was a football man. He knew football, played it and everybody had a lot of confidence in him."

To this day, many insist Baugh was the best overall player the sport has ever seen. He certainly was one of the game's most influential quarterbacks, and a major reason the sport looks like it does today.

Sonny Jurgensen

Vince Lombardi coached Bart Starr for nine years. And Lombardi, arguably the greatest coach in NFL history, thought the world of Starr.

Lombardi spent just one season with the fun-loving Sonny Jurgensen and was equally impressed.

"He hangs in there under adverse conditions," Lombardi said. "He may be the best the league has ever seen. He is the best I have seen."

That's heady stuff. Then again, Jurgensen's game warranted such praise.

Jurgensen played a remarkable 18 seasons—seven with Philadelphia and 11 with Washington—at a time when quarterbacks took a brutal beating. In the process, Jurgensen had a personal assault on the NFL record book.

Jurgensen, who was inducted into the Pro Football Hall of Fame in 1983, was named to five Pro Bowls. He also threw for more than 32,000 yards and 255 touchdowns, and was widely regarded as the greatest passer of his era.

Even at the age of 40 and in his final NFL season, Jurgensen won his third individual passing title.

"All I ask of my blockers is four seconds," Jurgensen once said. "I try to stay on my feet and not be forced out of the pocket. I beat people by throwing, not running. I won't let them intimidate me into doing something which is not the best thing I can do."

Sonny Jurgensen by the Numbers

5× Pro Bowl selection (1961, 1964, 1966, 1967, 1969)
2× Associated Press First-Team All-Pro (1961, 1969)
AP Second-Team All-Pro (1967)
Sporting News First-Team All-Pro (1961)
SN First-Team All-NFC (1964, 1966, 1967)
SN Second-Team All-Pro (1969)
NFL Championship winner (1960)
5× NFL passing yards champion (1961, 1962, 1966, 1967, 1969)
2× NFL passing touchdowns champion (1961, 1967)
NFL 1960s All-Decade Team
70 Greatest Redskins
Redskins Ring of Fame
Pro Football Hall of Fame inductee (1983)

Career Stats

Pass attempts: 4,262
Completions: 2,433
Percentage: 57.1
TD–INT: 255–189
Passing yards: 32,224
QB rating: 82.6

The Redskins traded quarterback Norm Snead to Philadelphia for Jurgensen in 1964. Jurgensen led the league in passing with the Eagles in 1962, but he also lived an extremely active nightlife and was injured for more than half of the 1963 season.

So the Eagles moved on.

"After they traded me, it was always a special game for me," Jurgensen said. "Anybody who tells you differently is lying."

Acquiring Jurgensen was quite special to the Redskins, too.

"Winning in 1964 is imperative," Washington coach Bill McPeak said at the time. "Jurgensen, at this stage of his career, is more advanced than Snead, and I think with the right supporting cast, he can take you all the way."

The Redskins never went all the way with Jurgensen. But they played some of the most entertaining football of the 1960s.

Jurgensen had a rocket for an arm and a big personality. Naturally, the games were never dull.

Washington had just one winning season during the seven years Jurgensen was the starter. That came in 1969, Lombardi's only season as coach.

Jurgensen led the NFL in passing attempts (442), completions (274), completion percentage (62 percent), and passing yards (3,102) that season. Washington also went 7–5–2 and had its best season since 1955.

But Lombardi was diagnosed with cancer and died before the start of the 1970 campaign.

Jurgensen played through the 1974 season. And even though he split time with Billy Kilmer that year, Jurgensen won his third NFL passing crown.

Jurgensen finished his career with an 82.62 career passer rating, the highest for any player in the "Dead Ball Era" (pre-1978). He also exceeded 400 passing yards five different times and threw five touchdowns in a game three times.

No, the Redskins didn't win as much as they would have liked during those years. But anyone who watched Washington during that time understands that was rarely Jurgensen's fault.

"I remember so many games," former Redskins tight end Jerry Smith said. "I remember a smiling face in the huddle, a person who lived life to the fullest, a man who wasn't afraid to express himself at a time when it simply wasn't in vogue.

"Every pass that man threw fit the situation. Fast, slow, curve, knuckleball, 70 yards, two inches. They were always accurate. If it wasn't complete, it wasn't No. 9's fault."

Joe Theismann

The end was painful, gruesome, horrifying.

Joe Theismann's first 11 years in Washington, though, were sensational.

And that's what Theismann likes to remember first and foremost.

Theismann had a memorable career, leading the Redskins to the Super Bowl XVII championship. He also was a two-time Pro Bowler and the NFL's MVP in 1983.

Much to Theismann's chagrin, though, his name will always be linked with that of New York Giants linebacker Lawrence Taylor.

Theismann suffered a compound fracture of his right leg after being sacked by Taylor during a *Monday Night Football* game in November, 1985. As Taylor pulled Theismann to the ground, Taylor's knee drove straight into Theismann's leg, breaking both the tibia and the fibula.

The Redskins were trying to run a "flea-flicker" play at the time. But the Giants—and Taylor—weren't fooled.

The injury was once voted the NFL's "Most Shocking Moment in History" by ESPN viewers. And Theismann, who was 36 at the time, never played again.

To this day, Theismann remembers the play like it was yesterday

"It was 10:05 PM. I can close my eyes and see the big Longines clock," Theismann said. "I remember everything that happened, all the people around me. I heard both bones break. It sounded like two muzzled gunshots over my left shoulder.

"From my knee down, the pain was excruciating. But it was such a short period of time. From my knee to my foot, my leg went completely numb. When I was transported from the gurney into the ambulance, they forgot to pick up my right leg and I remember asking the attendant, 'Can someone pick up my leg?'

"(At the hospital) they set up a TV for me with a coat hanger so I could watch the rest of the game. All the while they were working on my leg. The union was good, but because it was an exposed fracture, it was important to fight the infection…so the seriousness of the infection was more serious than putting the bones back together.

"It was a question of time whether the bones would heal. The bags of well wishes, people outside the window… it was surreal. And it helped—the encouragement. Now when someone has a fracture similar to mine, I call them up, talk them through it, and tell them what to expect going forward."

Up until that point, Theismann's career had gone better than he ever dreamed possible.

Theismann played three years in the Canadian Football League, then waited behind Billy Kilmer for four seasons.

Theismann finally got his turn in 1978, but the Redskins were a mediocre 32–32 during the first four years he was in charge. Finally in 1982, Washington broke through.

The Redskins went 8–1 in that strike-shortened season, then Theismann led Washington to a 27–17 win over Miami in Super Bowl XVII.

Joe Theismann by the Numbers

2× Canadian Football League All-Star selection
2× Pro Bowl selection (1982, 1983)
Associated Press First-Team All-Pro (1983)
2× United Press International All-NFC (1982, 1983)
UPI Second-Team All-NFC (1979)
Super Bowl champion (XVII)
1982 NFL MVP (Maxwell Club)
1983 NFL MVP (AP, Pro Football Writers Association, Newspaper Enterprise Association)
AP NFL Offensive Player of the Year (1983)
Pro Bowl MVP 1983)
Walter Payton Man of the Year (1982)
70 Greatest Redskins
Redskins Ring of Fame
College Football Hall of Fame inductee (2003)

Career Stats
Pass attempts: 3,602
Completions: 2,044
Percentage: 56.7
TD–INT: 160–138
Passing yards: 25,206
QB rating: 77.4

Theismann guided the Redskins back to the Super Bowl the following season, but they lost to the Los Angeles Raiders 38–9.

Two years later, Theismann's career was over following one of the most grotesque plays in league history.

"In June of 1986, I went out and tried to show the team that I could do the things that I did before," Theismann said. "Mentally, I felt like a tough individual. I was going to overcome everything. I did physical therapy, treatments, trying to come back, but was never able to.

"I showed up at Redskins Park, and there were 13 doctors, and Lloyd's of London insurance people there. I went on the field to work out for an hour, and after 10 minutes of running around and throwing the ball, I turned around and everyone was gone. I jogged inside and said, 'I'm not done yet.' They said, 'Oh yes, you are.' That aspect of my career was over."

Theismann set several Redskins franchise records, including most career passing attempts (3,602), most career passing completions (2,044), and most career passing yards (25,206). He also threw for 160 touchdown passes and 138 interceptions.

When Theismann's name is discussed today, though, usually the first topic is that horrific broken leg. And he's just fine with that.

"I spent 15 years in pro football before I got seriously hurt, so we use that as the line of demarcation," Theismann said. "I broke my right hand twice, dislocated my left elbow, tore up my left knee, broke one bone in my right leg in 1972, had my front teeth knocked out, had a sciatic problem shortly after getting into the game, had turf toe, hip pointer, a broken collarbone, cracked ribs, concussions—a myriad of things.

"But if you ask if I would go back and play the game—in a heartbeat. I knew that I had chosen a profession where I'd be beaten, battered, and bruised. Instead of complaining, I knew it was part of the job description. You're going to be sore. You're going to ache."

Theismann was certainly proof of that.

★ ★ ★

No. 8:
Denver Broncos

John Elway most certainly deserves to be discussed among the game's all-time greats. He won a pair of Super Bowls and an MVP, and was a nine-time Pro Bowler.

But to date, Peyton Manning has played just three years in Denver. And Craig Morton—like Manning—lost his only Super Bowl appearance with the Broncos.

Again, this is a top-notch trio. But it's not at the level of the threesomes above it.

John Elway

For Green Bay Packers fans, it was a horrifying moment that might just haunt them forever.

For John Elway, it was a time he had thought might never arrive.

On January 25, 1998, Denver Broncos owner Pat Bowlen stood inside Qualcomm Stadium in San Diego. Bowlen hoisted the Lombardi Trophy and yelled, "This one's for John."

Elway had just propelled the Broncos to a 31–24 win over Green Bay in Super Bowl XXXII. And after falling short in three other Super Bowls, this was Elway's time.

"Elway was the sentimental favorite and all that stuff," said former Green Bay Packers safety LeRoy Butler. "Everybody was cheering for him and wanted him to win a ring before he was done.

"I get all that. But that game still drives me nuts. There is no way we should have lost that game. We were on our way to becoming a dynasty."

Yes, those Packers—who were trying to win consecutive Super Bowls—were definitely headed toward a dynasty. Instead, Elway's Broncos prevailed that night, then repeated themselves in Super Bowl XXXIII.

In the 16 years since, New England is the only team to win back-to-back Super Bowls.

"As NFL players go, I was truly one of the lucky ones," Elway said during his Hall of Fame enshrinement. "I got to play my entire career in the same city. I got to play in the greatest football town in America, and for the greatest fans. And to top it off, I got to play for the greatest owner in sports."

Elway took a wild road to Denver.

Baltimore made Elway the first pick in the 1983 draft. But Elway had no interest in playing for the Colts—a traditional loser—and tried forcing a trade.

Elway, who had been drafted by the New York Yankees, threatened to play baseball. Finally, the Colts relented and traded Elway to Denver for offensive lineman Chris Hinton, a first-round draft choice, and backup quarterback Mark Hermann.

Hall of Fame quarterback Terry Bradshaw was one of many that ripped Elway's handling of the situation.

"You should play baseball," Bradshaw said at the time. "He's not the kind of guy you win championships with."

For several years, that appeared to be the case. But no one was blaming Elway.

Denver's defense was mediocre, at best. The Broncos never had a serviceable running game.

Yet Elway led Denver to AFC Championships in 1986, 1987, and 1989. The most dramatic of those titles came in 1986, when Elway engineered what's simply known as "The Drive."

With the Broncos trailing host Cleveland 20–13, Elway engineered a 15-play, 98-yard touchdown march that tied the game with just 37 seconds left in regulation. Denver then prevailed in overtime 23–20.

After each of those three AFC Championships, though, Denver came up short in the Super Bowl.

The New York Giants rolled past Denver 39–20 in Super Bowl XXI. The following year, Washington routed the Broncos 42–10 in Super Bowl XXII. And San Francisco destroyed Denver 55–10 in Super Bowl XXIV.

"I said my career would have been complete without a Super Bowl victory," Elway said. "I obviously said that without ever experiencing the feeling."

Throughout the early 1990s, Elway had to wonder if he'd ever win a Super Bowl. Buffalo took control of the AFC, winning the conference four straight years. Dallas was the NFL's new bully, winning three Super Bowls in four years.

And Denver was going nowhere fast, posting a mediocre 49–47 record during the 1990–95 seasons (.510).

But the latter years of Elway's career proved to be the most successful.

After going 13–3 in 1996, the Broncos lost their opening playoff game. But Denver rebounded with a vengeance the following season.

The Broncos went 12–4 in the regular season, went to the playoffs as a No. 4 seed, then won a pair of road games on their way to Super Bowl XXXII.

Green Bay was an 11-point favorite to repeat as Super Bowl champions. But behind a 157-yard, three-touchdown rushing effort from running back Terrell Davis, the Broncos pulled off one of the most stunning upsets in Super Bowl history.

Many called it the greatest Super Bowl ever played. And by the end, thousands of fans were chanting, "Elway, Elway, Elway."

"After that game on the field, I kept asking myself, 'We actually won a Super Bowl?'" Elway said.

Amazingly, the Broncos won it again the following year.

Denver began the 1998 season 13–0 and finished the year as the No. 1 seed in the AFC. Denver then cruised through the postseason, highlighted by a 34–19 rout of Atlanta in the Super Bowl XXXIII.

In the previous Super Bowl, Denver had designed its offense to highlight the unique skills of Davis. Against Atlanta, though, head coach Mike Shanahan put things in Elway's hands.

And even at age 38, Elway delivered, throwing for 336 yards and one touchdown, and winning MVP honors.

"I am just thrilled that we won," Elway said that night. "I'm thrilled to be a part of this team. This is what we play for, and to have this opportunity two years in a row is unbelievable."

John Elway by the Numbers

2× Super Bowl champion (XXXII, XXXIII)
Super Bowl MVP (XXXIII)
5× AFC champion (1986, 1987, 1989, 1997, 1998)
9× Pro Bowl selection (1986, 1987, 1989, 1991, 1993, 1994, 1996, 1997, 1998)
3× Associated Press Second-Team All-Pro (1987, 1993, 1996)
4× Pro Football Weekly First-Team All-AFC (1987, 1993, 1996, 1997)
AP NFL MVP (1987)
2× United Press International AFC Offensive Player of the Year (1987, 1993)
NFL 1990s All-Decade Team
Denver Broncos Ring of Fame
Denver Broncos #7 retired
Walter Payton Man of the Year Award (1992)
Pro Football Hall of Fame inductee (2004)

Career Stats
Pass attempts: 7,250
Completions: 4,123
Percentage: 56.9
TD–INT: 300–226
Passing yards: 51,475
QB rating: 79.9

Elway retired three months later. And he did so with virtually every Broncos record. Among them:

- Most total offensive yards: 54,882 (51,475 passing, 3,407 rushing)
- Most total touchdowns: 334 (300 passing, 33 rushing, 1 receiving)
- Most total plays: 8,027
- Winning percentage: .641 (148–82–1)
- Most career passing yards: 51,475
- Most career completions: 4,123
- Most career attempts: 7,250
- Most touchdown passes: 300

Elway was inducted into the Pro Football Hall of Fame in 2004. And he is widely considered one of the top five quarterbacks in NFL history.

"Best quarterback to ever play the game," said Mike Shanahan, Elway's coach during the Super Bowl championship seasons.

Added Elway: "I'd like to be remembered as a competitor. It may not look good for sixty minutes, but no matter what it looks like, I'll stay after it and try to win the football game."

For the most part, he did just that.

Peyton Manning

Many believed he was done.

His former team in Indianapolis had moved on. Several others didn't think the risk was worth the reward.

But betting against Peyton Manning has never been smart.

Denver took a risk and signed Manning—who missed the entire 2011 season following neck surgery—in March 2012. The three years that have followed have been among the most successful in franchise history.

While Manning has just three seasons in Denver, they've been so fruitful that he qualifies as one of the Broncos' greatest quarterbacks ever.

Denver has posted a 38–10 regular season record. The Broncos have won three straight AFC West titles and reached Super Bowl XLVIII, where they lost to Seattle.

"I think with Peyton, obviously there is not much he can add to his legacy," Broncos general manager John Elway said. "I do think that the one thing he can add is another Super Bowl championship.

"I think with where Peyton is, I said, 'You don't have to throw for another yard and you don't need to throw for another touchdown pass because your legacy is going to be one of the all-time greats.' Where he can really add to his legacy is to win a Super Bowl."

That's about the only thing Manning hasn't done in Denver.

Manning had a handful of suitors after the Colts released him back in 2012. But many were leery of a 36-year-old quarterback coming off a potentially career-ending injury.

But Elway—the greatest quarterback in Broncos history—chased Manning hard. And two of the finest quarterbacks in NFL history teamed up to chase a title.

"I realize I don't have 14 years left, by any means," Manning said on the day he signed with Denver. "This isn't something where I'm just building a foundation to do something in two years or three years. This is a now situation. We're going to do whatever we can to win right now. That's all I'm thinking about right now."

Added Elway: "My goal is to make Peyton Manning the best quarterback that's ever played the game, and he's got that ability with the football that he's got left. He's a guy that raises all boats. He's already made (his teammates) better, and they haven't met him yet just because of the type of person he is, his reputation and what he's done in this league. So, he's just going to have a tremendous effect on the Denver Broncos."

Manning has done that—and more.

Denver went 13–3 in the 2012 regular season. But the Broncos dropped a 38–35 heartbreaker to Baltimore in overtime in the AFC Divisional playoff. The Ravens then went on to win the Super Bowl.

One year later, Denver again went 13–3 and set an NFL record with 606 points. Manning also threw for an NFL-record 55 touchdown passes that season and won a record fifth MVP award.

But Denver's season ended in crushing fashion when it was routed by Seattle 43–8 in Super Bowl XLVIII. Manning set a Super Bowl record with 34 completions, but the Broncos didn't register a first down until the second quarter and didn't score until the third quarter.

"It's not embarrassing," Manning said afterward. "Embarrassing is an insulting word."

Manning and the Broncos were back at it in 2014, putting up video-game numbers and chasing the Lombardi Trophy.

Manning threw for more than 4,700 yards and 39 touchdowns. He also threw his 509th career touchdown pass early in the season, passing Brett Favre to become the NFL's all-time leader in that category.

Denver went 12–4 and once again won the division. But the Broncos' Super Bowl dreams were again shattered when they lost a home game to Indianapolis in the AFC Divisional playoff.

As stellar as Manning's career has been, he's gone one-and-done in the playoffs nine times overall, including two in Denver.

"It's just disappointing," Manning said. "Everyone would like to win their last game of the season."

Still, Manning's time in Denver has been remarkable.

In three seasons, Manning has thrown for almost 15,000 yards, 131 touchdowns, and just 36 interceptions.

Peyton Manning by the Numbers

Super Bowl champion (XLI)
Super Bowl MVP (XLI)
14× Pro Bowl (1999, 2000, 2002, 2003, 2004,2005, 2006, 2007, 2008, 2009, 2010, 2012, 2013, 2014)
7× First-team All-Pro (2003, 2004, 2005, 2008, 2009, 2012, 2013)
3× Second-team All-Pro (1999, 2000, 2006)
3× AFC champion (2006, 2009, 2013)
5× Associated Press NFL MVP (2003, 2004, 2008, 2009, 2013)
2× AP NFL Offensive Player of the Year (2004, 2013)
AP NFL Comeback Player of the Year (2012)
4× NFL passing touchdown leader (2000, 2004, 2006, 2013)
Indianapolis Colts all-time leader (career wins, passing touchdowns, pass attempts, pass completions, and passing yards)
NFL's all-time leader in career touchdown passes
Tied most Pro Bowl appearances by any player
Pro Bowl MVP (2005)
NFL 2000s All-Decade Team

Career Stats
Pass attempts: 9,049
Completions: 5,927
Percentage: 65.5
TD–INT: 530–234
Passing yards: 69,691
QB rating: 97.5

Manning's time in Denver has been short, but memorable. And it's why he's one of the greatest Broncos to ever play the position.

Craig Morton

It took until his third team, more than a decade after he first entered the NFL.

But Craig Morton finally found happiness. So did the Denver Broncos.

Morton failed in bids to become a franchise quarterback with both Dallas and the New York Giants. But when Morton was traded to Denver in 1977 at age 34, he miraculously revived his career.

Morton led the Broncos to Super Bowl XII, where Denver lost to Dallas, the team that had given up on him. Morton had five terrific seasons with the Broncos, and was eventually inducted into the team's Ring of Fame.

"When Craig came, I knew he had a heck of an arm and I knew he didn't have any legs," former Broncos standout wide receiver Haven Moses said. "But I figured I was going to catch a few more passes. I didn't anticipate what happened. I don't think either one of us saw that."

Who could have?

Morton was the Cowboys' first-round draft choice in 1965 and spent nine tumultuous years there. Morton backed up Don Meredith for four seasons, then led the Cowboys to Super Bowl V.

But Morton and Roger Staubach were pitted against each other in one of the greatest quarterback controversies in NFL history. At one point in the 1971 campaign, Dallas head coach Tom Landry had the two alternating every play.

But eventually, Landry went with Staubach and Morton was traded to the Giants.

Things didn't go any better there. Both Morton and Giants struggled, Morton fought with the media, and he was traded once again—this time to Denver.

At 34 years old, most anticipated Morton was nearing the end. But he discovered the fountain of youth in Denver.

Morton was the second-rated passer in the AFC his first year in Denver. And he won points for toughness, playing through a swollen left hip that needed to be drained.

Morton was named the NFL's Comeback Player of the Year that season. Morton was also named All-AFC by *The Sporting News* and led the Broncos to their first-ever Super Bowl.

Craig Morton by the Numbers

Career Stats
Pass attempts: 3,786
Completions: 2,053
Percentage: 54.2
TD–INT: 183–187
Passing yards: 27,908
QB rating: 73.5

The only negative was Denver's performance in the Super Bowl that season. Morton completed just 4 of 15 passes that day for 39 yards. He also threw four interceptions and was eventually benched.

Staubach, on the other hand, was brilliant, completing 17 of 25 passes for 183 yards and a touchdown while outplaying his former teammate.

"We couldn't do anything right," Morton said. "There was no reason to think we'd play that bad. We just gave the ball away too many times. They played well and they knew we couldn't run against them. They pulled the safeties up and blitzed all the time, and we didn't protect enough.

"I did call audibles and that was a mistake. The depressing thing is when you look back on the game, I don't know what you do. What you do is run the ball, and we couldn't do that. When we got in passing situations, they just came after us, and they beat me to death."

Morton led the Broncos back to the playoffs the next two years.

In 1978, Denver lost to Pittsburgh in the Divisional playoff. The following year, the Broncos lost to the Houston Oilers in the Wild Card round.

Amazingly, the best statistical year of Morton's career came in 1981 when he set career highs for passing yards (3,195), touchdown passes (21), and passing attempts (376).

But Morton threw just 26 passes the following season and retired before the 1983 campaign.

Morton finished his career with two Super Bowl appearances—one in Dallas and one with Denver. Morton was the first player to ever start a Super Bowl for two teams and is one of only 20 quarterbacks to play in multiple Super Bowls.

Morton never guided Denver to a Super Bowl title. But he did lead the Broncos to a level they had never reached before and helped put football on the map in Denver.

"Nineteen seventy-seven was a magical year that started Denver on the playoff ride with the Orange Crush (defense) and put Denver on the map as an exceptional football city," Morton said in the book *Game of My Life*. "That kind of changed the whole scenario of sports and what people thought about football in Denver."

★ ★ ★
No. 9: Oakland/ Los Angeles Raiders

The trio of Jim Plunkett, Ken Stabler, and Daryle Lamonica won three Super Bowls. They also helped the Raiders become one of football's dominant teams throughout the 1970s and 80s.

But while all three were excellent leaders, none is in the Hall of Fame.

Jim Plunkett

Jim Plunkett was left for dead.

The 1970 Heisman Trophy winner had drifted into NFL oblivion.

A series of injuries and uneven play had taken Plunkett from New England to San Francisco to the bench in Oakland. And in the late 1970s, Plunkett's NFL career was on the ropes.

But in one of the most improbable comeback stories in NFL history, Plunkett led the Raiders to championships in Super Bowls XV and XVIII. The Raiders were in Oakland for the first of Plunkett's Super Bowl victories, and in Los Angeles for the second.

"Many people felt I was washed up, and I wasn't sure they were wrong," Plunkett said.

With good reason.

Plunkett was the first overall pick in the 1971 NFL Draft by New England. But the Patriots had little talent, Plunkett took a beating, and knee and shoulder surgeries became commonplace.

After playing little in the 1975 season, Plunkett asked for a trade and was dealt to San Francisco. Things didn't go much better there, and the 49ers released Plunkett after just two years.

Plunkett was set to call it a career when Oakland owner Al Davis signed him.

After two years of mostly sitting, Plunkett got his chance early in the 1980 season when Raiders starter Dan Pastorini suffered a broken leg. What happened next was something out of Hollywood.

Oakland went 9–2 with Plunkett in charge and reached the AFC playoffs as a wild card team. Plunkett then led the Raiders to four postseason victories, including a 27–10 rout of Philadelphia. In the process, Oakland became the first-ever wild card to win a Super Bowl.

That season, Plunkett completed 14 of 18 passes for 261 yards and two touchdowns in a 34–27 AFC title victory over San Diego. Two weeks later, Plunkett

Jim Plunkett by the Numbers

Heisman Trophy (1970)
Pop Warner Trophy (1970)
United Press International AFC Rookie of the Year (1971)
Pro Football Weekly NFL Comeback Player of the Year (1980)
2× Super Bowl champion (XV, XVIII)
Super Bowl MVP (XV)
College Football Hall of Fame inductee (1990)

Career Stats

Pass attempts: 3,701
Completions: 1,943
Percentage: 52.5
TD–INT: 164–198
Passing yards: 25,882
QB rating: 67.5

threw three touchdowns—two to Cliff Branch and an 80-yarder to Kenny King—in the Super Bowl win over the Eagles.

Plunkett was named Super Bowl MVP and also received the NFL's Comeback Player of the Year award that season.

"Pastorini broke his leg, and I had my shot," Plunkett said. "Heck, I didn't even know I had it in me to go out there and play at a high level in this league."

Plunkett lost his starting job again, but was thrust back into the lineup in 1983 when Marc Wilson was injured. And once again, Plunkett made the most of it.

The Raiders went 12–4 that season and were the No. 1 seed in the postseason. Los Angeles then won its three playoff games by an average of 24.3 points and routed Washington 38–9 in the Super Bowl.

Once again, Plunkett did his part—and then some—throwing for more than 600 yards that postseason and posting a passer rating of 85.3.

"Our type of system was almost perfect for Jim," former Raiders coach Tom Flores said. "He was tall in the pocket, very powerful, a strong leader. The players liked him. They rallied around him and he just rose to the occasion, making big plays in big games."

Plunkett's career numbers certainly aren't breathtaking.

He had more interceptions (198) than touchdown passes (164) and a passer rating of just 67.5. But he also played in an era that wasn't particularly quarterback friendly and posted a stellar 8–2 postseason record.

Today, Plunkett remains the only quarterback in NFL history to have won two Super Bowls who isn't in the Hall of Fame.

"Obviously, it would be quite an honor," Plunkett said. "But my numbers are not like a lot of other players', especially with some of these current players, because it's more of a passing league now than it ever has been.

"So numbers-wise, not way up there, but probably ahead of some guys. And I got my rings, and I'm very proud of that fact as well. It was a long road and a tough road, and some people thought I was through, and I was fortunate enough to prove them wrong. You know, if I get in, I get in. If I don't, I can't worry about it."

Daryle Lamonica

Many across Packer Nation probably have forgotten—or never knew—just how close Lamonica came to playing for Green Bay.

Back in 1963, the Packers drafted Lamonica in the 12th round. The Buffalo Bills of the American Football League also took Lamonica in the 24th round.

When the Bills showed more interest, though, Lamonica went in that direction.

"The Bills were calling me every day," Lamonica said. "I got a call from a scout with Green Bay and he said that they would get back to me in a few days."

Years later, though, Lamonica discovered the Packers may have been more interested than he first thought.

"I was at the Touchdown Club in Washington, D.C., and Vince Lombardi sat right next to me," Lamonica said. "He said, 'Daryle, I'd like to ask you a personal question. How come you didn't sign with the Packers?

"So I told him the same story: that the Packers' scouting didn't really get back to me. He said, 'You know Bart Starr got hurt this year. You would have been my starting quarterback.' Still to this day, that's one of the best things a coach or person, with my great respect for him, has ever said to me."

Instead, Lamonica sat behind legendary Jack Kemp for four seasons in Buffalo. Lamonica then got his big break and was traded to Oakland before the 1967 season. Five decades ago, though, information was distributed in a far different manner than it is today.

"I was talking to somebody and he said, 'Hey, you have been traded to the Raiders!'" Lamonica said. "I said, 'Yeah, yeah, right. No way.' I had to call the Fresno Bee, my hometown paper, to find out that I was traded. I called my mom and she said that Al Davis had called and wanted me to call."

That call turned around Lamonica's career—and was a major reason the Raiders rose to glory in the 1960s. Lamonica was Oakland's starting quarterback the next six seasons, led the Raiders to the 1967 AFL Championship, and was named MVP of the league twice by various media outlets.

Lamonica was nicknamed "The Mad Bomber" by legendary broadcaster Howard Cosell for his propensity to throw deep and take plenty of chances. The numbers certainly support the nickname, as Lamonica averaged 14.9 yards per completion, throwing 164 career touchdowns and 138 interceptions.

Lamonica's 34 touchdown passes in 1969 remain a team record. And his 30 touchdown strikes in 1967 are second in Oakland history.

"Al Davis taught us that the offense could dictate to the defense by formation," Lamonica said. "We'd be able to get receivers in one-on-one situations, and we

Daryle Lamonica by the Numbers

3× AFL All-Star selection (1965, 1967, 1969)
2× Pro Bowl selection (1970, 1972)
3× Associated Press First-Team All-AFL/AFC (1967, 1969, 1970)
3× AFL champion (1964, 1965, 1967)
1967 AFL MVP (AP, United Press International, *Sporting News*)
1969 AFL MVP (UPI, *SN*)

Career Stats
Pass attempts: 2,601
Completions: 1,288
Percentage: 49.5
TD–INT: 164–138
Passing yards: 19,154
QB rating: 72.9

took advantage of that."

In Lamonica's first year as a starter, he led Oakland to a 13–1 record and the AFL championship. But the mighty Packers were waiting in Super Bowl II, and routed the Raiders 33–14.

Lamonica was just 15-of-34 for 208 yards that day. He did throw two touchdowns, but was also intercepted by Herb Adderley, who went 60 yards for a touchdown to give Green Bay an insurmountable 33–7 lead.

"We had a lot of young players," Lamonica said. "We faced a pretty tough opponent in the Green Bay Packers. I talked to Jerry Kramer and he said, 'Daryle, you had a big hurdle to get over. Right before the game started, the 'old man,' as they called Vince Lombardi, 'said that this was the last game that he was going to coach,' and he wanted to win one for the coach. He said, 'We were pretty well fired up.'

"They were a good football team. They had a great pass rush. We played them real tough to halftime. But we made a couple of errors and I threw an interception. I walked away from that game disappointed, but knowing that we had the potential to really play with the best of the best in the game. I knew that we had a chance to go on and do very well in the future."

Oakland remained one of football's dominant teams and reached the AFL title game the next three years under Lamonica. But Oakland suffered defeats to the New York Jets, Kansas City, and Baltimore—and each of those teams went on to win the Super Bowl.

"We were never able to close," Lamonica said. "I always felt bad about that."

Truthfully, Lamonica has nothing to feel bad about.

He was a three-time AFL All-Star and a two-time Pro Bowler. Lamonica was also a first-team All-AFL player twice.

It was a terrific run that simply lacked a championship.

Ken Stabler

Work hard. Play hard.

The NFL has never had a more fitting poster boy for that axiom than Ken "The Snake" Stabler.

Stabler led the Oakland Raiders to five straight AFC title games and a championship in Super Bowl XI, and was the NFL's MVP in 1974. In the process, Stabler was equally legendary off the field.

Throughout that era, the Raiders were seen as the outlaws of the NFL. And with Stabler's hard-partying ways, he was the perfect man to lead Oakland both on and off the field.

"We were the only team in pro football whose team picture showed both a front and side view," Stabler famously said.

Stabler also once uttered: "There's nothing wrong with reading the game plan by the light of the jukebox."

Or this classic: "All I wanna do is drive around in my truck and drink Jack Daniels...and they just don't understand."

Through it all, Stabler put together a brilliant career. And while Hall of Fame voters have always shunned Stabler, many insist his omission is one of the greatest injustices to any player in the last 25 years.

Stat geeks are quick to point out that Stabler had more interceptions (222) than touchdown passes (194). They'll scoff at his career passer rating of 75.3.

But Stabler won—and won often. And as one of the NFL's all-time gunslingers, the left-handed Stabler provided a bevy of highlight-reel plays and was one of the league's legendary bad boys.

Ken Stabler by the Numbers

4× Pro Bowl selection (1973, 1974, 1976, 1977)
2× Associated Press First-Team All-AFC (1973, 1974)
AP First-Team All-Pro (1974)
AP Second-Team All-Pro (1976)
1974 NFL MVP (AP, Newspaper Enterprise Association, Maxwell Club)
AP NFL Offensive Player of the Year (1974)
Super Bowl XI champion
NFL 1970s All-Decade Team
Led NFL in touchdown passes in 1974 and 1976

Career Stats

Pass attempts: 3,793
Completions: 2,270
Percentage: 59.8
TD–INT: 194–222
Passing yards: 27,938
QB rating: 75.3

"Just stay in the fast lane, and keep moving," Stabler wrote in his autobiography, *Snake*. "You cannot predict your final day, so go hard for the good times while you can."

The Raiders had plenty of good times with Stabler at the helm.

Stabler became Oakland's starter in 1973 and held the job for seven seasons before he was traded to Houston. In that time, Stabler went 68–25–1 for a sensational .729 winning percentage.

Oakland reached the AFC title game every season between 1973–77. And while the Raiders went just 1–4 in those games, they were always in contention for championships.

When the Raiders did win a Super Bowl title in 1976, Stabler set career highs for touchdown passes (27), passing yards per game (228.1), quarterback rating (103.4), and yards per attempt (8.17).

Those Raiders, under Hall of Fame head coach John Madden, were a well-oiled machine. And Stabler made the offense go.

In addition to winning NFL MVP honors in 1974, Stabler was named to four Pro Bowls and twice was selected as an All-Pro quarterback. Stabler was also named to the NFL's All-Decade team for the 1970s.

Through it all, Stabler partied as hard as anyone in the game. And he wasn't overly concerned about what others were saying.

"To be perfectly honest, I'm not going to change, because I don't know any other way," Stabler once said. "I'm going to live the way I want to live. I don't think it distracts me from doing what I want to do during the season.

"People say, 'You can't do those things as you get older.' Well, if I can't, and it hurts my game, I'll get out. But I'm not going to let football control my entire life. I play and I work as hard as I can, and in the offseason I do the things I like to do. That's not going to change."

Stabler never changed for anybody and was the one of the NFL's all-time rebels with a cause. And both he and the Raiders prospered because of it.

Stabler was a finalist for the Hall of Fame three times and a semifinalist six others. To date, though, he hasn't gotten the call.

"George Blanda was kind of my mentor," Stabler said. "George used to tell me the same thing all the time: 'You don't get many opportunities in this game. When you get your opportunity, be ready to play.'"

Stabler was. Which is a big reason the Raiders were a force throughout the 1970s.

★ ★ ★

No. 10: San Diego Chargers

Dan Fouts and Philip Rivers rank among the game's elite during their eras. Fouts is in the Hall of Fame, and Rivers will have a chance one day.

No. 3 John Hadl had a sensational run throughout the 1960s and early 70s, too.

But only Hadl was part of a championship team, helping lead San Diego to the AFL title in 1963.

Dan Fouts

Dan Fouts never reached a Super Bowl.

He actually played on more last-place teams (five) than first-place squads (three).

But few quarterbacks in the modern era of football did more to advance the passing game. And that's why Fouts was elected to the Pro Football Hall of Fame in 1993.

Fouts was also named the "Greatest Charger of All Time" in 2009.

"I can't say enough about Dan," former Chargers wide receiver Charlie Joiner said. "He is one of the greatest quarterbacks in NFL history and is definitely the best quarterback I ever played with."

Fouts was the fearless triggerman for "Air Coryell"—the high-powered, thrill-a-minute offense orchestrated by Chargers head coach Don Coryell. The sturdy, bearded Fouts looked like a lumberjack and played with no fear.

In the process, the Chargers became an offensive juggernaut and one of the most exciting teams the NFL has ever seen.

"Dan does not fit into any mold," Coryell said the night Fouts went into the Hall of Fame. "He will never be duplicated. He was special, very, very special.

"And my personal feeling when you add together all his personal abilities and his virtues, his accomplishments, he is the greatest quarterback in my mind that's ever played the game. In my mind, I know there's a lot of them, but that's how I feel."

Fouts was just the third player in NFL history to throw for more than 40,000 yards. He was the NFL's Most Valuable Player in 1982. He was a six-time Pro Bowler and a two-time Player of the Year in the AFC.

He also took a San Diego team with one of the NFL's poorest defenses to the AFC title game on two occasions and four consecutive playoff berths between 1979 and 1982.

Fouts retired with 42 team and seven NFL records. He threw 254 touchdown passes and passed for 300 yards or more in 51 games.

While Fouts wowed foes with his aerial exploits, he won just as many points for his fearlessness and brevity.

"Dan was intimidating simply because he would stand in there and take all (the punishment) a defense would give him," San Francisco coach Bill Walsh once said of Fouts. "If there was anybody who would stand strong right in the eye of a rush, it was Dan."

Former 49ers safety Ronnie Lott echoed those sentiments.

"He was a workhorse," Lott said. "Everybody talks about how (Chicago quarterback Jim) McMahon should have been an offensive lineman. Well, Dan would have been a great *defensive* lineman."

Fouts was just happy to ever get a chance to show his stuff.

Fouts' first few years in the league were inauspicious, to say the least. But when Coryell arrived in 1978, Fouts and the Chargers took off.

"There's no coach that has had as big of an influence on how offensive football is played today as Don Coryell," Fouts said. "The offense that became known as 'Air Coryell' led the NFL in passing seven of eight years. That statistical fact is unparalleled in the history of the game."

Fouts played in some of the most memorable playoff games in league history.

Dan Fouts

6× Pro Bowl (1979, 1980, 1981, 1982, 1983, 1985)
2× First-team All-Pro (1979, 1982)
2× Second-team All-Pro (1980, 1985)
Pro Bowl Co-MVP (1982)
NFL MVP (Pro Football Writers Association, Newspaper Enterprise Association, 1982)
NFL Offensive Player of the Year (Associated Press, *PW*, 1982)
2× United Press International AFC Player of the Year (1979, 1982)
San Diego Chargers #14 retired
San Diego Chargers Hall of Fame
San Diego Chargers 40th Anniversary Team
San Diego Chargers 50th Anniversary Team
NFL 1980s All-Decade Team
Pro Football Hall of Fame (1993)

Career Stats
Pass attempts: 5,604
Completions: 3,297
Percentage: 58.8
TD–INT: 254–242
Passing yards: 43,040
QB rating: 80.2

He threw for 336 yards and two touchdowns in a 34–27 loss to Oakland in the 1980 AFC Championship Game.

Then, in one the greatest playoff games of all time, Fouts led the Chargers past Miami 41–38 in the 1981 AFC Divisional playoffs. Fouts threw for 433 yards and three touchdowns in a game immediately dubbed the "Epic in Miami."

One week later, though, the Chargers lost in the AFC Championship Game in Cincinnati.

"He did not get (to the Hall of Fame) because of a championship team," Coryell said. "He is there because of him, all him…and that's special."

Fouts would likely dispute that fact. But there's no disputing he was one of the greatest quarterbacks of the last 30 years.

"It's been said that a pro football career is similar to a roller coaster ride," Fouts said. "I've gone from a pro prospect to a third-round selection to a rookie quarterback to a fledgling quarterback to a struggling quarterback to a promising signal caller to All-Pro almost to All-Pro, Player of the Year, to potential Hall of Famer, to aging superstar to ex-quarterback, to certain Hall of Famer to elected in the first year of eligibility," Fouts said. "As a roller coaster ride it has been too thrilling."

Philip Rivers

Every great thriller needs a villain.

Philip Rivers, the ultimate family man who has seven children with his high school sweetheart, doesn't fit the bill of your typical scoundrel. But across the NFL, that's exactly what he is.

Rivers has been one of the NFL's most successful quarterbacks over the past decade. But it's not just his right arm that drives foes nuts. It's also his motor mouth.

"What makes a good villain is that he has the opportunity to show his diabolicalness," Broncos linebacker Von Miller said. "He has the chance to pull it off, and he can beat you.

"(Rivers) does good stuff every time we play them. He is a really good player who has won a lot of games. Yeah, he bothers people because he talks. Everything little he does, he's going to let you know about it."

Denver defensive end DeMarcus Ware agrees.

"A lot of quarterbacks usually don't say much, but he'll talk," Ware said of Rivers. "If you hit him, he might say, 'Hey, that was a nice hit,' and pat you on the shoulder. That sort of (ticks) you off a little bit."

Rivers' play can certainly tick foes off, as well.

Rivers was the fourth overall pick in the 2004 NFL Draft. And after sitting behind Drew Brees for two seasons, Rivers was given the job in 2006.

He hasn't looked back since.

Rivers has been named to five Pro Bowls and led the NFL in passing yards in 2010. He tied for the NFL lead with 34 touchdown passes in 2008 and was the NFL's Comeback Player of the Year in 2013.

Rivers has piled up more than 36,000 passing yards and his 252 touchdown passes are just two off the team record held by Dan Fouts.

Just as importantly, though, Rivers has never missed a start. Rivers' current streak of 153 consecutive starts (including playoffs) ranks fourth all-time among quarterbacks.

"Love Rivers," Patriots coach Bill Belichick said. "[He's] really a football guy; very into it. He's very competitive, really smart, has a great understanding and feel for the game.

"He can attack the defense at all three levels, has great poise and presence in the pocket. He has deceptive mobility. He runs and is more active maybe than what he gets credit for, what you think he is. He's got a good touch on the ball, does a good job using all his receivers, gets the ball to the backs, obviously the tight ends, the receivers downfield on catch-and-run plays and on downfield routes. [He] reads blitz and those type of coverages well, gets the ball out in a hurry. He's been pretty good for a long time."

Rivers has been one of the game's top signal callers for nearly a decade now. But like so many other San Diego quarterbacks, Rivers hasn't been able to win a Super Bowl.

Rivers has more career wins (88) than any quarterback in franchise history. But postseason success has eluded him—which is why his name isn't discussed with the league's best.

The Chargers went 14–2 in the 2006 season, but lost their first playoff game that season to New England. The Patriots also defeated Rivers & Co. in the 2007 AFC Championship Game.

The Chargers were also ousted in the Divisional playoffs in the 2008, 2009, and 2013 seasons.

Rivers, one of the game's ultimate competitors, takes the losses harder than anyone.

"You don't want that feeling again," Rivers said of losing in the playoffs. "Playoff football is awesome. There is nothing better when it comes to the NFL. There is the NFL, and then there's the NFL playoffs. It's in a separate column."

Rivers, 33, still has time to win the ultimate game. But he also understands the clock is ticking—fast.

Those that know Rivers best would love to see him win a title someday. Right now, though, Rivers is fighting 31 other teams—as well as Father Time.

"He's a pure person: pure-hearted, pure spirit, pure emotion," Chargers center

Philip Rivers by the Numbers

5× Pro Bowl (2006, 2009, 2010, 2011, 2013)
NFL Alumni Quarterback of the Year (2010)
2013 NFL Comeback Player of the Year (Associated Press, Pro Football Writers Association)
NFL passing touchdowns co-leader (2008)
NFL passing yards leader (2010)
4× AFC Offensive Player of the Month (December 2008, December 2009, October 2010, September 2014)
2× NFL FedEx Air Player of the Week
San Diego Chargers 50th Anniversary Team

Career Stats
Pass attempts: 4,678
Completions: 3,025
Percentage: 64.7
TD–INT: 252–122
Passing yards: 36,655
QB rating: 95.7

Nick Hardwick says. "Everything you see on the field is him, coming out. He's fanatical about football, about life.

"How can you not love a guy who pours out every second of his life getting ready for the next football game?"

Rivers has given the Chargers plenty to love over the last nine years. The only thing missing is a Lombardi Trophy.

John Hadl

The name John Hadl will always make Packer Nation cringe.

Believe it or not, though, Hadl was one of football's elite quarterbacks for more than a decade in San Diego.

Hadl was a four-time AFL All-Star in San Diego. Hadl was named to a pair of Pro Bowls and was named to the Chargers' 50th anniversary team.

In Green Bay, though, Hadl's name is still cursed. That's because former coach and general manager Dan Devine traded two first-round draft choices, two seconds, and a third to the Los Angeles Rams in 1974 for the 34-year-old Hadl.

"The thing I've always said is I didn't make the trade," Hadl said. "I loved my time in Green Bay and really appreciated the people. But if anybody resents me, just remember, I didn't make the trade."

Hadl is right. And that alone would have made him a better G.M. than Devine.

For most of his career, though, Hadl was a terrific quarterback.

Hadl's was the AFL's leading passer in both 1965 and '68. He was also named MVP of the AFL's All-Star Game in 1969.

Hadl threw for nearly 27,000 yards during his 11 seasons in San Diego—nine of which he was the starter. He also threw 201 touchdowns and 211 interceptions.

"John was the man on those teams," former Chargers wide receiver Lance Alworth said. "He might not admit it now, but he was the man. He was always in control. He never got excited. He never lost his composure.

"He was always, 'Settle down. Let's get this done.' The receivers and backs might be saying (in the huddle), 'Throw it to me.' And John would say, 'Shut up. We can get this done if you guys will be quiet.' He had the respect of everyone in that huddle. He commanded respect and he gave his all."

Hadl may not have been the prettiest passer on the planet. But he was extremely effective.

The knock on Hadl, though, is he started just one playoff game with the Chargers.

"I played against (Joe) Namath and (Len) Dawson and the rest and I respected all of them," Alworth said. "But John was my man. He put the ball right where you wanted it. The balls didn't always look pretty, but they were right there, always very catchable."

Hadl was traded to the Los Angeles Rams before the 1973 season—and was named the NFC's Player of the Year that season. Hadl threw for more than 2,000 yards that season—a large number in that time—and 22 touchdowns while leading the Rams to the NFC West title.

Hadl lost his starting job the next season, though, which set things in place for his eventual move to Green Bay.

When the Packers started the 1974 campaign 3–3, Devine was feeling the heat of 3½ mediocre seasons. So he mortgaged Green Bay's future and sent five high draft picks to the Rams for Hadl.

John Hadl by the Numbers

4× AFL All-Star selection (1964, 1965, 1968, 1969)
Associated Press Second-Team All-AFL (1965)
United Press International Second-Team All-AFL (1965, 1966)
AFL All-Star Game MVP (1969)
2× Pro Bowl selection (1972, 1973)
AP First-Team All-Pro (1973)
1973 NFC Player of the Year (United Press International, *Sporting News*)
Rams MVP (1973)
San Diego Chargers Hall of Fame
Chargers 50th Anniversary Team
College Football Hall of Fame inductee (1994)

Career Stats

Pass attempts: 4,687
Completions: 2,363
Percentage: 50.4
TD–INT: 244–268
Passing yards: 33,503
QB rating: 67.4

To this day, it remains one of the most lopsided trades in NFL history.

"I still thought I could play at a high level," Hadl said. "But it just didn't work out that way."

No it didn't.

It quickly became apparent that Hadl wasn't the missing piece to put the Packers over the top. Hadl's play began to slip; his supporting cast was suspect, at best, and it was evident rather quickly that the trade was a disaster.

"We had a lot of nice guys and they worked awfully hard," Hadl recalled. "But we just didn't have a lot of talent."

That showed over the second half of the 1974 season. Hadl took over the starting job from Jerry Tagge with the Packers sitting at 3–5 and sparked a little life in the team by initiating a three-game winning streak.

Shortly thereafter, though, the bottom fell out. Green Bay lost its final three games of the season, averaging just 7.7 points per contest, and finished the year 6–8.

Devine then took off for Notre Dame and was replaced by Bart Starr. Hadl returned, though, and had perhaps his most dreadful year ever in 1975.

That season, he threw for 2,095 yards and completed 54 percent of his passes. But he had just six touchdown passes to 21 interceptions, and finished with a quarterback rating of 52.8 in Green Bay's forgettable 4–10 campaign.

That wound up being Hadl's final season in Green Bay. The Packers, though, felt the effects of the Hadl deal for years thereafter.

By giving up the ninth, 28th, and 61st overall picks in the 1975 draft and the eighth and 39th overall picks in 1976, the Packers went two years without bringing in top-notch young talent.

The result? A 27–47–2 record between 1976 and 1980.

"I don't even want to go there," Starr said when asked what the trade did for his chances to succeed.

Packers fans still look back at those numbers and shudder. Hadl isn't too happy about them either.

But the rest of Hadl's career was certainly a memorable one.

"He was a guy who made that league a better league," Chiefs Hall of Fame quarterback Len Dawson said of Hadl.

★ ★ ★
Acknowledgments

I'd like to thank my Packer Plus teammate, Martin Hendricks, for his assistance with the chapter on Bart Starr. Hendricks' research, knowledge, and history with both Bart and Cherry Starr dramatically improved the quality of this chapter.

I'd also like to give special thanks to Brett Favre for agreeing to write the foreword and Ron Wolf for writing the preface. Both men were instrumental in the Packers' return to glory a generation ago. And both shared stories of their remarkable highlights and experiences throughout the book. Thanks to that generosity, the readers were the true winners.

★ ★ ★
Sources

Most of the quotations found throughout this book were gathered from personal interviews between these players, coaches, and executives and the author. Many were provided specifically for this book. Others were selected from previous articles written while covering the team. Additional quotes and information came from various sources, which include the following:

Websites

Healthline.com

DetroitAthletic.com

ESPN.com

NationalFootballPost.com

Newspapers

LA Times

Denver Post

Baltimore Sun

★ ★ ★
About the Author

Credit: Gwen Holder Hornsby

Rob Reischel has covered the Green Bay Packers for the *Milwaukee Journal Sentinel's* "Packer Plus" since 2001. He has received 15 awards from the Wisconsin Newspaper Association for his writing and editing, and he is the author of *100 Things Packers Fans Should Know and Do Before They Die*, *Aaron Rodgers: Leader of the Pack*, and *Packers Pride*. He lives in Menomonee Falls, Wisconsin, with his wife, Laura, and their two daughters Mia (front) and Madison (right).